More praise for *Liberia's Women Veterans*

'Fresh. Daring. Artistic. Humane. Its breakthrough methods and a willingness to operate outside the box result in fascinating accounts of women who fought in Liberia's wars.'
*Christine Sylvester, University of Connecticut*

'Vastapuu not only offers a harrowing account of suffering as well as triumph over adversity, but also advances a truly innovative approach that makes this book highly relevant to a wide set of readers interested in questions of gender, violence and politics.'
*Roland Bleiker, University of Queensland*

# Politics and Development in Contemporary Africa

Published by one of the world's leading publishers on African issues, 'Politics and Development in Contemporary Africa' is an exciting new series that seeks to provide accessible but in-depth analysis of key contemporary issues affecting countries within the continent. Featuring a wealth of empirical material and case study detail, and focusing on a diverse range of subject matter – from conflict to gender, development to the environment – the series is a platform for scholars to present original and often provocative arguments.

Editorial board:

Rita Abrahamsen (University of Ottawa); Morten Bøås (Norwegian Institute of International Affairs); David Booth (Overseas Development Institute); Padraig Carmody (Trinity College Dublin); Neil Carrier (University of Oxford); Fantu Cheru (Leiden University); Kevin Dunn (Hobart and William Smith Colleges); Amanda Hammar (University of Copenhagen); Alcinda Honwana (Open University); Paul Jackson (University of Birmingham); Gabrielle Lynch (University of Warwick); Zachariah Mampilly (Vassar College); Henning Melber (Dag Hammarskjöld Foundation); Garth A. Myers (Trinity College Hartford Connecticut); Léonce Ndikumana (UMass Amherst); Cyril Obi (Social Science Research Council); Susan Parnell (University of Cape Town); Mareike Schomerus (Overseas Development Institute); Laura Seay (Morehouse College); Howard Stein (University of Michigan); Mats Utas (Uppsala University); Alex deWaal (Tufts University)

Published titles:

*Mobility between Africa, Asia and Latin America: Economic Networks and Cultural Interactions*, edited by Ute Röschenthaler and Alessandro Jedlowski

*Agricultural Development in Rwanda: Authoritarianism, Markets and Spaces of Governance*, Chris Huggins

Forthcoming titles:

*Food Aid in Sudan: A History of Power, Politics and Profit*, Susanne Jaspars

*Kakuma Refugee Camp: Humanitarian Urbanism in Kenya's Accidental City*, Bram Jansen

*Development Planning in South Africa: Policy Challenge in the Eastern Cape*, John Reynolds

*South Africa, AIDS and the Shadow of Biomedicine*, Isak Niehaus

*Infrastructure and Hybrid Governance in the Democratic Republic of Congo*, edited by Kristof Titeca and Tom De Herdt

*Slum Africa: Life and Governance at the Margins in Accra*, Paul Stacey

## About the author and illustrator

**Leena Vastapuu** is a postdoctoral researcher at the Tampere Peace Research Institute (TAPRI). She was born in 1983 in Mikkeli, Finland, and earned her doctoral degree from the University of Turku in 2017. In addition to Turku, Vastapuu has studied in Université Cheikh Anta Diop de Dakar, Sciences Po Lyon, and has acted as a visiting scholar at the Nordic Africa Institute in Uppsala as well as the School of Oriental and African Studies in London. Through her writing, teaching, consulting and voluntary work she tries to make sense of the world.

Born in 1988 in Helsinki, Finland, **Emmi Nieminen** is a visual artist (BA) specializing in comics and graphic storytelling. Her works mainly focus on human interaction and its imperfections and limitations in our daily lives. Characters living in Nieminen's universe all mean well, but tend to express themselves poorly. Nieminen's work has been exhibited in group and solo exhibitions in Germany, Italy, Taiwan and Switzerland, and has been published in various anthologies in Finnish, English and German. Currently, Nieminen lives and works in Tampere, Finland, and is part of the Tampere Kunsthalle collective. She has been nominated twice for the Sarjakuva-Finlandia award.

# Liberia's Women Veterans

War, Roles and Reintegration

**Leena Vastapuu**
**Illustrated by Emmi Nieminen**

**ZED**

*Liberia's Women Veterans: War, Roles and Reintegration* was first published in 2018 by Zed Books Ltd, The Foundry, 17 Oval Way, London SE11 5RR, UK.

www.zedbooks.net

Text Copyright © Leena Vastapuu 2018

Illustrations © Emmi Nieminen 2018

The rights of Leena Vastapuu and Emmi Nieminen to be identified as the authors of this work have been asserted by them in accordance with the Copyright, Designs and Patents Act, 1988.

Typeset in Plantin MT Std by seagulls.net
Index by ed.emery@thefreeuniversity.net
Cover design by Keith Dodds
Cover image: Young woman in Monrovia in 2012 © Leena Vastapuu

All rights reserved. No part of this publication may be reproduced, stored in a retrieval system or transmitted in any form or by any means, electronic, mechanical, photocopying or otherwise, without the prior permission of Zed Books Ltd.

A catalogue record for this book is available from the British Library

ISBN 978-1-78699-081-5 hb
ISBN 978-1-78699-080-8 pb
ISBN 978-1-78699-082-2 pdf
ISBN 978-1-78699-085-3 epub
ISBN 978-1-78699-086-0 mobi

*In memory of Ma (1986–2014), who is truly missed*

# Contents

| | |
|---|---|
| *Acknowledgements* | *viii* |
| *Preface : Liberia at war* | *xi* |
| Introduction: Hell is the absolute lack of being heard | 1 |
| 1. Auto-photographing rivers of insecurities | 21 |
| 2. Girl and women soldiers in Liberia's civil wars | 43 |
| 3. DDR: Disarmament, Disillusionment and Remarginalization | 85 |
| 4. Social rafting in post-war Liberia | 115 |
| 5. Let my children's future be alright | 147 |
| Conclusion | 169 |
| Epilogue: 'When I sing, I can forget about my problems' | 175 |
| *Notes* | *179* |
| *References* | *187* |
| *Index* | *205* |

# Acknowledgements

A huge number of scholars, practitioners and friends have contributed to this project in large ways and small. Unfortunately we cannot thank each by name, but would instead like to express our gratitude here in a collective manner. It is a true privilege and honour to have friends and colleagues like you around: thank you for taking part in this unbelievable journey.

In particular, Leena would like to thank her PhD supervisor Henri Vogt, whose encouragement and spot-on comments made it all possible in the first place. The research seminar at the Department of Philosophy, Contemporary History and Political Science at the University of Turku, facilitated in turn by Henri, Hannu Nurmi, Maija Setälä and Juha Vuori, provided the best possible intellectual and emotional harbour for the project, as well as comradeships that will last for a lifetime. My sincere gratitude to you all. I remain indebted to my second supervisor Mary Moran, who, among other things, provided many excellent comments and ideas for the final manuscript from across the sea. I also wish to thank the other readers of the project, Liisa Laakso, Annick T. R. Wibben and Gunhild Hoogensen Gjørv, as well as the anonymous reviewers of Zed Books. Your critical yet kind comments substantially improved the final output – as did the careful comments by Xavier Guillaume and Rune Saugmann Andersen for some of the individual chapters of the book. Furthermore, two amazing academics/activists/artists need to be thanked personally: Marjaana Jauhola and Saara Särmä. I only hope that one day I will be able to pay forward the intellectual, emotional and practical backup you have provided throughout these years. The recently established Feminist Peace Research Network (FPRN) also deserves praise -- and I cannot wait to see all the amazing things that will be done within it in the future. The final polishing of the manuscript was done at the Tampere Peace Research Institute (TAPRI), in the most supportive and warm atmosphere. Many thanks to all the colleagues and students at TAPRI, and especially to Tarja Väyrynen for providing me with the privilege to join the crew. From the start, Ken Barlow proved to be an ideal editor and Amy Jordan the most efficient production manager, whereas the final systematic editing for language and style was done by Adam Ulrich and Ian Paten. Thank you all.

The fieldwork periods in Liberia would not have been possible without the support and kindness of numerous individuals. First,

# ACKNOWLEDGEMENTS

I wish to thank everyone who donated cameras for the purpose of this study; you were indeed many in number – my deepest gratitude to you all. Leena Lindqvist: thank you for everything, and most of all your friendship. Special love to the Royal Turning Point Appreciation Society. Ilmari Käihkö, Jussi Laurikainen, Susanna Okker, Teemu Ropponen, Ulla Lydia Tarkka, Mirva Helenius, Heidi Lehto, Jan Elsner, Esko Nummenmaa, Anja Onali, Keijo Keskinen and the others from 'Finn House' and beyond: thank you. With great sadness we learnt of the sudden death of Markku Vesikko on 4 October 2016 in Monrovia. Markku was not only a treasure chest for his knowledge of Liberia, but, above all, a loving father, husband and friend who had the capacity to bring everyone together. Our thoughts are with you, Beatrice Zormaa Vesikko, and the whole family.

Glorious Neoh and her successor Jessica Doe proved to be the best possible research assistants one could ever ask for. In addition, Quita Saybay Tokpah was an invaluable help in Gbarnga. Thank you for everything. My gratitude also extends to the Neoh, Doe and Saybay families. Furthermore, I wish to thank Bartuah Gbor, Claudius Blamoh, Edwin Neoh, Emmanuel Carto, Emmanuel Sandi, Jessie King, Joyce Pajibo, Kofi Ayisa, Lyn and Jim Gray, Philip McKay, Olly Vick and all the staff members of FCA that could not be named here. Sire Sow, thank you for being such an amazing '*grand frère*' in Senegal so many years ago and for your methodological inspiration for this project.

Several institutions and trusts provided me with significant institutional and financial support. I remain indebted to Turku University Foundation, the National 1325 Network Finland, the Emil Aaltonen Foundation, the Finnish Peace Research Association, the National Graduate School of Political Studies (POLITU), the Doctoral Programme of Social and Behavioural Sciences of the University of Turku, the Nordic Africa Institute (NAI), the Centre of African Studies at the School of Oriental and African Studies (SOAS), and the Finnish Cultural Foundation. Special thanks to Inga-Britt Isaksson-Faris, Mats Utas, Michael Jennings and Zoe Marriage for your generous aid in making possible and facilitating the visits to NAI and SOAS.

The compassion and support of my family and friends kept me going even when it felt like I was biting off more than I could chew. Thanks, Mom, Dad, Juha, Keijo, my sister not by blood but by heart Katariina Rahikainen, and everyone else. To undertake the Metal Women project together with Mirja Kurri and Jaakko

Vastapuu was – and is – a rare privilege, but your endless encouragement and care are even more of a gift. Finally, my partner in life, the aforementioned Jaakko, your ubiquitous support, wisdom and love made everything possible. *Piur!*

Emmi is grateful for the financial assistance provided by Arts Promotion Centre Finland, Grafia – Association of Visual Communication Designers in Finland – and the Association of Finnish Illustrators. She would also like to thank the artists at Tampere Kunsthalle for the encouragement and professional and emotional support.

This book is dedicated to all you interviewees whose names we are not at liberty to share. The level of kindness, generosity and trust you have expressed throughout these years even in the most turbulent of times is a great reminder that hope is certainly not gone altogether, not now, not ever.

# Preface: Liberia at war

Liberia was plunged into an extended cycle of violence during the successive civil wars (1989–1997 and 2000–2003) which tore the country into numerous warring factions. To truly grasp the nature of these wars, one must look as far back as 1822, when the first Liberian-American settlers, some of them freed slaves, began to arrive in the area. The impetus of this immigration movement was the establishment of the American Colonization Society (ASC) in 1816, which 'had as its goal the separation of all black citizens from America' (Wander 1971: 57).

The independence of the country was declared on 26 July 1847, and by then it had become clear that the new immigrants had arrived to conquer the area – at least in a symbolic sense. Their True Whig Party held political power until 1980, when the first indigenous head of state, Master Sergeant Samuel Doe, seized power in a *coup d'état*, deposing Americo-Liberian president William Tolbert. However, it soon became apparent that Doe and his interim government, called the People's Redemption Council (PRC), were not only highly inexperienced – and thus vulnerable to various opportunistic influences – but also a brutal organization seeking political gain through violent means (Ellis 2001: 233). Doe and his National Democratic Party of Liberia (NDPL) won the first, allegedly rigged, national elections in 1985, and he was soon prepared to crush opponents whilst favouring his own ethnic group, the Krahn (Adebajo 2002: 28).

Liberia's first civil war began on Christmas Eve, 1989, when Charles Taylor, a former employee of Doe's government, launched an attack with his National Patriotic Front of Liberia (NPFL) against Doe's Armed Forces of Liberia (AFL) from the Ivory Coast (Ellis 2007). While Doe's forces were mainly composed of Krahn soldiers, the NPFL was affiliated with members of the Gio and the Mano ethnic groups. For the Western media, the civil war had thus become an example of ancient ethnic hatreds, even though the roots of the politicized 'tribalism' were for the most part only a decade old (Moran 2006: 16–17). Both Taylor's and Doe's forces committed large-scale human rights abuses, as would all warring parties in the coming decade.

During the first civil war, Liberian society and the international community were able to witness the constant birth of new warring factions owing to incongruities within the NPFL and the AFL. For example, the NPFL split in two when Prince Johnson, a former ally of Charles Taylor, formed his own group called the Independent National Patriotic Front of Liberia (INPFL).

In September 1990, Johnson's forces assassinated President Doe. The assassination was brutal – Doe was mutilated and his ears were sliced off. According to Prince Johnson, he was 'in perfect control' of the situation and thus it was likely to be his personal decision to videotape the incident and allow for its public distribution (Law 2006). Soon after, the Economic Community of West African States (ECOWAS) decided to intervene, mainly to prevent Taylor from gaining control over the capital, Monrovia. ECOWAS formed the Interim Government of National Unity (IGNU) and chose Dr Amos Sawyer as its president. Taylor decided not to cooperate with the IGNU, and the war crossed the border into Sierra Leone. By this point, hundreds of thousands of Liberians had been killed or wounded, about half of the population was displaced, and the country was in chaos (Gershoni 1997: 55).

The situation was further complicated by the birth of yet another guerrilla force called the United Liberation Movement of Liberia (ULIMO), consisting mainly of the former supporters of Doe's government (Ellis 1995: 170). In 1994, ULIMO split into ULIMO-K, led by Alhaji Kromah, and ULIMO-J, under the command of General Roosevelt Johnson. In addition, some minor forces had been formed in different parts of Liberia, such as the Liberian Peace Council (LPC), the Lofa Defence Force (LDF) and the Citizens' Defence Force (ibid.: 172–3).

After at least thirteen failed attempts, a fragile, temporary peace was eventually achieved with the implementation of the Abuja II Accord in 1997 (signed in August 1996). Presidential and legislative elections were held shortly thereafter in July 1997, with Charles Taylor and his National Patriotic Party winning over 75 percent of the vote (Kieh 2008: 156).

Between 1997 and 2000, most Liberians were offered a brief respite from war. During these three years the international community made many promises to support the rebuilding of the country, yet these promises were rarely fulfilled in practice (Bøås 2005: 83). There seem to be several interrelated reasons why the situation deteriorated and erupted into full-scale fighting on the border facing Guinea. Firstly, Taylor's government was unstable and he was unwilling to integrate former enemy soldiers into his armed forces (UNSC 2003). Secondly, a new rebel group was forming called Liberians United for Reconciliation and Democracy (LURD), which had the goal of overthrowing Taylor. Thirdly, the international community did not react in time to the human rights abuses and political harassment committed by Taylor and his regime.

From the beginning of the millennium onwards, LURD and AFL, now under the command of Charles Taylor, were fighting each other mainly in Lofa County next to Guinea, with little ground being gained by either side. Hence the second Liberian civil war had begun. In 2002, a new guerrilla group called the Movement for Democracy in Liberia (MODEL) had assembled its forces with the goal of overthrowing Taylor (ibid.). MODEL gained support from the Ivorian army and France. In addition, the United States and the United Kingdom supported the rebel movements in their fight against Taylor's AFL. Taylor did not have enough military capacity to fight a two-front war, and had therefore no other option than to attend peace talks in Ghana in June 2003 (Bøås 2005: 86).

The peace negotiations were facilitated by the Economic Community of West African States (ECOWAS). Among the participants were representatives from the Liberian government, LURD, MODEL, eighteen political parties, and civil society organisations.[1] On 4 August 2003, ECOWAS launched its Mission in Liberia (ECOMIL), and a week later Charles Taylor handed over the presidency to Vice-President Moses Blah. The Comprehensive Peace Agreement (CPA) was signed between the participants on 18 August 2003 (UNSC 2003a; Government of Liberia 2003). On 19 September, the United Nations Security Council adopted Resolution 1509 (UNSC 2003b), which set out a mandate for the establishment of the United Nations Mission in Liberia (UNMIL), backed by a force of 15,000 United Nations military personnel. As agreed in the CPA (Government of Liberia 2003), the National Transitional Government of Liberia (NTGL) began its duties the following October, headed by chairman Gyude Bryant.[2]

The civil wars of Liberia were deeply intertwined with the wider Mano river region. The Mano river itself forms a section of the boundary between Liberia and Sierra Leone, and the events occurring on the other side of the river typically spilled over also to the opposing frontier (see, e.g., Hoffman 2011: loc. 503). Indeed, Charles Taylor played his cards on both sides of the border but was later tried in court only on his crimes in Sierra Leone. In May 2012, the Special Court for Sierra Leone found Charles Taylor guilty on eleven counts of war crimes and crimes against humanity for his role in the Sierra Leone civil war (SCSL 2016). At the time of writing, neither Charles Taylor nor any other warlords have been prosecuted for war crimes committed during Liberia's civil wars.

This book narrates these civil wars and their aftermath from the perspective of 133 women war veterans who reside in the towns of Ganta, Gbarnga, Kakata and Monrovia in Liberia. In doing so, it provides a new perspective on Liberian society both during and after the conflicts and complements the already-existing literature on the region. Furthermore, the book reaffirms the notion that each conflict environment has its own gender dynamics that need to be carefully considered in the disarmament, demobilization and reintegration phases. If these dynamics are neglected, as was the case in Liberia and as is exemplified throughout the book, girl and women veterans are typically left to fend for themselves.

# Introduction: Hell is the absolute lack of being heard

*Samuel*: The problem with the show is that there are no women. I mean, in a way that women used to be there. They only have their girlfriends here, just to have sex. But it wasn't so.

*Angela*: That is true.

*Grace*: This is a show, it is not perfect.

*Juliet*: The events that are taking place in the show, many are real even though there are mistakes as well. Many of these things were happening. But the big mistake is that there are no women except as lovers. They should have put women there, more women. Going to the frontline and leading women and men. That is a real mistake.

*Leena*: The kinds of girls and women you have in the movie, do people [former female and male soldiers] calculate them when I ask about the number of girls and boys, women and men in each faction?

*Angela*: No. They don't count them. They are just along [with] the male soldiers.

Under the piercing noise of the generator next door we barely hear each other, let alone the soundtrack of *Johnny Mad Dog* (2008), an award-winning movie on child soldiering in Liberia by Jean-Stéphane Sauvaire.[1] The racket of the generator does not matter too much, though, since all but Grace have seen the film before, and they can explain the unclear scenes to her. In addition to myself and Grace, who was first captured by Charles Taylor's AFL and later its opposing force LURD in the second Liberian civil war, wartime commanders Samuel and Juliet are present, as is Angela, who spent some five years on the war front with three different factions fighting in Liberia's first civil war. Now, at my request, these former child soldiers are gathered here to review a film. It is one of those extremely sweaty July afternoons in a Monrovian shanty town, and there is neither window nor fan to carry the stagnant petrol-filled air from the tiny room. It is time to begin.

After a good two hours – we have had to pause the film a few times to fill up the generator and get some fresh air – the moment of judgement has arrived: how was the movie? Good entertainment, all the reviewers conclude. But everyone also agrees on the fact that there is one big mistake in the script if comparing the film to how 'it used to be in wartime': women actors are only given roles as lovers, victims and sexual objects. No girl of women soldiers, let alone commanders, are present in the movie.

Yet it is often precisely from movies, TV series or other forms of popular culture that we gain our modest understanding of the realities on the frontline. Over and over again the (white) male soldier is placed at the centre of these pieces, typically framing him as the rescuer; the hero; the survivor. However, among those individuals having witnessed warfare first-hand it is rather rare to find someone who would disagree with the famous phrase 'war is hell'.[2] But if hell can additionally be described as the 'absolute lack of being heard', as Mikhail Bakhtin (1986: 126) insightfully argued three decades ago, can it also be understood as the absolute lack of being *seen*? To be invisible, overlooked, just air in the eyes of the people around? And then again, how devastating can it be to first experience one form of hell on the frontline and then go through another as a forgotten war veteran in the immediate post-war period? To not be accepted as someone who has survived hell?

Scholars such as Nordstrom (1998), Lorentzen and Turpin (1998), Mazurana and McKay (2001; and McKay and Mazurana 2004), Shepler (2002) and Coulter (2009) have led the way in revealing the lived experiences of the often-forgotten girl and women soldiers of various parts of the Global South. Popular studies on child soldiering (e.g. Rosen 2005; Honwana 2006; Singer 2006; Wessells 2006; Gates and Reich 2010; Özerdem and Podder 2011; Drumbl 2012) also typically recognize the roles of girls in the ranks, albeit, in many instances, in thin separate sections that emphasize sexual abuse. Nonetheless, systematic inquiries about the realities of female war veterans in the Global South that are based on first-hand research data gathered more than ten years after the end of the conflict are, according to my knowledge, extremely rare. If, however, we wish to learn about the long-term impacts of warfare and the numerous post-war reintegration programs on former female soldiers' lives, and hence be better equipped to address the needs of girl and women war veterans in the future, it is necessary to collect first-hand empirical data from various environments around the world.

This book reviews *the Liberian civil wars and their aftermath from the perspective of women war veterans*, thus providing one data set for increasing our understanding of girl and women soldiering in the Global South. The leading roles in this project are played by a variety of extremely brave and resilient individuals, such as Angela, Grace and Juliet, all of whom we met above. Their roles are backed up by a number of supporting actors similar to Samuel. Since the category of girl is highly contentious in Liberia, as is briefly discussed in what follows, and as all the research participants in this project came of age during the wars or at least in the post-war period, I have chosen to utilize the terms of *girl and women soldiers* or *female soldiers*, depending on the context. What is common to all the 133 women war veterans interviewed for this research project is that they took part in either one or both of Liberia's civil wars (1989–1997 and 2000–2003) in various capacities, thus acting as (child) soldiers.[3]

When discussing child soldiers and their post-war trajectories, it is important to remember that the vague categories of childhood, youthhood and adulthood are anything but universal (e.g. Abbink 2005: 5–6; Clark-Kazak 2009: 1308–9; Christiansen et al. 2006). Formally, the Children's Law of Liberia treats any person under the age of eighteen as a child (Government of Liberia 2011). In the Revised National Youth Policy, on the other hand, youth is considered to be between the ages of fifteen and twenty-five (Youthpolicy. org 2014), whereas some religious groups in Liberia understand anyone under the age of thirty-five as youth. The definition of 'youthhood' can thus vary enormously from person to person in Liberia and beyond (e.g. Utas 2008), and age should be considered more as a social construction than a bare number. This problematic and its gendered implications are further touched upon in Chapter 4.

## Challenging the taken-for-granted

The research data for this book were gathered between the autumn of 2012 and the summer of 2014 – nine to eleven years after the end of the last Liberian civil war. During these two years, I undertook three separate field research trips to four counties in Liberia, spending a combined length of five months in the country, and set out to answer the following questions:

- What kinds of roles did girl and women soldiers undertake in Liberia's civil wars? (Chapter 2)
- Were these roles recognized in the Disarmament, Demobilization and Reintegration (DDR) programs

implemented after the wars? And if they were, how did these programs succeed in their tasks? (Chapter 3)
- In which types of positions and roles do women war veterans find themselves in today's Liberia? What are some of their coping strategies? (Chapter 4)
- What kinds of aspirations and dreams do these women have today? (Chapter 5)

As I demonstrate in Chapter 1, choosing the most accurate research methods in the social sciences is often a tricky task, but especially so if the *life-worlds* (Husserl 1970) of the research participants differ radically from those of the researcher. I had realized already in the planning stages of the project that I would always be a true outsider in relation to Liberian women war veterans – owing not only to our cultural differences and personal histories, but also to our radically different living environments, social class, and trust in the institutions and societal structures of our daily lives. If I were only to use conventional social scientific research methods, such as structured or semi-structured interviews alone, I would inevitably come to practice a form of epistemic violence (Spivak 1988) through the process of formulating the research questions/themes for the interviews to be conducted. In the words of James Davies (2010: 13), the challenge was that 'those aspects of reality which sit beyond the reach of the specified method, by being seen as methodologically inaccessible, are somehow depreciated in their empirical existence'. Indeed, maybe the actual goal of being 'scientific' might produce 'incomplete knowledge and, by extension, unscientific results?' (Brigg and Bleiker 2010).

Hence the question was: how could the level of epistemic violence be diminished as much as possible in this specific context? If 'traditional' empiricism – the view that seeks to separate the observer and the observed – was not sufficient in this case, maybe I needed to turn towards *radical empiricism*, which 'denies the validity of such cuts and makes the interplay between these domains the focus of its interest' (Jackson 1989: 3; James and Perry 1912). Instead of trying to 'purify subjectivity' through the selected methodological choices, maybe I should consider 'how far methods mould subjectivity' (Davies 2010: 13)?

With these epistemic challenges in mind, I accidentally came across some non-academic visual experiments I had carried out in Dakar a few years earlier (see Chapter 1), and began to contemplate the possible use of photography in studying 'the Other'. I soon learnt about an ethnographic method called *auto-photography*, in which the researcher conducts exploratory interviews and chooses key interviewees from this group, distributes cameras to key participants, asks them to take photographs in line with predetermined themes, and carries out individual photo-elicitation interviews.[4] In these interviews, the photographs are placed one by one in front of the photographer/interviewee, who explains why she decided to take the photograph in question and what the insights of the picture reveal about the provided theme. I decided to give this research approach a chance: it was radical, different, and, most importantly, it was something that seemed to have the potential to provide space for the research participants themselves to describe their life-worlds to me in a non-imposing manner. In addition, with this method, the research participants would not be forced to discuss painful and traumatic issues against their will.

My first field research trip took place in 2012, when I headed to Liberia with a suitcase packed with donated film cameras. Being aware of the dangers of 'victimcy talk' (Utas 2011: 218), I had decided to try to locate research participants mainly from outside the NGO sector and managed to find a woman who would accommodate me for the first month of my stay. The house was situated in a very poor neighbourhood in the capital city of Monrovia, and I soon came to learn that my caring and generous landlady was operating a small-scale drug business from the house. In addition to selling small commodities, she occasionally prepared 'eggnog' spiced with cannabis. This clever, albeit risky, move allowed her to gain some extra income, but also created a small-scale security network since the house had become a favourite hangout spot for the local youth. In an area where armed robberies frequently took place and the police were seen as more of a danger than a security provider, it was certainly wise to have numerous eyes watching over the house. It was in this house I first got to know some former child soldiers. After observing my behaviour and asking about my intentions for a while, several young war veterans began to approach me themselves. Through the contacts provided by these individuals, I was later able to locate the majority of the research participants residing in the various shanty towns of Monrovia. An enormous help in the task of finding research participants was also Pastor Jessie King, who put me in contact with Quita Saybay Tokpah and Philip McKay, both of whom were crucially important in locating individuals from Gbarnga and Ganta. Furthermore, Edwin Neoh kindly brought together a large number of women veterans in Kakata. A small group of interviewees in Monrovia was also gathered with the generous aid of Emmanuel Carto from Concern Worldwide Liberia.

Glorious Neoh acted as a highly committed and thorough research assistant for the first two field research periods in 2012 and 2013. When Glorious later began her nursing studies, her job was undertaken by another priceless assistant, Jessica Doe. Not only did these women sometimes act as my translators, but, most importantly, they were also cultural guides and trusted sisters, who would patiently explain many unwritten cultural rules concerning everything from the right way to wash laundry to how to use the correct hand signals for getting around using the public cars and motorbikes. It was with the assistance of Glorious, Jessica and Quita that I conducted the 133 exploratory interviews in Monrovia, Kakata, Gbarnga and Ganta (see also Chapter 1).

On the one hand, the purpose of the first round of interviews was to systemically map basic information about the participation of girls and women in the various warring factions operating in Liberia's civil wars. On the other hand, another goal was to locate key interviewees to represent the various forms of female soldiering in the country. The aim was to find representatives from different ranks and factions, as well as interviewees from the diverse living environments in which these women had ended up in the post-war period. After the selection process, the key participants were requested to photograph their lives under the themes of *My current realities* and *My aspirations/ dreams* – a process that produced thousands of pictures and extremely fascinating photo-elicitation interviews. To systematize these data, I transcribed all the interviews (exploratory interviews and photo elicitation interviews) and used the NVivo program to code them into three sections: life prior to the war(s), life during the war(s), and life after the war(s). Within these large sections, numerous subthemes arising from the interview data were coded, and systematic background statistics drafted (age, group, rank, reason for joining, reason for leaving, etc.), to which I refer in what follows.

In addition to these data, I organized countless informal discussions with former boy and men soldiers, community elders, and women and men prostitutes as well as group discussions with local journalists (one group); prostitutes (three groups); and a village meeting in close proximity to the town of Gbarnga.

Being a woman war veteran in Liberia carries a very strong stigma. Although most of the interviewees were graciously welcomed home by their families after the war(s) (see Chapter 3), the overwhelming majority have shared their histories as soldiers with very few individuals. Some have even hidden their past from their partners, and many are worried about possible consequences for their children if information about their veteran status were to spread further. Therefore, all the research participants' names are pseudonyms. In addition, and unusually for the auto-photographic methodology, no photographs can be found in this book. However, since visual components carry a crucial methodological value in the research project (see Chapter 1), it would have been a shame not to include *any* visualizations in the book besides the front cover. The photographs taken by the research participants are in and of themselves components that not only bring to light some aspects of social life in Liberia which might otherwise be difficult to perceive, but are also elements that 'record the visual perceptions of those who made them' (Wagner 2006: 57).

For these overlapping reasons, I approached Emmi Nieminen,[5] a renowned comics artist and illustrator, who kindly took up the challenge of creating illustrations for the book that are based on the photographs taken by the research participants, but are also produced in a manner that blurs individual identities. Owing to the significant number of photographs, we decided that Emmi should have some artistic freedom in combining various types of pictures. The illustrations marking the beginning of each new chapter have therefore been inspired by the photographs the research participants have taken themselves to describe their experiences and aspirations under the given chapter title.

## Women war veterans as social rafters

In the chapters that follow, Liberian women war veterans are understood as social rafters. By drawing from and redeveloping the concept of social navigation (Vigh 2006a, 2006b, 2009), it is argued that the 'tactic agency' (De Certeau 1984; Utas 2005b; Vigh 2006a) of these social rafters is severely limited in comparison with their more fortunate peers. In this endeavor, the Liberian street milieu is understood as a complicated (in)security environment, an interconnected system of rivers and rivulets where each small stream has its specific task in the production of (in)securities. Hence, time and again, social rafters are forced to resort to peculiar and potentially dangerous arrangements in order to feel safe and secure, arrangements that are scrutinized in different sections of this book.

Although the living environments of these social rafters are extremely challenging, each period of chaos entails a seed of hope.

Indeed, my initial suggestion was to use 'Hope is not gone altogether', an expression used by Veral at the very end of her exploratory interview in the town of Gbarnga in 2012, as the title of this book. As we will later come to learn, Veral was a multitasker and fighter in the first Liberian civil war who was captured and forced into a very abusive relationship with a well-known commander. During the time of our latest encounter in the autumn of 2013, Veral still suffered from some severe physical and mental injuries from the war that were affecting not only her own well-being, but also her relationship with her fiancé and children. Despite the numerous hardships she had encountered (and was still encountering) Veral had managed to find some kind of peace within herself and persuasively argued that 'hope is not gone altogether' since she still had 'life inside' her.

This book draws heavily on the vast empirical material but inevitably some theoretical key concepts are woven in among the empirical findings. In addition to social rafting, a crucial theoretical concept and methodological signpost in the project is *curious contrapuntalism*. Curious contrapuntalism can be described as an imaginary map which guides both the writer and the reader in the task of situating the rivers of (in)securities flowing to the oceans of the world. Curious contrapuntalism represents a postcolonial feminist worldview; a way to critically observe and challenge overlapping and constantly evolving social realities. In essence, the approach combines Cynthia Enloe's concept of curious feminism with Edward Said's contrapuntal reading. Like social rafting, curious contrapuntalism builds upon existing academic work, but it also adds new layers to the theoretical insights of prominent scholars from postcolonial feminist theory, and, most importantly, from the empirical findings from Liberia. In this research project theory has been tested in a specific empirical context, and when reasoned inadequate, further developed to bridge the gap between theory and practice.

*Curious feminism*, developed by the celebrated feminist IR scholar Cynthia Enloe, is the starting point of curious contrapuntalism. Enloe defines feminist curiosity as a 'curiosity that provokes serious questioning about the workings of masculinized and feminized meanings. It is the sort of curiosity that prompts one to pay attention to things that conventionally are treated as if they were either "natural" or, even if acknowledged to be artificial, are imagined to be "trivial," that is, imagined to be without explanatory significance' (Enloe 2004a: loc. 1973). In other words, employing 'a feminist curiosity means asking questions about things that others hoped they would just take for granted' (Comfort 2011: 41), such as why are we discussing 'cheap labour' instead of 'labour made cheap' (Enloe 2004a: loc. 40–41). Or what, in fact, do loaded terms such as 'natural', 'tradition' or 'always' mean in the specific context at hand (ibid.: loc. 26–32)?

The other foundation block of curious contrapuntalism, *contrapuntal reading/method*, borrowed by Edward Said from 'Western art music',[6] overlaps with Enloe's feminist curiosity in many ways. Like the latter, the former encourages the reader/observer to challenge the 'taken for granted'/'the natural' by trying to tease out the unwritten stories and realities behind the text at hand (Said 1994: 78–80). Said (ibid.) urges us to 'read back' the text and attempt to see the story behind the story; to critically ask why we are told certain details while some other seemingly important particularities are left out. By trying to understand what kind of power structures we take for granted and by being curious about the forces that keep the powerless in their precarious positions, both Said and Enloe encourage us to be wary of power at all times and side with the most unprivileged (Said 1996: 32–3; Enloe 2004a). In addition, Said and Enloe argue that power and nationalisms are always interrelated and are therefore deeply suspicious of projects disguised in nationalistic uniforms. As an alternative, they call for international secular humanism, for worlding social realities and human experiences, and for seeing the world as a shared, common place for all individuals and peoples. It can thus be argued that curious contrapuntalism is a dear sister of peace research, whose initiator, Johan Galtung (1969: 17), stated that for a peace researcher there cannot be any home country but the world.

To be an intellectual in today's world is therefore a challenging and energy-consuming task (Enloe 2004a: loc. 29–34) that requires, among other things, undertaking continuous curiosity (Enloe 2013); treating 'every day as a new day at school' and thus considering oneself an amateur rather than a professional (Said 1996: 82); observing who is taken seriously and why (Enloe 2013: loc. 137) and, overall, developing a 'global intellectual posture' that dares to question power even when it might be personally or otherwise risky (Said 1996; Biswas 2007).

In the rest of the Introduction, I detail Enloe's and Said's theoretical insights and add some components from feminist postcolonial theory in order to pave the way for a profound definition of curious contrapuntalism. The Introduction ends with an invitation to the reader to practice curious contrapuntalism during the process of reading the book. Indeed, the overall aim of the chapter is to create a composition that allows for the reader/spectator to become a vulnerable observer (Behar 1996) with a curious attitude who both recognizes the dangers of dominant narratives but also reflects critically upon their own subject position within the research/reading process at hand. Instead of offering a straightforward and well-detailed map, curious contrapuntalism is understood here as a multi-layered world atlas of plots, narratives and perspectives that does not aim to simplify and generalize, but rather make visible the streams and islets that are typically zoomed out on and considered as 'insignificant' or 'trivial'. It is maintained throughout the book that complexity does not have to mean chaos, but, when analysed with contrapuntal curiosity, it can rather be understood as a colourful and fascinating patchwork.[7]

## Practicing feminist curiosity as a researcher

Cynthia Enloe developed the concept of feminist curiosity at the beginning of the new millennium when she was frequently invited to speak to various types of audiences in different parts of the world. While planning her lectures, Enloe realized that she would need to present concrete examples of how feminist analyses could contribute in making complex social realities more approachable. She became 'curious about curiosity and its absence' (Enloe 2004a: loc. 39) and the power structures that were leaning on our enduring absence of curiosity (ibid.: loc. 44). Why, for example, is sewing work in textile factories in the Global South typically undertaken by women (Enloe 2000a: 162)? And why are so many of the celebrated fashion designers men? Who, on the other hand, has the incentive and power to reproduce the idea that women are 'in their nature' more peaceful than men?

Enloe (2013: loc. 578) maintains that the everyday may be opened anew from a very revealing perspective by asking the simple question '"Where are the women?" — in the history of colonialism and anticolonialism; in the international textile industry; in the political economies of rubber, sugar, tea, and bananas; on and around military overseas bases; in the growing tourism industry; and in globalized domestic work.'

As Enloe indicates, girls and women are only placed in supporting roles in the majority of studies and popular presentations about child soldiering. This is problematic since girls may comprise up to 30 percent (McKay and Mazurana 2004: 115) of the world's

300,000 child soldiers (Singer 2010: 93) – a number that is evidently contested and impossible to verify. Even the figure of 30 percent may be an underestimation since girls are made invisible on multiple, overlapping grounds. Although girls and women do not always take roles on the frontlines, they indeed *are* there in the battlefields and their surroundings; for instance, as cooks, cleaners, camp followers, sexual slaves, girlfriends, and teen mothers (see Chapter 2). This kind of ignorance is not only problematic for academic reasons but might additionally have very dire consequences when different types of support initiatives, such as the Disarmament, Demobilization and Reintegration (DDR) programs, are planned and undertaken (see Chapter 3). It is time to take girl and women soldiers *seriously*.

Young girl and women soldiers are part of masculinist military structures that cannot be ignored when trying to understand their realities in the forces and in the post-war periods. On many occasions, Cynthia Enloe has directed her feminist curiosity towards militarism, and defines it as an *ideology* embraced by an institution, person or community that contains a set of core beliefs: (a) that armed force is the ultimate resolver of tensions; (b) that human nature is prone to conflict; (c) that having enemies is a natural condition; (d) that hierarchical relations produce effective action; (e) that a state without a military is naive, scarcely modern, and barely legitimate; (f) that in times of crisis those who are feminine need armed protection; and (g) that in times of crisis any man who refuses to engage in armed violent action is jeopardizing his own status as a manly man (Enloe 2002: 23–4).

Related to and intertwined with the ideology of militarism, *militarization* is a complicated socio-political process in which the core beliefs of militarism are carefully implanted in a certain society, community or organization (ibid.: 24). In the ensuing chapters, I will, for instance, explore the militarization of the international aid industry in Liberia (see Chapter 3) as well as post-war Liberian society in general (see Chapter 4).

To end this short introduction to the insights of feminist curiosity, a few remarks have to be made on what it means, in practice, to take 'mundane' individuals and different types of research materials *seriously* (Enloe 2013). First, it entails taking into account multiple and possibly surprising sources of information alongside official data, such as people's behaviour models and casual conversations within powerful institutions (Enloe 2004a: loc. 69). Second, it grants considerable evidential value to fictional literature, personal memories and ethnographies alongside 'traditional' scholarly articles and official documents. A simultaneous reading of these different sources can produce 'thickly local' and at the same time 'broadly comparative' understandings of a certain phenomenon (ibid.: loc. 2238; Enloe 2013: loc. 787); an analysis that has the ability to concurrently investigate both structures and culture (ibid.: loc. 1055). This does not, however, mean that all research material should be given equal status. Rather, the aim is to understand different materials as complementary information sources concerning a certain phenomenon. All in all, it can be summarized that Enloe's views about simultaneous reading closely resemble Said's contrapuntal method.

## Worlding texts with the contrapuntal approach

Edward Said (1935–2003) was not only an eminent scholar and well-known activist, but also a classically trained musician. He fell in love with classical music as a young boy and nurtured this affection throughout his life. Said's affinity trickled down to his academic work and inspired the development of the method he labelled *contrapuntal reading* (see, e.g., De Groot 2005).

In the world of music, the term counterpoint was first utilized in the fourteenth century 'to describe the combination of simultaneously sounding musical lines according to a system of rules'.[8] These rules targeted at composers have fluctuated from extreme strictness to more flexible versions and are still a constant topic of debate. Nevertheless, some common features can be traced from these variegated rules. Roger Bullivant (1984: 501), for example, remarks that in counterpoint all voices are potentially equal; individual parts form a continuum so that when one voice ceases, another will carry on; and several scales and keys can exist concurrently. For a non-musician, the explanation provided by Benjamin Boretz (2001: 177), who cites the Montpellier Codex, might be useful:

> It is hard to write a beautiful song. It is harder to write several individually beautiful songs that, when sung simultaneously, sound as a more beautiful polyphonic whole. The internal structures that create each of the voices separately must contribute to the emergent structure of the polyphony, which in turn must reinforce and comment on the structures of the individual voices. The way this is accomplished in detail is what I am calling 'counterpoint.'

Said introduced the term contrapuntal for the first time in his essay 'Reflections on exile' (originally published in 1984). As the title of the essay indicates, the text revolves around the concept of an *exile*, who, according to Said, has a tendency to see 'the entire world as a foreign land'. This capability of having an original vision creates a 'plurality of vision'; 'an awareness of simultaneous dimensions'; a chance to reflect upon and compare experiences from various environments concurrently – in essence, a state of being in the world that is *contrapuntal* (Said 2000: 186).

However, Said's fullest elaboration on contrapuntal reading can be found in *Culture and Imperialism* (1994). According to Said (ibid.: 36), a contrapuntal perspective is needed because: '[W]e must be able to think through and interpret together experiences that are discrepant, each with its particular agenda and pace of development, its own internal formations, its internal coherence and system of external relationships, all of them co-existing and interacting with others.'

Instead of offering a precise methodological toolbox on how contrapuntal reading can be practiced, Said has unfortunately scattered his ideas on the matter throughout *Culture and Imperialism*. This is one of the weakest points of his elaboration, as Wilson (1994) also remarks: Said seems to believe that practical examples are enough in their own right. Therefore, we are left with no alternative than to turn our attention to these examples.

> In practical terms, 'contrapuntal reading' as I have called it means reading a text with an understanding of what is involved when an author shows, for instance, that a colonial sugar plantation is seen as important to the process of maintaining a particular style of life in England. [...] In reading a text, one must open it out both to what went into it and to what its author excluded. [...] In addition, one must connect the structures of a narrative to the ideas, concepts, experiences from which it draws support. Conrad's Africans, for example, come from a huge library of Africanism, so to speak, as well as from Conrad's personal experiences. [...] This is, perhaps, to overstate the matter, but I want to make the point that far from Heart of Darkness and its image of Africa being 'only' literature, the work is extraordinarily caught up in, is indeed an organic part of, the 'scramble for Africa' that was contemporary with Conrad's composition. (Said 1994: 78–80)

The purpose of contrapuntal reading is thus to attempt to find a path behind a text; to 'read back' by contextualizing the text and its author; to try to understand what is taken as a fact and what is being excluded; in essence, its purpose is to provide equal space for individual voices that are overlapping and intertwined, yet unique.

Contrapuntal reading has mainly been utilized in literature studies, Said's home discipline. However, Aamir Mufti[9] (2005: 477) remarks that many possible uses of contrapuntality in academia and beyond remain unexplored. Geeta Chowdhry (2007) continues Mufti's line of reasoning by exploring the possible applications of contrapuntal reading in the discipline of IR. She argues that the method might 'engender the articulation of exiled voices' in the discipline (ibid.: 103). Contrapuntality, Chowdhry maintains, should not be mistaken as an appeal for postmodern plurality where each voice is given equal status, but rather should be treated as an attempt at 'worlding' and historicizing the texts, institutions and practices (ibid.: 105). According to Chowdhry (ibid.: 106), 'a contrapuntal story about IR narrates a different international relations into existence, one in which the experiences and histories of the privileged are read against the histories of the dispossessed and marginalised.' In a discipline that tends to place enormous weight on institutions, states and power structures, that 'outsources' the political to social movements by claiming to be value-free (Seppälä 2017), and is self-referential to the extent that has been described by Henri Vogt (2008: 366) as 'intellectual group masturbation *par excellence*', this is certainly a welcome approach.

## Curious contrapuntalism as a theoretical backbone

While there seem to be numerous similarities between *curious feminism* and *contrapuntal method*, as presented in the previous sections, some differences can also be found. Most importantly, whereas Enloe seeks to examine social realities mainly by emphasizing and exploring the life-worlds of women, Said's analytical starting point is in (post)colonialism. In addition, Enloe concentrates especially on societal phenomena and everyday lived experiences while Said applies contrapuntal reading and analysis mainly to textual material. I do not find these differences problematic, however, but rather exciting and beneficial: in a *contrapuntal* spirit Enloe's and Said's in and of themselves beautiful narratives can reinforce and interconnect with one another, hence producing a beautiful contrapuntal whole. Nevertheless, since the approach developed here has both a feminist and postcolonial background, I find it is essential to finalize *curious contrapuntalism* by adding some insights from postcolonial feminists themselves.

Both Cynthia Enloe and Edward Said led scholarship in their respective fields and beyond. As rare as it is to find a book in the field of feminist IR without a reference to Enloe, it is just as difficult to find one in postcolonial studies without Said's name. Postcolonial feminist theory strives to combine these fields of inquiry by inserting race into mainstream feminist theory and by bringing feminist perspectives into postcolonial theory (Lewis and Mills 2003: 3). Postcolonial feminism, sometimes referred to as Third World feminism, gained ground in the 1980s when black feminists in particular began to question the universality of the feminist movement of the time. Feminists of color (e.g. Moraga and Anzaldúa 1981; hooks 1982, 1984; Davis 1983; Lorde 1984; Amos and Parmar 1984) argued that Western feminism had imperialistic roots, was in essence racist, and therefore did not manage to capture the multifaceted challenges faced by women of color in various social environments. As Amos and Parmar (1984) state in their powerful article 'Challenging imperial feminism': 'There is little recognition in the women's movement of the ways in which the gains made by white women have been and still are at the expense of Black women' (p. 5), whose experiences are measured 'against their own, labelling it as in some way lacking, then looking for ways in which it might be possible to harness the Black women's experience to their own' (p. 11).

The debates that had mainly dealt with the injustices faced by the black women in the West/North soon spread to tackle the experiences of the women of the Global South. Already in the early 1980s, Adrienne Rich had argued against universalistic claims on womanhood by raising the question of 'politics of location'. Rich maintained that she herself, for example, as a white North American feminist, needed to take responsibility for her whiteness and geographical background as 'points of location' that shaped her 'ways of seeing' and 'ideas of who and what was important' (Rich 1985: 9–13).

A critique of the ways of seeing, defining and analysing the 'Third World Woman' was also central to Chandra Talpade Mohanty's highly influential article 'Under Western eyes' (1984).[10] Mohanty identified some of the main problems in the Western feminist discourse about women of the Global South. First, she challenged the notion of global sisterhood, wherein women were seen as a singular category of analysis bound together by shared oppression.

In this discourse, as victims of male violence, as dependants, without considering specific historical, economic and social surroundings such as class, these ahistorical bodies could be saved only by development (ibid.: 337–43). '*Development* here becomes the all-time equalizer' (ibid.: 343, emphasis in original) that places gender 'over and above everything else', thus producing 'ahistorical, universal unity between women based on a generalized notion of their subordination' (ibid.: 344).

Mohanty also confronted the methods typically used to demonstrate the global subordination of women. Relying primarily on numbers (e.g. what percentage of women wear the veil) and on 'universal' concepts (e.g. marriage, sexual division of labor, reproduction), these methodological choices once again ignored the historical and cultural specificities and treated superficially similar situations as identical (pp. 346–8). Mohanty concluded that it is 'only in so far as "Woman/Women" and "the East" are defined as *Others*, or as *peripheral*, that (Western) Man/Humanism can represent him/itself as the center. It is not the center that determines the periphery, but the periphery that, in its boundedness, determines the center' (p. 353, emphasis in original).

In this book, the dichotomy between 'centre' and 'periphery' is investigated on two complementary levels: the 'centres' are the West/North and the masculine boy/man soldier, and their opposing, often neglected 'peripheries' are the Global South and the feminine girl/woman soldier. As important as it is to investigate the 'peripheries' themselves, it is just as important to ask what these margins can narrate and reveal about the various types of centres.

'The ghost of black feminism', as Carbin and Edenheim (2013: 243) fittingly describe it, also made an impact on the so-called mainstream feminism. The fear was that concerns about race, class and ethnicity, for instance, could weaken the understanding of gender as the number-one source of inequality, and in this way threaten the existence of feminist theory itself. *Intersectionality* – the understanding that different forms of oppression such as gender, race, class and disability often intersect and have a tendency to reinforce one another – seemed to provide a bridge between the two opposing camps, and soon became a standard concept adopted by the majority of feminist scholars and activists regardless of their scholarly background (ibid.: 243–4). Although the roots of intersectionality are deeply interwoven with the histories of the anti-slavery movement, black feminism and postcolonial feminism, the term itself was first coined in the field of law by Kimberlé Crenshaw in 1989. By exploring three court cases from an intersectional viewpoint, Crenshaw (1989: 166) came into the conclusion that:

> If any real efforts are to be made to free Black people of the constraints and conditions that characterize racial subordination, then theories and strategies purporting to reflect the black community's needs must include an analysis of sexism and patriarchy. Similarly, feminism must include an analysis of race if it hopes to express the aspirations of non-white women. Neither black liberationist politics nor feminist theory can ignore the intersectional experience of those whom the movements claim as their respective constituents.[11]

As a method of analysis, *curious contrapuntalism* is both postcolonial and feminist and therefore necessarily intersectional. It strives not to generalize and simplify, but rather to practice curiosity towards the life-worlds and social surroundings of individuals who are discriminated against on multiple grounds, but who, nonetheless, manage to survive in various rivers of insecurities and even find occasional joy in their daily encounters. Using these locally situated life stories, similarities and patterns are then outlined and some forms of generalizations can be made. In this book, however, these conclusions are not primarily drawn about women in general or even about Liberian women. What can be traced through curious contrapuntalism are the current lives and aspirations of women war veterans in Liberia. In this manner these layers narrate a story of post-conflict Liberia that can then be contrasted and compared to other existing stories about the state of the country today, as well as to the realities of (women) war veterans in other parts of the world.

Finally, a few words on the importance of visuality and visuals must also be included in this section, since looking, visualizing and seeing have always been at the centre of postcolonial feminism. The representations of the black female body in Western artwork, popular culture and journalism are deeply embedded in the legacies of colonialism, race and sexuality (see, e.g., Willis and Williams 2002). In addition to visual objectification, the black history entails the politics of the 'gaze'. bell hooks (1992), for instance, remarks that slaves were often denied their right to gaze and were punished for doing so at the wrong time. She emphasizes, however, that the 'oppositional gaze' can never be truly tamed: 'Spaces of agency exist for black people, wherein we can both interrogate the gaze of the Other but also look back, and at one another, naming what we see' (ibid.: 116).

The 'gaze', then, is always informed by the life-world (Husserl 1970) and the politics of location (Rich 1985) of the spectator.

Against this historical background, the 'politics of location' would have inevitably caused huge challenges for this project if photographs taken by the respondents had been placed here in their original form. Perceiving and understanding are always limited by the previous knowledge and values of the spectator, and photographs can 'speak' very little without substantive explanatory notes (see also Chapter 1). We, the author and illustrator, believe that this dilemma can partly be overcome with carefully planned and executed illustrations that strive to combine both the visual and verbal sides of the auto-photographic interviews conducted about a certain social phenomenon.

## Conclusion

Throughout this Introduction, I have sought to exemplify that curious contrapuntalism is a combination of two types of curiosity that aim to render the mind and senses susceptible to observing the world's phenomena in a novel and stimulating way. The goal of curious contrapuntalism is in essence normative – to side with the 'subaltern' – by teasing out the various forms of discrimination against these 'Others'. In this task, not only academic material but also products of popular culture and street knowledge are taken seriously.[12] Whereas both Enloe and Said concentrate largely on textual analyses and oral histories, however, in curious contrapuntalism *curiosity also materializes via visual representations*. These representations can be found in the photographs produced by the research participants, in the photo-elicitation interviews, as well as in the visualizations scattered throughout the book. In addition, it must be understood that all shades of information are not treated as equals, but rather as complementary and overlapping interpretations of the same phenomenon.

When observing the world's phenomena (such as girl and women soldiers of Liberia) with a curiously contrapuntal attitude, it becomes evident that the issues and bodies that might at first appear 'meaningless' or 'insignificant' can actually be the most important things to investigate; not only in and of themselves, but also in order to comprehend the forces and powers that have condemned these matters as 'meaningless'. In what follows, the exploratory and photo interviews of Liberia's women war veterans form the basis – in music terminology the thematic subject or the *soggetto* (Sachs 2001: 558) – for a feminist contrapuntal understanding of these women's post-war actualities. In this composition, official documents, formal interviews, academic texts and even novels, folktales, poems, pictures and local gossip are mirrored and compared to this underlying *soggetto*. The role of the researcher and illustrator is that of composers, whose *state of being in the world* and *politics of location* profoundly influence the final output. The guidelines of the composition, nonetheless, are not drafted in absolute freedom by the composers, but are deeply embedded in the academic community's underlying 'contrapuntal rule' of academic integrity. Finally, it is up to the audience – the reader/observer – to evaluate the quality and value of the final composition.

# 1
# Auto-photographing rivers of insecurities

More than a quarter of a century ago Gayatri Spivak (1988: 66) posed her famous question 'Can the subaltern speak?'. After critically examining the works of Marx, Gramsci, Foucault and Deleuze, among others, Spivak's answer was 'no' – at the end of the day, the subaltern cannot speak if academics and other intellectuals continue to scrutinize the 'Other' only through their own 'universal' paradigms. According to Spivak, these paradigms tend to have two implicit problems. On the one hand, the heterogeneity of the subaltern mass is not recognized. On the other hand, the intellectual is considered – falsely – as someone who can 'speak for' the subaltern. Drawing upon the work of Michel Foucault, she thus argues that intellectuals (herself included) inevitably practice epistemic violence when they force the subaltern to speak the language of the dominant elite or remain virtually unheard. Spivak's essay has provoked a fair amount of criticism, due also to the author's complicated use of language, yet has continued to be seen as one of the most influential texts in postcolonial studies (see, e.g., Didur and Heffernan 2003). One reason for this success may be that her main concern remains pertinent throughout the spectrum of social sciences: how can we investigate the 'Other', the 'subaltern', without imposing our implicit ontological and epistemological preconceptions on the subjects and topics we are trying to comprehend?

In this chapter, I explain and justify the main methodological choices of this book by suggesting that the auto-photographic research approach can provide a useful alternative for shifting agency from the researcher to the research participants, hence amplifying the voices of the 'Others'. I am certainly not arguing that this research approach would somehow magically solve the problems of representation, nor that any research setting could ever be value-free. However, I do claim that when the auto-photographic method and the photo-elicitation technique are brought together as a methodological set in a *curiously contrapuntal* spirit, they carry the potential to reduce epistemic violence, especially in risky environments. Moreover, this methodological combination might prove useful in places where cultural biases and unequal power relations between the researcher and research participants may unintentionally distort research results.

## Visualizing the 'pain of others'

The ethical struggles related to observing and visualizing pain are anything but new. For example, in Book IV of Plato's (2012) *Republic*, there is the story of Leontius, the son of Aglaion, who comes across dead people lying at the executioner's feet. Leontius feels both a desire to stare at the corpses, but is also disgusted and abhorred by the sight. He covers his eyes and struggles for a time, but finally gives in to the desire to see and forces his eyes wide open. Leontius rushes towards the corpses, shouting: 'Look, ye wretches, take your fill of the fair sight.' It is apparent that Leontius is going through an emotional struggle. He has both the human desire to observe, to know what is really happening around him, but at the same time he realizes that not looking would most likely be more ethical and respectful towards the 'Other'.

Whenever I present my research project to individuals and audiences from various educational and institutional backgrounds, the ghost of Leontius seems to somehow loom in the background. 'Can I see the pictures?'; 'Oh, it would be so interesting to explore the photographs'; 'You just have to put at least some pictures in your book – how can we otherwise know that they exist?' are just some of the various comments concerning the photographs taken by the research participants. Indeed, it seems that although visuals have recently been granted a considerable amount of attention – for example, in critical international relations theory[1] – the *production of visuals* as a *research method* still remains in the margins of the discipline. Therefore, I have decided to begin my methodological introduction by further explaining and justifying the often challenging and complicated visual choices made in the course of the project at hand.

To begin with, the reader might find it surprising that only illustrations, but no photographs, are presented in a book that champions the auto-photographic research approach. This is in essence an ethical choice since being a woman war veteran in Liberia typically entails a very strong stigma. To give an example, one late evening in November 2012 I received a phone call from Monrovia. It was from Juliet, a former frontline fighter who now sounded anxious and asked me to 'tell the BBC'[2] to take her picture off the Internet. Juliet had just found out that a close-up photograph of her holding an AK-47 was online. According to Juliet, the picture was taken during the second Liberian civil war from a helicopter that had suddenly appeared above her. The helicopter disappeared as quickly as it had arrived, and Juliet had already forgotten the whole incident. But now, when she found her face in a picture in the international news, she remembered the incident again. Juliet was extremely worried that this 'BBC effect' might prevent her from traveling abroad. Moreover, she was concerned about the stigma the photo might still cause for her and her children, some nine years after the war had ceased. I thus promised Juliet that I would see what I could do and call her back at the first possible opportunity. Soon, however, it became evident that my abilities were very limited in this matter. The picture was already on countless personal websites, news sites and blogs. Because of this and a few similar incidents, I have therefore decided to be extremely cautious in publishing any photographs of the interviewed women.

In addition to research ethics, utilizing visuals that entail the 'pain of others' (Sontag 2003) in a respectful but truthful manner is always a very problematic question (e.g. Butler 2010; Möller 2009, 2013). In addition to various types of media actors, the 'security–development nexus' (Duffield 2001) also relies on images of pain to gain the general public's attention for generating funding for humanitarian projects in the Global South (e.g. Wilson and Brown 2009; Calain 2013; Kotilainen 2016). Thus, like Leontius some two thousand years ago, the everyday observer of today also constantly encounters horrifying images without really considering the ethical implications of choosing to look at the suffering bodies or turn one's head away. When the current visuals of suffering are examined through the lens of *curious contrapuntalism*, however, it quickly becomes apparent that pain is made visible in the global North under a strict double standard. As David Campbell (2004: 64) remarks: 'When dead bodies do feature in the media, they are more often than not bodies of dead foreigners. And more often than not, images of dead foreigners are little more than a vehicle for the inscription of domestic spaces as superior.' In other words, the ethical standards of presenting suffering entail complex moral choices that might, on the one hand, cause empathy and therefore spark social responsibility and action, but, on the other hand, might also further deepen the enduring postcolonial and gendered divisions between 'us' and 'them' (Kleinman and Kleinman 1996).

## The auto-photographic research approach

Considering all the ethical challenges that images of pain contain, the logical question is: why bother with visual methods at all? Why not undertake more conventional social science research instead, the kind that relies mainly on research data produced with methods such as interviews, participant observation, censuses and surveys?

As is briefly mentioned in the Introduction, my interest in photographic methods did not emerge in academia, but in another West African country, Senegal. When I had returned to Dakar for the first time after having lived for six months in one of the city's neighborhoods, I decided to ask my local friend Sire to take over my camera and photograph his daily activities. I did not expect much from the photos, especially since this was the first time Sire had used a digital SLR camera. In addition, I had already taken thousands of pictures of my small home district, called Santhiaba, and was quite convinced that he would bring back pictures similar to those that I already had in my possession. Later that same evening, Sire came back with well over a hundred pictures on the camera. The photographs revealed that I had been right in assuming that the surroundings were already familiar to me. However, at the same time it was evident that I had been completely wrong about the insights of the pictures; in front of my eyes I saw the everyday lives of Santhiabans in a way I had not understood them before. I was able to see Sire's whereabouts during an ordinary day and witness the ways in which he navigated Santhiaba and its surroundings. In addition, the themes and details he considered fascinating and worth photographing were in many instances totally different from my own set of pictures. I was also astounded at the way individuals looked at Sire through the lens of the camera; somehow, it seemed that I was able to see through Sire's eyes.

This incident came to mind a few years later when I tried to find a suitable way to collect data for my future dissertation. While flipping through old photographs in Finland, it occurred to me: maybe through auto-photographic research data I would be able to 'see' as the 'Other', as had been the case in Senegal. In addition, by giving cameras to the interviewees and asking them to take pictures of their daily realities and aspirations, it would be the research participants rather than myself who would set the agenda for the interviews. Finally, I also figured that the method might provide a visual access and therefore some form of understanding of insecure places and environments that I could not frequent for security reasons.

Hence, from the autumn of 2012 to the summer of 2014, I spent a combined period of five months in Liberia during three separate field research trips. With the help of my research assistants, I conducted some 160 exploratory interviews and distributed thirty-five cameras to chosen key interviewees in the towns of Monrovia, Kakata, Gbarnga and Ganta. Many cameras were broken in the process and a few were stolen. Furthermore, I decided to discard some material either because the profiles of the interviewees did not match the research setting (e.g. age of the interviewee) or the data seemed unreliable (e.g. contradictory information about their own movements within the warring factions). In the end, I had accumulated 133 exploratory interviews and twenty-five photo-interviews. For the purpose of this chapter, I have chosen three cases from these data to focus upon.

Research interviews entailing a photographic component have been used in academia for decades. The method was first described by John Collier Jr (1957), a documentary photographer who had been involved in a multidisciplinary research project investigating the relationship between the environment and mental health in Canada in the mid-1950s. As part of this project, Collier photographed the living surroundings of a number of chosen research participants. The resulting pictures were placed in interview situations that Collier (ibid.) labelled in his article as *photo-interviews*. When this initial experiment seemed to produce deeper information than 'ordinary' interviews previously had, the practice of *photo elicitation* spread, and Collier's later works (Collier 1967; Collier and Collier 1986) became standardized introductions to visual anthropology and sociology (Harper 2002: 14).

Building on the methods and ideas of John Collier, some anthropologists began to question their own subject positions within their research settings in the 1960s and 1970s. It was understood in a very intersectional manner that, among other things, the researcher's race, gender and social position had a deep impact on what was studied and which methods were chosen (Thomas 2009: 2). A revealing example of the impact of subject positions can be found in my own experiences in Santhiaba. The photographs I had taken sometimes differed radically from the pictures taken by Sire, since we had an utterly dissimilar understanding of what was interesting in that particular social environment.

After the findings of John Collier Jr, the next significant developmental step in participatory visual research came about in 1966, when film and communications scholar Sol Worth and anthropologist John

Adair launched an experimental collaborative research project in North America. Worth and Adair gave 16mm film cameras to Navajo Native Americans, taught the research participants to utilize the cameras and edit film, and asked them to film their living surroundings. The scholars maintained that their method was able the capture the 'Navajo' ways of experiencing the world. Although some critics argued that Worth and Adair's work was placing too much emphasis on ethnic and racial differences at the cost of other social identities, their research was nevertheless an important benchmark in the development of auto-photography as a visual method (Thomas 2009: 2).

There are numerous variations within the field of participatory photography (see, e.g., Balomenou and Garrod 2015), such as photovoice (e.g. Ruby 1992); photo essay (e.g. Grusky 2004); photo-interview (e.g. Vila 2013); photo-communication (e.g. Dinklage and Ziller 1989) and pluralist photography (Bleiker and Kay 2007). Therefore, for the sake of clarity, I have decided to utilize the term 'auto-photographic research practice' to describe the methodological combination of participant-generated auto-photographs and photo-elicitation interviews. Thus, I use the term 'auto-photography' to refer to the process in which the research participants of this project have taken photographs of their *everyday realities* and their *aspirations*. By 'photo-elicitation' I mean the step in the interview processes in which I have placed the participant-generated photographs one by one in front of the interviewee/photographer, who has provided me with detailed insights into each picture. Together, these two steps form the auto-photographic research approach.

Within the various strands of participatory photography, it is typical to include selected participant-generated photographs in the final publications. For the ethical reasons described above, including photographs in this book was not an option. In a somewhat opposite manner, some writers, such as the celebrated photographer/essayist Susan Sontag (1977, 2003), have addressed the challenge of visualizing the 'pain of others' by choosing not to include any visuals whatsoever in their oeuvres. Nonetheless, I find the alternative of not including any visual material in this book unsuitable for various reasons.

First and foremost, in a project that relies so heavily on data gathered with visual methods, it would somehow seem devious to report research results only in written format. In addition, providing yet another output that treats and favours words as the only 'proper mode of explanation, as *the* tool of thought', as Nick Sousanis (2015: 54, emphasis in original) remarks in his outstanding graphic novel

*Unflattening*, would have denied the indisputable power of visuals of various kinds. A telling example of this power is that the quality of information gained from adding visual material to a research interview, an important detail already emphasized by Collier (1957), seems to have a physical basis in human biology. To simplify, the brain's capacity seems to be utilized more thoroughly when visuals (photographs; paintings; cartoons, etc.) are presented alongside verbal information. This could possibly explain why a 'visual interview' can produce not only deeper information than a verbal interview alone, but also information of a different kind (Harper 2002: 13). Finally, placing illustrations inspired by the actual research data alongside the textual material also represents a *curiously contrapuntal* statement. How we navigate, raft and make sense of the world around us is fundamentally tied to all the senses the individual has in her possession, yet we, the members of the academic community, tend to report our research results almost exclusively through words. The illustrations in this book can therefore be thought of as a tentative attempt to reach behind the textual, an experiment that strives to understand this world of ours as a multidimensional entity in which we simultaneously utilize all our available senses.

### From social navigation to social rafting

> I talked to sailors who had got safely away in boats after the seas had made their ships founder. But the men knew little about rafts. A raft – that wasn't a ship; it had no keel or bulwarks. It was just something floating on which to save oneself in an emergency, until one was picked up by a boat of some kind. [...] 'But you can't navigate a raft', he added. 'It goes sideways and backward and round as the wind takes it'. (Heyerdahl 1984: 23-4)

In this book, the security environment of Liberia's women veterans is understood as a web of rivers, streams and rivulets where droughts and floods occasionally occur, and where a steady rivulet might suddenly turn into a bursting stream. In these (in)secure rivers, the interviewees of this project can be thought of as managing and surviving through *social rafting*, a term that builds upon the popular idea of social navigation, but also differs from it in terms of intentionality and resource availability.

The two main building blocks of social navigation are tactic agency and navigation. In her article 'Innocents ou coupables?

Les Enfants-soldates comme acteurs tactiques', Alcinda Honwana (2000; see also 2005) suggested that child soldiers exercise a form of tactical agency. By borrowing the distinction made by Michel de Certeau (1984: xix) between a tactic and strategy – where a strategy is understood as being produced by 'subject of will and power' that can be separated from the immediate environment (e.g. the strategy of an enterprise in a city), and a tactic is understood as an always time-dependent and institution-free action (e.g. moving about in a city as an individual) – Honwana argued that although coming from positions of extreme feebleness, child soldiers are tactical agents in De Certeau's sense. This means 'a specific type of agency that is devised to cope with the concrete, immediate conditions of their lives in order to maximize the circumstances created by their military and violent environment' (Honwana 2005: 49). Navigation possibilities in these types of social environment are bounded, but do, however, exist, Honwana (2000: 78) concluded.

The most-cited theorist on social navigation is possibly anthropologist Henrik E. Vigh (2006a: 51; see also Vigh 2006b), who applied the concepts of tactical agency and navigation to explaining the lives and struggles of marginalized youth in Bissau, the capital of Guinea-Bissau. Vigh's young research participants explained to him that in the hardships experienced by urban, marginalized youth, the way to get by was through *dubriagem*, an ancient Portuguese word still used in Guinea-Bissau today. By combining tactical agency with *dubriagem*, and with the clarifications provided to him by his research participants, Vigh developed the term social navigation to describe urban youth's survival strategies in Bissau, where 'possibilities and life chances are limited in the extreme' (p. 56). Since then, the term has gained wide support, especially in youth and conflict studies, but as Vigh (2009: 419) himself notes: 'despite its increasing popularity, the concept is most often used in an unspecified and misunderstood manner – it is generally not well defined!'

Interestingly, anthropologist Mats Utas (2005b) applied both the concepts of tactic agency and social navigation in his article 'Victimcy, girlfriending, soldiering: tactic agency in a young woman's social navigation of the Liberian war zone' on the manoeuvrings of 'Bintu', a young Liberian woman who participated in Liberia's first civil war in various capacities. By carefully following her whereabouts and social relations during the war, Utas (ibid.: 426) came to the conclusion that 'a more robust analysis of women's lives in the war zone requires seeing women as something other than mere victims devoid of agency, or alternatively as "fully free actors", but rather as tactical agents engaged in the difficult task of social navigation'. In this regard, I completely agree with Utas: we certainly need to avoid simplistic victim narratives and address individual experiences in all their complexities within specific social environments. Nevertheless, since the combination of cunning, sense of rationality and utmost intentionality that Bintu seemingly possessed in her manoeuvrings was extremely rare among the interviewees (as forty-three of the participants stated that they joined the forces willingly, I do not recognize a pattern of victimhood in my data), I find that the concept of social navigation might not be best suited to address the agency of these women in today's Liberia. Therefore, I tend to agree with Chris Coulter (2008: 68), who compares her own research findings among Sierra Leone's young women soldiers to the approach Utas takes in his piece as follows:

> Whereas Utas wanted to problematize the predominant notion of women as victims in humanitarian discourse, I, on the other hand, have been more interested in examining local social relations and my informants' position in them. Although I do acknowledge that some of my informants may at times have chosen to become fighters or lovers to commanders, it is crucial to emphasize the structural constraints circumscribing those choices; sometimes, the only choice was between becoming a fighter/lover or dying, which is not really much of a choice, more a matter of bare survival. Here, I find Aretxaga's concept of choiceless decisions useful precisely in its subtle double critique: it at once questions women's passivity and victimization while also challenging the liberal belief of agents' free choice (Aretxaga 1997: 61).

Hence, in this specific research setting, I have chosen to rename the concept of social navigation *social rafting*. Although social rafting also understands individuals as tactical agents in De Certeau's sense, it differs from social navigation by emphasizing the importance of the resources available at any given time in the specific social surrounding. Thus, in social rafting, the material of the raft, the scale of the stream and the level of professionalism certainly matter: sometimes the journey can be calm and enjoyable, whereas at other times the ride can prove fatal to an inexperienced or badly equipped rafter. To simplify: when one cannot navigate without some sort of technical knowledge and the possibility of steering the vessel at hand, it is impossible to stay afloat on a ramshackle raft hastily put together using odd pieces and objects lying around.

By describing the situation of women war veterans of Liberia in terms of rafting rather than navigating, the available resources, professional capacities of a specific rafter and geographical challenges (Korf et al. 2010) can be better addressed in each particular situation. While, for example, a professional white-water rafter has all the skills and capacities imaginable to modify and change her equipment to match her personal skill level on the one hand, and the scale of the rapid on the other hand, a victim of a sudden flood may sometimes have to grab hold of anything she can – be it a tree branch, a jerrycan or a wooden door passing by. Far from being able to navigate in the water, sometimes a rafter has to put all her energies into staying afloat and trying not to sink into the dark waters looming below the seemingly calm surface.

Finally, it is impossible to escape the postcolonial connotations embedded in the word navigation itself. As Jamal Eddine Benhayoun (2006) indicates in his book *Narration, Navigation, and Colonialism*, the seventeenth- and eighteenth-century tales of great European sea voyages to faraway destinations in Africa and beyond, for example, were not only favorite adventure stories of the time, but also acts of reinvention and a colonial exercise in which colonialism was 'sustained and empowered by the double practice of narration and navigation' (ibid.: 20). Relatedly, as Liberia's history as a country is deeply intertwined with the founding of the American Colonization Society in 1816, with its aim of relocating free people of color to their 'native homeland' on the west coast of Africa, an area that would later be renamed Liberia, utilizing the concept of navigation in this research setting might certainly yield undesirable connotations. From this historical perspective, it is perfectly sensible to discuss social navigation when referring to narratives and actions that individuals have directed mainly at the global aid community, narratives such as the one Utas (2005b) investigates in his article, but doing so is less sensible if trying to understand and unravel social relations and structures on a more general level in today's Liberia.

## Amy, Teta and Priscilla as social rafters

In the summer of 2014, I was exposed to a very concrete example of social rafting while in West Point, one of Monrovia's numerous shanty towns. When arriving there one early morning, I found many of the respondents devastated and ill: a flood had occurred the previous week. Not only had the water entered a number of houses, it had also taken many of the ramshackle buildings out to sea. Floods are very typical during the rainy season in the world's rainiest capital, but since West Point is situated on a narrow peninsula between the Mesurado and Saint Paul rivers, floods and huge waves can potentially have extremely devastating effects on the area. Some of the residents had lost almost all their possessions and were aided by their street sisters and street brothers; others were sleeping rough under their *lappa* clothes with their children. Many suffered from colds and other infections since they were not able to warm themselves at night. Individuals and families were collecting a piece of cardboard from here, another from there, a third from a friend; receiving clothes from benevolent neighbors and friends, buying food on credit and trying to contact whoever they thought might be of help. Indeed, their actions and manoeuvring on that particular morning can probably best be described as social rafting.

Thus, to survive as a disadvantaged individual in post-war Monrovia's various slums requires, among other things, social skills, intelligence and luck, as well as the ability to smartly manoeuvre through the various obstacles thrown up by the constant lack of resources. As we will come to learn in the chapters that follow, the various skills that the (young) soldiers learnt on the frontlines during the war(s) are highly valuable, even today.

In order to further illustrate how social rafting is understood in this research project, let us take a quick look at the cases of Amy, Teta and Priscilla, all of whom participated in Liberia's civil wars in different capacities. Amy acted as a fighter and commander in both civil wars, whereas Teta and Priscilla participated in the second war – the former in combat service support tasks and the latter in frontline fighting. After the fighting ceased, all three women ended up living in one of Monrovia's numerous shanty towns. Although the next chapter is dedicated as a whole to describing and detailing the recruitment, participation and experiences of girl and women soldiers in Liberia's civil wars, I hope to demonstrate through these three cases both the applicability of the auto-photographic research approach and the concept of social rafting in this specific research setting.

Amy, the oldest of the three, had been very lucky as a young girl before the war began, since she had been given a chance to help a 'Congo woman' with her housekeeping duties.[3] Amy's tasks included a massive amount of household chores, but she became literate in return, and learned all the other necessities that being 'civilized' required (Moran 1990, 2006; see also Chapter 5). However, her newly acquired skills soon turned against her when she was captured in 1990 during a visit to her parents' village. As a literate and in many ways capable sixteen-year-old young woman, she attracted the attention of the leaders of the National Patriotic Front of Liberia (NPFL) and was captured. Later, when the group divided into two, Amy chose Taylor's forces and ended up commanding her own unit comprised of around fifty young women and men. Altogether, she spent more than ten years in various warring factions in both civil wars.

While Amy enjoyed the short lull between the two civil wars during the final years of the century, Teta decided to run away from her home. Her aunt, the owner of the house, had recently realized that Teta's beautiful young body could be used as a commodity and had therefore forced Teta to perform sexual services for those willing to pay enough. Being forced into prostitution, Teta escaped the house at the age of fifteen and ended up on the streets of Monrovia, and, in the following months, as a 'general's wife' in the Armed Forces of Liberia (AFL). Besides 'loving business', Teta's wartime combat service support duties (see Chapter 2) included cooking, cleaning and porter services, as well as selling looted goods on Monrovia's street corners for the benefit of her 'bush husband's' unit.

In the first year of the new millennium, Priscilla's house was attacked in war-torn Monrovia. Priscilla's parents were brutally executed in front of her and the ten-year-old girl was captured by members of the Liberians United for Reconciliation and Democracy (LURD). Priscilla was trained as a fighter and headed to the frontline with her AK-47 and her new boyfriend, whom she had decided to start 'loving to' during the training phase of her service. In addition to having a 'regular' relationship, this move was also a clever security arrangement for Priscilla, as it provided protection against the possibility of being raped by random male soldiers from her own unit.

My first encounter with Teta happened in a small room in a Monrovian slum, a room that had cardboard walls and was owned by a shopkeeper living in the same 'zinc round'. The shopkeeper, Pa Chea, allowed idle youth to spend time in that room; sometimes they bought liquor or other commodities from him, and other times he just liked to have them around to provide company. In addition, by allowing these youngsters to stay in his shop, he created a small-scale security network and a resource base should he one day need some services. It took time and numerous encounters to get Teta to trust me, but finally she agreed to taking a camera along and photographing her daily activities and aspirations. Through Teta's pictures, it became evident that she was a small-scale drug dealer who saw prostitution and selling drugs as her only sources of livelihood. She had been in jail numerous times, lived in a tarpaulin house that was almost collapsing, and most of her family members had either abandoned her or were dead.

In many ways, Priscilla's realities resemble those of Teta. Like Teta, Priscilla also earns the greater part of her income from a combination of petty drug business and prostitution; her living conditions are deprived; and she does not have good relationships with her remaining family members.

Both Teta and Priscilla are extremely underprivileged, even in the Liberian context. Their *rafts of survival* can therefore be thought of as collections of random pieces of junk that they have hastily assembled together. Teta and Priscilla have no proper steering mechanisms on their rafts, let alone the resources or know-how to significantly improve their vessels. Both Teta and Priscilla are nonetheless experts when it comes to manoeuvring their own rafts of survival in their personal rivers of (in)securities. That is why an outsider or someone from an upper social class who visits these specific rivers would most likely be in trouble if only given Teta's or Priscilla's raft on which to survive. It is therefore important to keep in mind that these women are definitely not only victims, but also social survivors with a sense of pride who manage to endure the storms of life.

In comparison to those of Teta and Priscilla, Amy's raft is a bit more stable and sophisticated. After the second civil war, Amy succeeded in subscribing to a Disarmament, Demobilization and Rehabilitation (DDR) program in three separate locations with weapons she had hidden in different phases of the civil wars (see also Chapter 3). From the money acquired through these processes, she was able to save a few hundred US dollars and build a small zinc house on an abandoned strip of land in the capital. Today, the community is one of the numerous slum areas of Monrovia. Even though Amy's living environment seems very poor in her pictures – for instance, the majority of residents defecate into plastic bags and throw them into the nearby swamp – she is still doing rather well in comparison to Teta and Priscilla. As became evident from Amy's set of pictures, she has a very modest shop attached to her 'zinc round' that she shares with her youngest daughter. From there, a random passer-by can purchase a shot of *gana gana*, local 'whisky' made from fermented cane juice; a cigarette 'from China'; a roll of toilet paper; or occasionally a small bottle of 'egg-nog' spiced with cannabis leaves. Amy has also acquired some crooked benches where customers and random individuals can 'lecture' about everyday life or enjoy the overtly distorted *hipco*-music that is constantly blasting from her precious boom box. These arrangements not only provide a small income, but are also a source of security for Amy and her daughter, since the customers have an incentive to keep the business going.

## Strengthening the rafts of survival

During my second field research visit in 2013, I was struck by the complexity of security arrangements one has to master as a poor person in Monrovia. During my previous field trip in Liberia, I had lived with two families residing in different shanty towns of the capital, and found Glorious as my research assistant from another of these households. Thus, when organizing my second research trip, Glorious and I had planned to live in the house she had just rented for herself and her daughter in one of the disfranchised neighborhoods of the capital. This way we could easily coordinate our work and maybe locate new interviewees from that particular neighborhood. However, because her sister had suddenly come to visit Monrovia, we had to alter our plans at the last minute since four people could simply not fit in one double bed.

Then, just two weeks into my second field research trip, I met Glorious one morning with a deep look of worry on her face. The previous night, armed robbers had entered the house next to hers, killing one person and wounding two others. The quarter's unofficial 'security guards' caught one of the robbers, killed him, and threw his body into the river. When the policemen came to the quarter later that morning, none of the residents confessed to having known the person who executed the robber. Afterwards, the 'security guards' were celebrated as heroes since nobody trusted the police anymore. Because of these events, Glorious had slept for only a few hours and was extremely worried about the safety of her household since she could not afford an iron door at the moment. Even though she had made an agreement with a bunch of young boys that they would be her 'street brothers' and come to her help anytime, she no longer felt safe and secure. Although I was extremely worried about Glorious's and her daughter's safety, at the same time I felt relieved that I had not been living in her house as we had originally planned. I realized that if I had been there, our house would definitely have been one of the favoured targets in the slum since no other white residents lived in the neighborhood. In this way, as a researcher seeking to be as close to her interviewees as possible, I would not only have put myself in danger, but also Glorious and her daughter.

How, then, can one deal with security issues in an environment where the police and other authorities are anything but trustworthy if one cannot afford concrete walls or an iron door, let alone private security services? To stay afloat in this type of river of (in)security, human relations are key; the 'wealth is in people' (Bledsoe 1980), as the example of Glorious reveals.

Social networks can have two faces, however. Once I met Teta while she was still in the process of taking photographs. She was worried because her right hand was completely swollen and had two deep cuts in it. Because of this injury, she was unable to finalize her set of pictures. She nonetheless asked me to photograph her damaged hand on her behalf, since 'you people need to know what is going on in our country today'. Teta explained that the reason for her condition was her current boyfriend, who had beaten her up for some trivial reason. Similar instances were also familiar to Priscilla, who, while viewing the picture of her current boyfriend, explained that he was frequently violent towards her, mainly out of jealousy. Interestingly, neither of the men had complained about the fact that their girlfriends were forced to turn to prostitution for their everyday necessities, but instead had problems with 'outside boyfriends'. They seemed to be fine with 'professional promiscuity', a quite normal profession in their particular neighborhoods, but even the rumor of 'intimate promiscuity' was enough to provoke a violent attack.

There are countless explanations for why so many battered women cannot end their abusive relationships (see, e.g., Ferraro and Johnson 1983; Rhodes and McKenzie 1998). Although some of these reasons are relevant in the case of the interviewed women, an interesting practical reason for the fact that the numerous Tetas and Priscillas of Liberia stay with their violent partners is the need to increase their everyday security – to strengthen their rafts of survival. To put it simply, a disadvantaged woman who is in a relationship with a well-respected and street-smart man is generally much safer and better off than someone who is either single or with someone who is incapable of 'providing for' his family – be that with income, or, as a minimum, increased physical security. The apparent flipside is that, in return for general safety on the streets, numerous women need to endure occasional violence inside their homes. Amy, on the other hand, can afford to be picky when it comes to partners since she does not need a boyfriend to strengthen her raft of survival. Her security is sufficiently guaranteed by the fact that a huge group of young men and women from her neighborhood utilize her small shop as a local 'entertainment spot' and have an incentive to keep the business going by keeping it secure.

The threat of violence in these neighborhoods is abundant, even in the daytime. On one occasion during Amy's interview we had to stop the discussion to fetch her twelve-year-old daughter from the local police station. The daughter had had a violent quarrel with a drunken man who apparently was not agreeing to take responsibility for the baby that Amy's daughter was now carrying. In order to free her daughter, who now also carried bruises on her swollen body, Amy had to provide the police officer with US$20 as a 'contribution', and promise that she would keep her daughter next to her in the future.

Many disputes in these areas are drug-related. Cannabis is produced in Liberia and can be found in various forms practically anywhere in the country. One portion, or 'wrap', of marijuana on the street market costs around twenty US cents. In addition, West Africa is one of the transit points for smuggling heroin and cocaine to Europe and North America.[4] Many of the interviewees of this book, such as Teta and Priscilla, have 'gained' from the spillover of this trafficking in the form of cheap heroin. In the slums of Monrovia, a portion of *tar-white* (brown heroin that is usually smoked through a metal pipe made from foil) costs about US$1.1, whereas a gram is sold for approximately US$14. Among the research participants, cocaine usage is rather rare since one gram can cost as much as US$50.[5]

Teta's set of pictures was extremely revealing about the realities of substance abusers in Monrovia. In addition to having taken detailed photographs of the users of different kinds of narcotics, she gave detailed accounts of how those drugs were consumed, what they cost, and what effects they had. In many of her pictures, former child soldiers, obviously now adults, were completely high on drugs, leaning on the walls with an empty look in their eyes. While observing one of these pictures, Teta explained: 'They are all ex-combatants. Some of them fought, some of their families were killed, some people lost their legs; they are all traumatized.'

Although Liberia has just recently reformed its legislation on drug and substance abuse (Legislature of Liberia 2014), severe weaknesses prevail in the law enforcement sector (US Department of State 2014). As illuminated in the following chapters, corruption is ubiquitous and police officers are deeply distrusted; in some of the pictures taken by the interviewees there are Drug Enforcement

Agency (DEA) officers in uniform consuming the drugs they had confiscated that night. In the following excerpts, Teta and Priscilla exemplify some of the everyday worries of substance abusers in the shanty towns of Monrovia.

> *Leena* (L): What is happening in this picture?
>
> *Teta* (T): We were thinking about the police in this picture. When I went inside the room, they all looked sad and so I asked them: 'But what has happened?' And they told that it will not be easy today since the police is arriving.
>
> L: But how were you able to tell in advance that the police were coming?
>
> T: Someone called them! It is funny [laughing] but also serious. Because when the policemen come, they can capture you and take your picture in the station. After, they will ask money from you: 40, 30, 20, 10, 15 USD. It all depends. So when they are coming, everybody is in worry. You see, me and you it is not the same [gives me her hand]. Now smell my hand. Smell it? So if they smell the drugs on you, next they will ask you to show your teeth. You can also tell from the teeth if a person is smoking.
>
> [...]
>
> *Leena* (L): Priscilla, the last time I was here, you had your small business. Can you tell me once again what happened with your bucket? Why don't you have it anymore in your pictures? [Priscilla had had a small bucket that she carried around on top of her head. It contained cigarettes, matches, candies and, on occasion, drugs.[6]]
>
> *Priscilla* (P): The police people came and took my bucket. They said that I've got drugs in the bucket.
>
> L: Did you have [at the time]?
>
> P: No. But they took it and beat me and put me to jail. I spent two days there and then my boyfriend came and freed me [paid a bribe]. They took my bucket, took my small money, turned me around and took my picture.
>
> L: But why?
>
> P: They took it to tell people that I am a drug seller. If you will pay, they can take your picture off the wall.

> *Jessica (research assistant)*: The reason they are putting these pictures up is that if they are taking your picture three times, the first two times someone can come and free you with some money. But with the third one they will carry you straight to South Beach [central prison in Monrovia with a very bad reputation]. That is where armed robbers, the rapists, the murderers, all those are kept.

After hearing Teta's and Priscilla's stories about the pictures, I visited two local police stations in different slums and had a meeting with the heads of the stations. On both of their office walls were numerous photographs of mostly young men and women, with handwritten captions on each picture stating 'drug addict', 'armed robber', 'thief', 'prostitute' and so on. In addition, one station head asked for 'a kind contribution' in order to receive some information on Liberian street drugs. In Teta's words, the situation was indeed 'funny but also serious'.

## Street sisters and brothers as security providers

> [Street brothers and sisters are] the people that can protect us in the street. If somebody is beating me, he comes and fights with me. If somebody is cursing to me, he can come and put his mouth there.
> *Priscilla, Monrovia*

All the research participants took numerous pictures of their 'sisters' and 'brothers'. At first I did not give the issue much thought, but then I started to wonder how this was possible. Where did all these sisters and brothers come from? After all, many of the interviewees had in fact lost contact with their families and some were orphans. When inquiring about the matter, it soon became apparent that the majority of sisters, brothers and even mothers were not biological relatives, but 'street sisters', 'street brothers' and 'play mothers'. These were individuals who would take care of each other in times of need by providing one another with food, shelter, small favours or advice, among other things. Together, they formed small-scale security networks, huge rafts of survival that were sturdier than the fragile rafts of vulnerable individuals alone. Basically, the more *wealth in people* (Bledsoe 1980; see also Chapter 2) one had, the better one's chances of managing different types of daily struggle.

These types of informal security arrangements have been well theorized in the context of Africa. For example, *patrimonialism/ neopatrimonialism* (e.g. Pitcher et al. 2009), *clientelism* (e.g. Van de Walle 2014) and *bigmanity* (e.g. Utas 2012) have become standard concepts when trying to unveil the informal power relations ubiquitous on the continent. AbdouMaliq Simone's (2004) idea of *people as infrastructure* is a fresh take on the issue since it captures not only human relations themselves, but also 'the ability of residents to engage complex combinations of objects, spaces, persons, and practices'; conjunctions that 'become infrastructure – a platform providing for and reproducing life in the city'. Simone emphasizes that the critical question for researchers and policymakers is that of how to 'practice ways of seeing and engaging urban spaces that are characterized simultaneously by regularity and provisionality' (ibid.: 408). In other words, how can one make sense of, truly understand, these multilayered infrastructures of spaces, objects, people and their social relations? How can one unravel the life-worlds of individuals and their social arrangements, arrangements such as *street sisterhood* or *rafts of survival*?

The auto-photographic research approach seems to provide the researcher with ways of seeing and understanding what might at first glance appear to be invisible or inaccessible life-worlds. Firstly, the method can facilitate communication in which neither the interviewer nor the interviewee can easily dictate the topics of conversation. Secondly, the method can provide access to possibly dangerous arenas, and ultimately provoke understanding beyond verbal encounters: seeing is believing, but seeing is also understanding. Let me provide a final practical example from the interview material.

In one of Priscilla's pictures there is a small child, probably about two years old, posing for the camera in a beautiful print dress in front of a dilapidated thatched wall. Her eyes filled with joy, Priscilla explained the context of the photograph in her photo interview session.

*Priscilla* (P): This is my [street] brother's baby here. The other people, I don't really know them.

*Leena* (L): What is the child doing?

P: She is playing on the ground. That is why I took the picture.

*Jessica (research assistant)*: What are you thinking of when you see this picture?

P: If I will have a good home someday, that is how I want to take care of my children.

L: And how is that?

P: I will bathe him, feed the baby, see that he is not sick, make sure that the baby has a good health.

L: So you want a baby one day?

P: Yes. That is why I took the picture.

L: When you look at the picture, how do you see her future?

P: Well, the baby's mother ran away and left the baby with her father. Nobody really knows where she went. We are the ones who can take care of the baby, especially me, I am the one taking care of her.

L: So how do you see this girl's future?

P: I hope she will have a good future.

L: What is a good future?

P: She will have her own house, her own car, a job, she will be working and helping people.

As the example hopefully demonstrates, street sisters and street brothers help one another, not only in acute crises, but also in smaller and bigger everyday challenges. Nobody forced Priscilla and her friends to take the baby under their care, but they did so out of humanity, out of kindness and solidarity. Like the majority of biological siblings, they watch each other's backs and give advice, or if needed they can very concretely fight by their sides. Also, like 'ordinary' siblings, they can have arguments over trivial matters, gossip or just share good times. It must be highlighted here that regardless of all their enormous daily struggles, numerous pictures taken by the interviewees reveal situations of joy and laughter, of good times shared with loved ones.

## Conclusion

At the beginning of this chapter I quoted Gayatri Spivak (1988: 66), who asks: 'Can the subaltern speak?' In this chapter, I have examined Spivak's concern through auto-photographic research data produced by Amy, Teta and Priscilla, three young women veterans from Liberia's capital, Monrovia. By explaining the historical background and application of the *auto-photographic research approach* in this research setting, and by detailing some of the main concepts of the project, such as *social rafting* and *street sisterhood* in relation to the experiences of these three women, I have aimed to prepare the reader for the following, more empirical chapters.

By working with the highly disenfranchised yet extremely persistent interviewees of this project, I have come to the conclusion that maybe the 'subaltern', the 'Other', cannot speak the language of the dominant elite, but that is not a problem of the subaltern mass, but rather of the ignorant scholar. It is, and should be, the struggle of the privileged person to examine her own *life-world*, to critically scrutinize her own ontological and epistemological assumptions, if that is what it takes to achieve a better understanding between the scholar and the 'Other'. I have tried to exemplify that one manner to lessen epistemic violence (ibid.) in projects carried out in dangerous environments, such as Monrovian slums, and at the same time a promising way to amplify silent voices, can be found in such non-conventional methodological choices as the auto-photographic research approach. Pictures in this specific context, and with these particular individuals, indeed tend to be worth a thousand words – at least when the contents of these photographs are clarified by the photographers themselves. It seems that the 'subaltern' can speak to the arrogant observer via pictures; the 'subaltern' can visualize.[7]

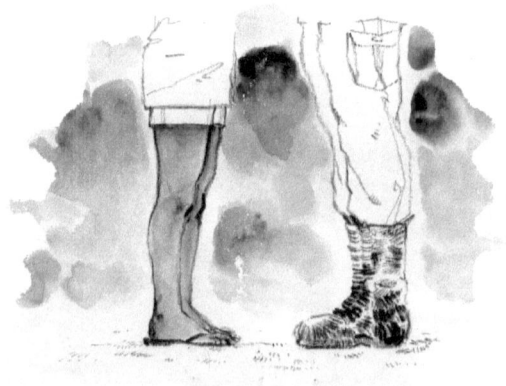

# 2
# Girl and women soldiers in Liberia's civil wars

If we wish to understand the lives of Liberia's women war veterans today, it is essential to gain at least a basic understanding of their wartime actualities.[1] Participating in the everyday realities of the fighting forces meant a profound shift in the lives of these women; a shift that often left behind permanent physical and psychological scars. For instance, when the basic security structures provided by families, communities and friends suddenly vanished, individuals needed to create new security networks – novel rafts of survival – often from scratch. In order to persist in the dangerous rivers, the individual needed wits, persistence, social skills and, indeed, luck.

In this chapter, these wartime actualities are examined in three main sections. First, I discuss young women's reasons for joining the fighting forces in Liberia. Most of the interviewees were forcibly abducted, whereas those who enlisted voluntarily can be further divided into three main groups according to their stated motives: revenge, peer pressure/material benefits and everyday injustices. Obviously, these reasons formed a complex motivational whole for many individuals who decided to join the ranks, but all interviewees were nevertheless able to specify the main motive for their participation. There was no difference between urban or rural areas in terms of motivational patterns or recruitment tactics.[2]

The roles of women and girls in the forces are detailed in the second part of the chapter under the main categories of combat service support, fighting and commanding. Time and again, girl and women soldiers of the Global South are simply lumped together as 'vulnerable groups', such as Women Associated with the Fighting Forces (WAFF), war-affected women, sex slaves or camp followers.[3] The reasoning behind these very vast categories is that women and children are typically supposed 'presumptive noncombatants', whereas men are treated as 'presumptive combatants' (Carpenter 2003). In this section, I reassess the usage of sex/gender-based categories and argue that a classification that is based *first* on duties/ranks and *second* on sex/gender is often better suited for addressing girl and women soldiers' multiple roles within the various fighting forces of the Global South. I maintain that in addition to providing an enhanced analytical accuracy, this terminological turn has important policy implications. Indeed, if the actual roles of girl and women soldiers are correctly understood in the specific conflict environment, their needs can also be better served in the post-war period.

The third main section of the chapter concentrates on systematic inequalities inside the Liberian factions. I argue that the intersecting structures of social exclusion, such as gender, age and class, were only partially present *inside* the forces. For this purpose, I have teased out three main categories of exclusion that affected girl and women soldiers' statuses inside the forces: rank, sex/gender and human relations.[4] These three categories are handled separately in the chapter, yet with awareness that all of them must be understood as an intersecting, contrapuntal whole. Throughout the chapter, the voices of the interviewees form a type of *soggetto* (see Chapter 1) that is compared with and reflected against general theories of women and (girl) child soldiering, as well as empirical evidence from other conflict surroundings.

## Joining the forces

Many young women are forced to become soldiers, but some do make the decision voluntarily. Nevertheless, the notion of volunteerism can be contested when considering the push and pull factors behind individual decisions to enlist – push factors being the circumstances that drive individuals away from their communities, and pull factors being those (imagined) conditions that lure civilian girls and women into the armed forces. Brett and Specht (2004) have found environmental, personal and case-specific reasons for children to become soldiers. These may include: problems in school or in the family environment, insecurity and lack of income (push factors); and the need to find shelter, food, financial support or a more secure environment (pull factors). If there are many of these push and pull factors affecting an individual decision to enlist, the nature of volunteerism can be questioned.[5]

Two-thirds of the interviewees stated that they joined the ranks unwillingly after being abducted (67 percent).[6] The young women who took the initiative and actively decided to take part in the war(s) can further be divided into three main groups: those who joined because of 'disadvantages' (lack of food, shelter, protection or other necessities: 15 percent), those who joined to avenge the death of someone they held dear (11 percent), and those who joined owing to peer pressure and/or to gain material goods (7 percent).

It has been estimated (Specht 2006: 34) that an unusually high number of young women in Liberia joined the ranks with 'feminist motives', such as becoming equal with men. The present research material, however, does not support this line of reasoning. I maintain that the interviewees of this project have not sought to become equal with men in a Western single-sex manner, but rather, after their service in the ranks, hoped to construct an updated *dual-sex system* in which both sexes have their particular rights and duties as women and men.[7] As in Rwanda (Burnet 2012) and elsewhere, numerous Liberian women and girls did not become heads of households or members of fighting forces in order to get rid of the patriarchal structures of the society, but simply because they had no other options. In this 'accidental' manner, these young women began to question the gender roles society had previously placed upon them. Quoting Jennie Burnet (ibid.: 13), who writes on the Rwandan case: 'These women were clearly not passive victims, but neither were they intentional gender revolutionaries.'

All in all, it can be summarized that in each 'voluntary' recruitment there were several push and pull factors that created such an attractive whole that an individual finally made the decision to join. The push factors include bad living conditions or family relations, lack of essentials (food, safety, social networks), peer pressure and willingness to avenge. Examples of the pull factors entail possibilities for protection, benefits (e.g. food, money, drugs or clothes), revenge and honour.

Abduction and the first few weeks in the forces

In practice, there were no safe places for children and youth in Liberia during the civil wars: they were captured from their homes in both rural and urban areas, from streets, marketplaces, fields and schools. Places where many young people gathered, such as video clubs or entertainment centres, were particularly attractive for kidnappers since they offered the chance to abduct numerous youngsters at one fell swoop. Sometimes even a refugee status or residency at a camp for internally displaced persons (IDPs) did not offer safety. For instance, Frances, who later carried an RPG (rocket-propelled grenade) launcher, was captured at the age of fifteen from an IDP camp in Montserrado County during the first Liberian civil war alongside twenty girls and twenty-five boys.[8] She received six months of training and spent altogether four years on the frontline with NPFL. In her exploratory interview in 2012, Frances explained that 'those people made us smoke gunpowder and drink liquor to make us active on the frontline, to catch our enemies ... they made us do so many things during the revolution.'

The majority of the abducted young women suffered sexual abuse during their time in the forces (see Box 2.1). 'They showed me life' was an expression that was normally utilized when a girl was forced to lose her virginity. Nevertheless, it must be noted that not everyone suffered sexual abuse, and it was also a common practice to begin a relationship; to start 'loving to' a soldier or commander in return for protection – a behavioural pattern that might partly be explained by Graham's Stockholm Syndrome Theory (covered in detail in the second part of this chapter).

---

### Box 2.1 The abduction of Hawah

I was stopping with my mother at the age of fourteen. We were in Gbatala. This is during the second war now, because me, I was small during the 1990 war. When we were going, they were fighting behind us. It was on the 24th of August, when the people attacked our home. They [Taylor's ATU] were having a base there, Gbatala base. So that is how we started running and they were behind us. We were going to Monrovia. I was the only big girl and my mother was pregnant at that time. I was having our load: our bags and pots, my clothes and my older brother's clothes. I was having them. And they nearly caught my late brother because of me, because I was small and I was having our load. When I was walking, my ma told me that I should leave the load and my late brother. But I said no, and so we started going. When we reached one of the hottest area, the soldiers came with a pickup and they said 'you there with a bag'. That is how they took the bag from me, held the bag and put it down.

They put me in the car. My mother told them that please put my daughter down. And they told my mother: 'If you are talking, we will fire you!' True story! They told her: 'Either you want your daughter's or your own life.' That is how they carried me and brought me to Totota. We left the car and they tied my hands! At the age of fourteen. They tied my hands. The man said: 'If you cry, we will kill you.' And that is how they carried me away to another village. Far away. At that time I didn't know about life. I assure you, I didn't know about life.

> So I said to them: 'please let me go, I only want to go back to my ma'. At that time my mother was already going because the soldier boys were behind them. So the man said that the only way for me to go back to my ma would be for me to become his woman. I said: 'I don't know about man business.' At that time I was at the fourth grade. And they said that you cannot go to your pa or you will die. And I said: 'Please don't kill me.'
>
> So they put me in a certain house. I was in the house and I didn't want to be there. I was just there crying, crying, crying. He returned in the evening and that is how he forced me. [silence] He showed me life. He forced me and he showed me life. That whole day I was bleeding. My stomach. [silence] I was feeling pain! I started crying. And I said: 'I'm begging you, don't kill me!' He said: 'I'm not going to kill you. I will take care of you, you will be my woman now.' I said that I didn't want to be his woman and asked him to carry me back to my ma.

After suffering the traumatic experiences of being abducted and often sexually assaulted, girls and women had to be indoctrinated into the fighting force. Typically, no specific indoctrination rituals took place with abducted young women, but rather the indoctrination was performed via physical and psychological violence and an overall atmosphere of fear. Michael Wessells (2006: 57) notes that although 'child soldiers are sometimes portrayed as having been programmed or brainwashed, this term can be misleading since child soldiers undergo self-guided, internal changes in adapting to their new situation. [...] Cut off from their previous lives, they learn to put their past behind them and reconstruct themselves in the context of the armed group.'

Indeed, rather than being forcefully 'brainwashed', girl and women abductees in Liberia had to rapidly adapt to their new social environments – to master the rules of the armed forces and understand the meaning of ranks and social networks. As Singer (2006: 72) writes, the overall purpose of indoctrination is 'to create a sort of "moral disengagement" from the violence that children are supposed to carry out as soldiers'. This process typically begins immediately, when children are still at their most vulnerable stages after having been recently disconnected by force from their civilian networks (ibid.).

## Injustice

Many of the interviewees stated that their main reason for joining the ranks were 'disadvantages', an expression that can be understood to mean injustices. These included a lack of food, shelter, protection or other necessities. One of the most interesting of these reasons was the need to protect oneself from sexual and other types of violence. Oretha, for instance, was raped by three men in 1991 in Gbarnga, the capital of Bong County. She got angry and tried to find a way to become a fighter, but did not manage to convince any general of her abilities on the frontline. Two years later, Oretha got involved in a relationship with a man who convinced her that becoming a fighter was not the right solution. The couple had a baby a year later, and in 1994 the war reached their area. Not long after their first unsuccessful attempt to flee, the escapees fell into the hands of some fighters for AFL, and, once again, Oretha was raped. After having been forced to witness this violence against Oretha, her boyfriend was executed, but the one-month-old baby girl and her mother were spared. Oretha explained in her interview that at this point she had had enough. She did not want to be a victim anymore. Hence, she volunteered in NPFL and finally took up a position as a bodyguard for a woman commander. When I asked Oretha if the desire for revenge was among her main motives for volunteering, she forcefully denied it, and explained that her only reason for enlisting was the need to protect herself and her baby against all the injustices happening around her.

When the first civil war escalated in Liberia, most of the wealthiest people were either able to leave the country or at least send some of their family members away, typically to the USA or another safe environment.[9] However, some families who would have had enough financial resources to flee, decided to stay. Among those who lingered on were Angela and Angeline, twins, whose father had held a high position in Doe's government. During the spiral of violence that finally led to Doe's assassination in 1990, government officials were tracked down and executed. Among the victims was the father of the then fifteen-year-old twins, who was tortured and killed in front of his family in 1990. The rest of the family was saved only because of Angeline's 'country name', which she shared with one of the assaulters; Angeline's namesake convinced the others that it would bring him bad luck to kill the rest of the family. Because of this connection, he also decided to secretly accommodate the family in his own house instead of leaving them in their now unsafe family home in one of the upper-class residential areas of Monrovia.

In the course of the following year the twins lost their sister in a relationship dispute. Furthermore, the rest of the family was prevented from returning to their family home by relatives who claimed that the widow no longer had any rights to the house. Along with their mother, Angela and Angeline struggled to get by with hardly any money at all, and finally decided that their best option would be to run away, join the war and try to find resources from the warfront. Thus, in 1991, Angela volunteered in INPFL and headed to Kakata with her AK-47, whilst Angeline stayed in Monrovia and acquired a gun through her boyfriend, a member of the ECOMOG forces. In 2012 Angeline explained her situation: 'There were other girls and we all had to fight for our lives. Because the men that we all went to, they were not there to protect us. So we were forced to hold guns at that time to be able to protect ourselves. [In 1994] my ECOMOG boyfriend went back to his country. Myself too, I left Monrovia, I went to Cape Mount and joined ULIMO-J, and later changed the group to NPFL.'

Maybe surprisingly, the twins did not contend that avenging the death of their father was among their main motives for joining the war. Nonetheless, for many Liberian girls and women it was precisely the wish to avenge the death of a loved one that led them to take up arms.

### Revenge

> I was fourteen years old. I was fourteen when I took a gun to pay my family debt, I never took a gun for freedom. And I killed. I never joked with them, I fucked with them. I was on the frontline. Sometimes when I left the frontline, I knew the tribe that killed my family. And the people that killed my people, they were Gio people. And I killed them. I used to go from village to village and I damaged people's lives.
> 
> *Ciata, Monrovia*

In both Liberian civil wars, there were numerous young women who volunteered in the forces seeking revenge for someone beloved. These loved ones included family members, friends, spouses, and in one instance even a village chief. The wish to avenge is yet another factor that does not fit neatly into the picture of a peace-seeking Liberian mother,[10] nor does it correspond with the contested humanitarian and journalistic discourses in which women are portrayed as naturally nonviolent. Indeed, it seems that those who violate this 'universal truth' are analysed in detail in comparison with their male counterparts.[11] These misconceptions have fortunately been shaken in recent decades in academic research,[12] yet the continuing media attention given to women perpetrators of violence seems to indicate that gendered stereotypes of violent behaviour are extremely persistent.[13]

Some Liberian girls and women were forced to witness extreme violence, such as the dismembering or beheading of family members, acts that both traumatized them and prompted them to seek revenge. These brutal deeds happened in both wars and among all factions. For instance, when I first met Theresa, the oldest of the research participants, and asked her to share her life story with me and my assistant Glorious, she stated that she joined the first civil war in order to avenge the injustices she had experienced. When we inquired about the details of these injustices, Theresa simply stated that there was too much unjustified violence around her. It was evident that Theresa felt uncomfortable sharing these experiences with us and I wanted to respect her decision. Later that evening, however, Theresa and Glorious had a private discussion. It was only then that Theresa felt relaxed enough to explain in detail the circumstances that led her to join the war.

In early 1991, at the age of twenty-five, Theresa was pregnant with her third baby. She and her husband were residing in Monrovia, where Theresa was practicing her profession as a nurse. The family had recently understood that the Krahn ethnic group in particular was now under threat, and since both Theresa and her husband were from this group, they decided to seek refuge in different places. Theresa and her two children went to hide on the premises of what was then a Lutheran church, but soon discovered that there was no food available there; they were only provided with tea for several days. As a consequence, Theresa and her children went to seek shelter at the American embassy, but the lack of resources was as evident there as it had been at the Lutheran church. Later, when Theresa went to meet her husband at a secret location, the couple fell into the hands of Taylor's NPFL. Theresa's husband was beheaded in front of her, but she was finally freed after being harshly interrogated. Soon after, Theresa gave birth to her son, asked her mother to take care of her three children, and went to INPFL's leader Prince Johnson and asked to be given a gun. Johnson questioned her for a while about her motives for joining the ranks, but Theresa convinced him that she only wanted revenge for her husband. She fought for approximately one and a half years for INPFL, but decided then to leave the forces, since 'Prince Johnson was killing everybody. It was insane. There were different, different forces that were fighting each other. So when the tension was hot, I decided to drop my arm into the river and so I became a civilian.'

Peer pressure/Advantages

Only very few of the interviewees directly stated that their decision to enlist was affected by the possibility of gaining different types of material goods from the 'war business', but many nevertheless indicated that they had heard of such behaviour. This reveals that rumors about girls' and women's motives for joining the forces were omnipresent, but it also indicates that the research participants were possibly reluctant to state that acquiring benefits was among their main reasons for joining the war. Nonetheless, on the basis of my data, I cannot agree with Irma Specht's (2006: 16, 35) argument that 'gaining red shoes' or similar luxury items would have been among the key motives for young women to participate in the Liberian civil wars. First, all but one of the interviewees who affirmed that the possibility of acquiring goods affected their willingness to join the ranks also had other reasons for their decisions. For instance, it was common that these girls were severely ill treated at home (a push factor) and consequently spent a good deal of their time on the streets with friends. Upon hearing rumors of the basic goods that soldiers in the ranks could receive, many individuals calculated that it would be in their best interests to join the forces.[14] Related to this, in the heat of the second civil war in particular, it was not uncommon to also see civilians participating in the 'looting business', thus not making it worthwhile to join solely for benefits. For example, Wlejii, later a cook, porter, washer and the lover of a LURD general, was captured in 2003 whilst looting goods from a Monrovian supermarket with a group of friends.[15]

The following story of Chantal is a revealing example of the complex realities that the push and pull factors together created in individual decisions to take up roles in armed groups in Liberia. On the brink of the second civil war, Chantal was twelve years old when she and her friends noticed a group of soldiers who had rented a whole apartment close to her home. When she approached the inhabitants, she was physically abused. However, she was also attracted to the lifestyle the soldiers seemingly had. With their trendy clothes, proud postures and peer support network, they left an indelible mark on Chantal's mind, a very strong pull factor that eventually drove her to volunteer in AFL. But there were also numerous push factors. At the time, Chantal was living with her father and stepmother, who forced her to undertake most of the housework. If she did not perform her duties well enough, she was severely beaten – of her numerous scars, many date back to this time. In her own words she was also a 'rude girl', apparently someone who revolted against her parents, as is common for children going through puberty. Chantal's biological mother was not present much – another push factor – and Chantal had just given birth to her first child. She was not capable of or interested in nurturing her baby, and therefore Chantal's biological mother had agreed to take the baby under her care. As a consequence of these compounding factors, Chantal had, in her own words, 'lost hope in life already' and decided to take part in the war.

Sara, in turn, was the only woman who stated that she joined the troops *only* because of 'benefits'. At the age of thirteen, she spent a lot of time with her friends loitering on the streets of Voinjama, the capital of Lofa County. It was 1999, and a certain type of hairband had just come into fashion. Sara had managed to acquire one of these hairbands and was once again hanging around with her friends when a group of youngsters approached her and stole her brand-new hairband. This was not the first time an incident like this had taken place, and Sara got very angry and frustrated; she had had enough. Therefore, when Sara's friends told her that as a soldier these things would not happen anymore, she went to Gbatala base and volunteered in Taylor's special forces ATU, received US$150, and took a position as her male commander's bodyguard.

Young age, peer pressure, street realities and an unstable environment created a vicious circle. Armed groups were able to utilize these vulnerabilities by either creating fantastical notions of a soldier's life filled with endless resources and peer protection networks, or by luring young people into places from which there was no return. But, as we come to learn in the second main section of this chapter, the actualities of warfare proved to be quite the opposite of glamour and delight for most young women entering the frontlines.

### Girls' and women's roles and duties in the ranks

Liberia's girl and women soldiers are typically placed in categories such as 'Women Associated with Fighting Forces' (WAFF), 'Children Associated with Fighting Forces' (CAFF) or 'camp followers' when referring to unarmed women.[16] Therefore, the majority of the interviewees of this book could thus be regarded as being both WAFF and

CAFF, for they are females who took part in the war(s) while being under eighteen years of age. Nevertheless, I find these categories problematic for four interrelated reasons. The first is terminological: how should we define a girl soldier since she is both a CAFF and a WAFF? Should priority be given to gender or age? Moreover, all three of the categories mentioned above neglect the multitude of roles women and children normally undertake in wars, and in this way totally overlook individual duties/ranks. The third reason why I find these categories problematic is more practical: when women and children are being treated as ensembles instead of individuals, the post-war assistance provided to 'CAFFs', 'WAFFs' and 'camp followers' consequently lacks detail and provides assistance based on large-scale generalizations. And finally, these types of highly gendered terminologies seem to build up gender stereotypes instead of dismantling them. It is also remarkable that since one's individual rank is the most important attribute when estimating the status of a woman soldier in the West/North, categories such as WAFF seem to be yet another way of othering conflicts that are taking place 'somewhere out there' in the Global South.

For these overlapping reasons, I have chosen not to utilize concepts such as WAFF, CAFF or camp follower in my analysis. Instead, I will employ categories based on young women's stated duties in the forces: combat service support tasks (55 percent), fighting (37 percent) and commanding (8 percent). As we will see in the sections that follow, girl and women soldiers in Liberia were not just 'second-class soldiers', but active, dynamic and resilient individuals who played vital roles in the warring factions of Liberia.

### Combat service support: managing daily life within the forces

> For me, I was in a cooking department in the government troops. We were cooking for them, taking care of them – if some of them were wounded, we fixed hot water and massaged their bodies and other things to stop the pain. Sometimes we gave them sponge baths.
> *Marthaline, Monrovia*

> For since men who are well treated by one whom they expected to treat them ill, feel the more beholden to their benefactor.
> *Machiavelli*, The Prince

While WAFF is the general term normally utilized for women participating in the fighting forces regardless of individual military ranks, the non-armed women who take part in the war economy are usually discussed as camp followers. As Cynthia Enloe (1983) remarks, this type of woman is treated as an outcast; someone who is trailing behind the male soldiers, trying to reap any small profit the men in khaki could possibly provide. 'Skirts dragging in the battle-field mud, she tags along behind the troops, selling her wares or her body, probably at an unfair price' (ibid.: 1–2; see also Enloe 2000a).

As is the case with the terms WAFF and CAFF, the expression 'camp follower' therefore also easily undermines the enormous importance these women have in the everyday lives of soldiers. A parallel can be drawn with being a housewife in the civilian sphere of life: someone who is considered responsible for maintaining the domestic order without receiving a salary from these duties. Like housewives with their families, 'camp followers' also play a massive yet often formally unrecognized role in caring for the well-being of the troops. A telling example of the importance of non-armed staff is that in the United States military, for instance, only 15 to 20 percent of military personnel take part in combat activities, thus leaving the majority of military employees to serve in combat service support tasks (Mazurana and Eckerbom Cole 2013: 203). Further, again in the US Army, military cooks are not just 'cooks' or 'camp followers', but 'Culinary Specialists' entitled to the same war veteran benefits as any other armed or non-armed soldiers (US Army 2014). For these multiple reasons, I have opted to place the non-armed girl and women soldiers under the category of combat service support, a term that is widely used in military discourse all around the world. This category emphasizes the importance of this personnel to the factions rather than separating them into the distinct category of 'camp followers'.[17]

In Liberia's civil wars, the responsibilities in combat service support included: cleaning and washing services; finding water and food supplies through legal and illegal means; cooking; carrying munitions and other equipment; maintaining weaponry; nursing; entertaining the troops and providing mental as well as physical 'comfort' to frontline soldiers. Physical comfort entailed sexual services that were most often, but not always, forced. Sexual abuse was prevalent inside all the warring factions in both civil wars. To protect oneself against the hazardous rapes of male soldiers, the best strategy for some non-armed women was on the one hand to begin a relationship – to become a 'bush wife' – with the most high-ranking soldier possible. On the other hand, however, these kinds of 'love affairs' were very often involuntary and many women were obliged to follow their bush husbands to the frontline and be ready to provide any services they might require (see, e.g., Box 2.2).

Although the majority of the interviewees deeply despised their abusers, some described feelings of love towards their bush husbands, even if the relationship was initiated by force (see also Coulter 2009). One psychological explanation model for this seemingly irrational behaviour pattern might be found in the 'Stockholm syndrome' and particularly in Graham's Stockholm Syndrome Theory. Even though the model can undeniably be criticized for imposing another Western psychological explanation on the distant 'Other',[18] I nonetheless wish to include the 'theory' here as I have not managed to find anything else as fitting in its explanatory power.

The Stockholm syndrome was coined as a term in 1973 to describe and explain the complicated and perplexing relationships between four hostages and their two captors. During their captivity in a bank vault in Stockholm, the employees being held hostage started to express empathy and become emotionally attached to their kidnappers, thus acting in a way that seemed irrational to outsiders and officers trying to negotiate with the captors. This illogical behavioural pattern, which occurs in some hostage situations, later became known as the Stockholm syndrome, and ever since has become a popular, yet somewhat disputed, concept for describing similar types of behaviour.[19]

In 1987, Dee Graham argued that the 'Stockholm syndrome' could be found among individuals in various types of situations involving an abuser and a captive. Among the nine groups she investigated were, for example, concentration camp prisoners, cult members, battered women and physically and/or emotionally abused children. According to Graham, bonding with an abuser happened in these diverse groups when four precursors co-existed. These were: 1) a perceived threat to survival and the belief that one's captor is willing to carry out that threat; 2) the captive's perception of some small kindness from the captor within a context of terror; 3) isolation from perspectives other than those of the captor; and 4) a perceived inability to escape. This extension of the Stockholm syndrome was later renamed Graham's Stockholm Syndrome Theory (Graham et al. 1994: loc. 802–912).

All Graham's precursors were present in various degrees in the Liberian warring factions. The lives of girl and women soldiers were constantly under threat and escaping the forces was often impossible or at least extremely risky. The commander of one's faction, in accordance with the general guidelines provided by the Chief of

Staff, set the rules for the community that individuals had to adapt to while putting aside some of their previous beliefs about community life. When in this context of terror a captor (e.g. a bush husband or commander) then performed small acts of kindness, these deeds sometimes created a very strong bond between the captor and the captive – between the patron and the client. In Desire's exploratory interview from 2012, we find an apt description of the messiness of the emotions she held towards her abuser.

> So he told me that the first thing to do was to plait his hair. You know, at that time some of them were having bushy hair! And I went there to do it but I was not able. He told me that if I would not plait his hair, he would kill me. So we were there. We were there. And he and I fell in love. Because we were there, what to do. Because if I didn't do it, they would kill me. So I was there with them. And then our boys from this side too, they came to attack them. He held me. Mostly the boy, the man, I was with, he was really good. Yes. The commander, he was very good.

In practice, the feeling of love was often deeply related to the circumstances many unarmed women found themselves in; they sought shelter and protection, and in accordance with Graham's Stockholm Syndrome Theory, 'fell in love with', or, in the Liberian vernacular, started 'loving to' a person who could provide these necessities to them. The circumstantial nature of this type of affection manifests itself in the fact that the majority of wartime relationships broke down at the end of the conflict. Finally, however, it must be emphasized that although Graham's Stockholm Syndrome Theory seems to offer at least a partial explanation for the emotional bonds between some bush husbands and their 'wives', more empirically informed research on the phenomenon is certainly needed.

All in all, the backup provided by soldiers performing combat support tasks was indispensable for the armed factions in Liberia, as it is for fighting forces all over the world. Nevertheless, when inquiring in interview situations about the number of men and women, boys and girls in each faction, these individuals were most often sidelined by former commanders or fighters (women and men). It was only when I asked about the exact number of 'cooks', 'cleaners' or 'girl-friends' following the troops on a day-to-day basis that these de facto soldiers were considered.

### Fighting: a sense of respect

For most women, acquiring a gun meant increased safety among the troops. People with their own weapons were well respected and generally treated better than non-armed soldiers. Nevertheless, many had to maintain their (unwanted) relationships even if possessing a weapon had already strengthened their rafts of survival.[20] After receiving a gun and being trained to use it, narcotics also entered the scene. By providing them with narcotics, the 'fighters were made brave' and the break-away from civilian life was further enhanced. Naturally, however, drugs and other substances were also used in order to increase camaraderie within the group as well as for the sheer pleasure of getting high and 'forgetting about everything'.[21]

In addition to relationships, physical protection was regularly sought from 'magic', *juju*. For instance, *bulletproofing* was performed by cutting small wounds into a soldier's skin and rubbing gunpowder into the cuts. Sometimes the gunpowder was also mixed with low-quality crack cocaine, resulting in a mixture called 'brown brown'. These kinds of rituals were typically performed by special *medicine men* who received payment for their services. Sometimes, however, commanders 'bulletproofed' their soldiers themselves if a medicine man was not available for some reason.[22] A few of the interviewees also brought up their experiences with cannibalism. Two of them were first assigned as cooks in Taylor's AFL and were regularly ordered to use human organs to prepare 'special soups' that some commanders thought would bring special protection against enemy forces.[23]

*Juju*, and cannibalistic practices in particular, have been given a lot of attention in the media coverage of Liberia's civil wars. Cannibalism certainly took place in Liberia, but it is hard to estimate how widespread the phenomenon was. On the basis of my research data, I argue that the rumors were many, but actual acts of cannibalism were limited.[24] Furthermore, in their portrayals of Liberia's 'rebel soldiers', the media placed heavy emphasis on the outfits worn by young male soldiers. With their wigs, skirts, bras and wedding gowns, they intrigued Western observers and were seen as something inexplicable, yet more proof that Liberia was indeed the true 'Heart of Darkness', a place where the rules of 'ordinary warfare' did not apply.[25]

Whilst this explanation was, for the most part, considered satisfactory in the popular media, anthropologist Mary H. Moran (1995) provided a historical and insightful analysis of the phenomenon in her article 'Warriors or soldiers? Masculinity and ritual transvestism in the Liberian civil war'. Basing her arguments on personal ethnographic fieldwork, as well as Enloe's views on militarism and masculinity (e.g. Enloe 1983), Moran presented three versions of idealized masculinity in Liberia: the warrior, the soldier and the commando. She argued that whereas the indigenous *warrior* 'as a construction of ideal masculinity takes a diversity of forms among indigenous Liberian cultures' and can include feminine articles such as bras or negligees alongside traditional masculine weapons' (p. 79), its Western-originated counterpart, the *soldier*, 'was presented as disciplined, progressive, and committed to the betterment of the nation and the protection of its people' (p. 78). In her article, Moran exemplified how the newly adopted masculine ideal of the soldier became ever more unpopular in the course of the 1980s and was replaced by that of the indigenous warrior, who was 'free to play with gender identity' (p. 80). Finally, the most recent model of militarized masculinity, and accordingly Liberia's military fashion, was the *commando*, a character drawing its inspiration from the American film industry. Moran maintained that the peculiar styles of Liberia's male soldiers could be explained by a type of collision of these three masculine role models in the course of the first civil war. This peculiar melange produced a cacophony of styles and outfits resulting in 'Schwarzenegger and Stallone in wigs and wedding dresses' (p. 82).

When placed in this chaotic context, it is probably not surprising that the military fashion of Liberia's women combatants also began to intrigue Western observers. Young women fighters were portrayed as real-life action heroines, lustful sex symbols who were literally ready to crush their opponents with their AK-47s. Black Diamond in particular, a photogenic LURD commander, attracted Western journalists:

> Black Diamond could be the prototype for an action hero, a sort of African 'Lara Croft.' She's all sleek muscle and form-fitting clothes, with an AK-47 and red beret. She has a bevy of supporting beauties, equally stylish, who loiter nearby, polished fingernails clutching the cold steel of semi-automatic weapons. (Itano 2003)

> A 22-year-old woman in embroidered jeans, a bright top and heeled shoes sips a soft fruit drink through a thick smudge of lipstick. Meet Black Diamond, one of the most feared woman fighters in Liberia's civil war. (Reuters 2003)

As Western observers, we rarely question the presumption that women soldiers should be willing and ready to wear masculine clothes.[26] Women in uniforms are not seen as performing acts of ritual transvestism, as was the case with 'bizarre' Liberian male fighters wearing women's clothes (Moran 1995: 83).[27] Hence, when young women with 'polished fingernails', 'heeled shoes' and 'form-fitting clothes' entered the frontlines in Liberia, they were easily labeled as 'African Lara Crofts'[28] instead of professional soldiers. But what, then, did the women war veterans of Liberia themselves say about their wartime outfits?

They first remarked that the 'fashion plays' of women did not normally take place on the frontline, but in lulls between battles. Indeed, playing with styles and attire does not end in times of war, as one the respondents explained to me. Especially for those soldiers being based in urban areas, it was often possible to purchase fashionable clothes and underwear sold from huge packages imported from abroad. A former AFL and LURD fighter, Juliet, for example, very vividly described one incident in 2003 when she was 'in red T-shirt, blue jeans being white inside and black hair tie', longing to see her friends again and 'crying for peace'.

Some of the interviewees also clarified that a soldier wants as a minimum to look 'decent' on the battlefield, if at all possible. For instance, Mariama, one of LURD's girl commanders, was extremely pedantic about her wartime attire and did not allow other girls to wash her clothes because the results did not satisfy her. She explained that jeans in particular had to be properly cleaned since she sometimes had to wear the same pair for several weeks on the frontline. Jeans were the only outfit imaginable for the rural battles, Mariama explained, because 'being in jeans meant that you had many pockets where you were able to put your bathing soap, toothbrush, towel and everything. Because anywhere you went fighting, when the night caught you and when you were sleeping there, you had your small small things on you.' Once on base, however, Mariama was very willing to 'play' with fashionable clothes originating from abroad. I heard similar practical arguments about frontline attire again and again; jeans were chosen because of their durability and practicality. Hence, wartime female fashion in Liberia can be partly explained by practicalities and the very basic human instinct to look attractive among one's peers, but can also be seen as a natural way of soldiering in a *dual-sex* system. Whereas Western observers, who are born and raised in *single-sex* systems, seem to take it as a natural fact that respectful women soldiers ought to be seen in masculine loose-fitting khakis and combat boots, Liberia's girl and women fighters did not have these limitations, and indeed took it as their right to dress and be seen as *female* soldiers whenever it suited their purpose.

In practice, colour codes were used to differentiate the various fighting factions from one another. In the second Liberian civil war, for example, Taylor's soldiers (AFL) used to wear either red, yellow or orange T-shirts and hairbands; LURD forces put on brown T-shirts; and the members of MODEL dressed in green T-shirts or other brightly coloured clothes if green was not available. These simple 'uniforms' were normally provided by the commanders of the unit, but they occasionally ran out. The lack of uniforms caused problems, especially in the rural battles, since it was difficult to tell which fighter fought for whom.

The training varied from very well-organized six-month-long training periods to twenty-minute sessions on how to dismantle and fire a gun. Longer training phases usually took place on training bases in either mixed-sex or all-female groups. When a soldier changed or was forced to join a new faction, she normally received new training according to her upcoming assignment. If, for example, a person was intended to be a bodyguard for someone important (up to Charles Taylor), she would then receive special training to perform that duty.

For many, the reality of being a fighter proved far from glamorous. Juliet, who described her wartime uniform above, was captured in 1997 at the age of thirteen after being betrayed by her friend. First she was fighting for AFL, until an unsuccessful attack took place, and thus she became a fighter and later a commander for LURD. In her first photo-elicitation session, Juliet wanted to explain her life as a frontline fighter through some pictures she had taken for the interview. It is interesting that Juliet, probably unconsciously, shared these experiences using the present tense instead of the past tense. This signifies the importance of Juliet's past experiences in her life today, more than ten years after the last civil war. In addition, there is a sense of coaching in the interview – Juliet is very clearly trying to educate me on the realities of a 'bush war'.

In one of Juliet's photographs, there is a rope with a knot in it. The rope is tied to a pole under a zinc roof, and seems to serve no specific purpose. Maybe it is normally utilized as a clothesline; maybe it has some other unknown function. We had the following discussion while looking at the photograph.

> *Juliet* (J): In this one I just imagined. [silence] Because in the wartime you have certain areas in the bush where they train you to do these things. Sometimes they use ropes. So when I saw this thing [silence], then I remembered. Sometimes when you are hiding from the people who are firing at you, your enemy, you

can hide from them [with the help of ropes]. Later, you use the ropes to come down.

*Leena* (L): So you were learning this when you were trained?

J: No, they don't teach you these things. But they teach you to use signals, like putting a rope in a certain way as a sign to go somewhere. Like choosing the right road to go to. You know?

L: Yeah. What other kinds of things did you learn? And can you use some of these skills even today?

J: Yes, yes.

L: What kinds of things? What did you learn?

J: Oh, I learned so much but now you cannot use it. Because we are not fighting anymore, now are the normal days.

In her photo set there was also a photograph of the 'bush' dominated by deep green grass. In the middle of the photo there is a lonely palm tree, whereas the upper right-hand corner is dominated by two small concrete buildings next to each other. The area is definitely very moist and fertile, at least in the rainy season. Juliet explained her reasons for photographing the scenery as follows.

J: In this picture, I imagined the time in the bush. Because sometimes when you see one house here, the other would be far away. And there is sometimes water, like small waters in between the houses [there is a small area of water like this in the picture as well]. And you have to cross the water like that. And you have to drink the water. And you have to crawl.

L: How did you feel when you had to do it?

J: Well, you know, when you are running away from the enemy … The people are firing at you. You have to go to the bush. And you have to go across the dirty water and drink it. At that time we used to drink any kind of water.

L: When you were there, were you afraid?

J: Yes, you are trying to find a way to meet your friends. Because in the bush you cannot fight as a group, you have to go one-one, or sometimes two-three. Because if you go as a group, sometimes the people can find you. You are making a lot of noise and all that.

L: And when night fell, how were you able to sleep?

J: You just have to lay down on the grass and sleep. Even if the rain is falling, that is what you have to do. And all kinds of lice and animals can come, but what to do?

L: Yeah. Sometimes when you saw a house [like that in the picture], did you go and take it over?

J: Yes. If there is nobody there, you can just go in there to sleep.

L: And if there were people …?

J: You can just go in there and say, please, can I come. And as long as they know that you are a soldier, they open their door for you. And they can ask you to come inside.

L: So they were kind?

*Glorious (research assistant)*: Yes, but they were also afraid.

J: Yeah.

L: Sometimes you stole from them?

J: No.

L: But if you didn't have any food, you just drank the dirty water – how were you able to find food?

J: In the bush you are able to see a plantain, banana, you can cut it down. And sometimes you can go to some people and cook in their kitchen. And then you can eat. Or sometimes, you just drink water and that is all. If there is no food. Or sometimes, you eat ripe fruits that you can find from a tree.

L: How about if you needed to wash your clothes?

J: Then you just need to wait until you reach the base.

L: And if you menstruated?

J: Then you just go to the creek and wash yourself.

L: But you had some kind of a cloth or something?

J: Yeah. Sometimes you have your pack bag and you have things there. Or you have a *lappa* with you and you can tear the *lappa* and use that.

L: Were there some other kinds of problems? Like coldness? Or sickness?

J: Yeah. Sometimes the leeches are all over your skin, or you are having a cold, all that. Sometimes you can come to Monrovia with money and buy some pain tablets: malaria medicine and all that, but there are always too few of them. And the medicine will always be spoiled as well when it's wet and cold. Or sometimes you can take it and you don't know if you will still be sick tomorrow.

L: If your friends were very sick, did you carry them with you?

J: Yes, no way you can leave a person if it isn't his time to die! If a person dies, you just have to leave him there.

L: Yeah. You have to, because there are no other opportunities. And what other things can you think about when you see this picture?

J: What I think now, what I told you about, drinking the dirty water and all. Sometimes we were so hungry. And we used to lay down anywhere.

L: Yes. It is not a life for human beings. How were you able to tell if a person who came was an enemy or not?

J: We had a sign and the enemy had a sign. For example, cutting a banana leaf in a certain way. Or waving in a certain way. And sometimes you can leave some signs on the ground for your own people, secret signs, and so you know that this is a road your people had passed.

L: So you had all kinds of signals you agreed on before? And so you knew where to go and if it is safe or not?

J: Yeah, yeah.

L: Did you ever make mistakes on the signs?

J: No. You cannot make mistakes.

If the circumstances were physically demanding, there were also enormous psychological burdens to carry. Most of the research participants were forced to witness extreme violence, be targets of ferocious acts, and, as fighters or commanders, also be ready to commit atrocities. Many of the women were unwilling to discuss the atrocities they themselves had committed and simply stated that they were forced to kill or do 'wicked things'.[29] However, some women gave detailed descriptions of the violent acts they committed. Whilst the details of these atrocities are not relevant here, the circumstances in which one changes from a victim to a perpetrator remain pertinent. The story of Evelyn provides an apt description of this process.

Evelyn joined the first Liberian civil war in the northernmost county of Liberia, Lofa, when she was fourteen years old. She was at home in her village when some members of NPFL entered the small farm and started harassing her family. The intruders expressed anger over the small amount of rice the family had managed to produce that year since 'at that time the rice business was very hard' (as the crop had been minimal throughout the country, the soldiers were eager to steal as much rice as possible for their own needs). When Evelyn's father revealed that he was the owner of the farm, he was immediately shot. After this, two of the intruders remarked that Evelyn's mother was pregnant and began an argument over the gender of the unborn baby. In order to discover which of them was right, the boys split open the stomach of Evelyn's mother and removed the baby boy from the uterus. In doing so, the rebels actually committed two murders, for the wound was so deep that it penetrated both the mother and the soon-expected son.[30] After witnessing these incidents, Evelyn was taken with the unit to a nearby town.

Evelyn's first duty was to act as a cook for the unit with another girl. The next morning, she was brought a dead dog and told that she should prepare it as food. She undertook the preparation but refused to eat the meat. After a quarrel, she was forced to eat it, and was told that she would be the one to sleep with the commander that night because of her stubbornness. Evelyn was horrified – she had never been with a man before – and expressed her concern by saying: 'Oh no. As for me, I don't know about life. When I was a child growing up, my mother put a rope on my waist and told me: "If you do man business, I will die".' Evelyn was nevertheless carried into a room inside the main building. Soon after, another dispute erupted between the boys about 'the law' that forbade the unit's members to have sex inside that particular house. For this reason, Evelyn was dragged into a nearby mosque and raped by three boy soldiers. In 2012 Evelyn described her feelings in the mosque as follows:

> At that time, I never knew about life. After they had done what they were doing, I saw blood coming out of me. When they had finished, my friends then took me from there and I began to have that kind of a bad heart saying to myself that: 'As long as they killed my ma and pa right in front of me and raped me, then I will stay with them until I will find somebody to pay my debt on them.' That's how I was with them. I spent more than a year with them.

After about a year, Evelyn met a 'woman general' (a mid-level commander) who asked her to join her unit. Evelyn decided to join the group, received military training, and was given a gun. As she explains:

> So myself, I was part of them and my heart was already cooked. So in the night when the WAC[31] girls then came, they brought liquor, they brought opium, and started to smoke and to drink. So that is how myself, up to now, I'm still smoking and drinking. That is how we started fighting until we attacked Bomi highway. When we attacked Bomi highway, I saw somebody passing and then the same things these people did to my ma and pa, I did the same to that person too. I commanded the women and our children and took everything from them. I replaced my slippers, I replaced my clothes, and that's how I was doing my fucking cat [that is how I was harming them]. We were there until they killed our big man; the man commander, and that's how we became vampires on our own. That is how we came in town here. And that is how I was assigned with my new commander [a notorious NPFL general].

Evelyn's descriptions of the violent acts she both witnessed and committed are nothing abnormal in the context of Liberia's civil wars. Even the process that she went through, that of changing from victim to perpetrator, is typical in the context of my data. What is peculiar, nonetheless, is that Evelyn herself often points to the fact that her 'heart became cooked', or that she somehow became accustomed to the moral community around her – again a behaviour pattern that at some level seems to fit with Graham's Stockholm Syndrome Theory. Evelyn began to live according to the rules of this new community, and, little by little, she started to commit atrocities similar to those that she herself had previously endured, thus becoming a ferocious fighter equipped with a 'cooked heart'.

### Commanding: only for the strongest and bravest

> I was able to go on the frontline, I was able to be there with [a male commander called] Foot to Foot, and I was able to fire just like the way the men were doing it. Anywhere they went, I went there. So they saw that the other women were not fit. The other girl, they called her Snake in the Grass, they took the ring [signifying rank] from her and gave it to me. So that's how I became a commander for the girls.
> *Mariama, Monrovia*

In the Liberian civil wars, all-female units were called Women's Artillery Commandos/Women's Auxiliary Corps (WAC), and the girls and women commanding these groups were given the title of WAC commander. As the term WAC suggests, most female commanders had only girl and women soldiers in their units, but there were also some commanders with male fighters under their command. In practice, however, the term WAC commander was mostly used to differentiate female commanders from their male colleagues. Interestingly, the A in the abbreviation WAC in the Liberian context is sometimes referred as 'Artillery' and other times as 'Auxiliary'. During World War II, there was a heated debate in the USA about the involvement of women in the ranks. In 1941, the US War Department created a group called the Women's Army Auxiliary Corps (WAAC) that would be a 'separate, supplementary, parallel adjunct of the military establishment' (Permeswaran 2008: 97). Again, women soldiers were not considered 'real soldiers', but a kind of supplementary support unit. Against this background, perhaps it is not surprising that all-female units in Liberia were not simply called, for example, 'Women's Army Corps'.

All major fighting factions in the Liberian civil wars had girl and/or women commanders. The eleven former girl and women commanders I interviewed were affiliated with AFL (in both the first and second civil wars), ULIMO, NPFL, LURD and MODEL. In the interview situations, interviewees often used the terms commander and general interchangeably, which makes it difficult to understand and estimate military structures from the perspective of girl and women soldiers. However, some of the respondents clarified the relationship between a commander and a general by explaining that a general had several commanders under her own command. In practice, while a general received her orders directly from the chief of staff, the commanders' orders typically came from the generals. At least in LURD and Taylor's AFL, female generals were called WAC directors, the heads of all the female units. WAC directors received commands directly from the chief of staff and had assistant WAC directors under their command.[32] One WAC director explained her and her male counterpart's relationship as follows: 'We were working like a wife and a husband who have their [soldiers as] children.'[33] On the other hand, two of the commanders I interviewed took their orders directly from the chief of staff, but nevertheless did not define themselves as WAC directors or generals, but 'only' as WAC commanders.

Commanders were not chosen based on age, but on their ability to perform on the frontline. Commanders were offered their positions if they proved to be brave, resilient and fearless. In addition to physical ability, charisma and leadership skills were also essential. According to Juliet (interview 2013), trust also played a huge role in becoming a commander:

> *Juliet*: Leena, it is like that in the war, when they see that you are active and sexy [charismatic], people will always put you in a position of a big person. Because you are active and you have a certain way of talking to the people, that is why the other people will always want to be behind you.
>
> *Leena*: Okay. So you will take your place.
>
> *Juliet*: Yes, so people can tell that this is our commander, this is our leader. So people can come to you and tell you that I want to follow you.
>
> *Leena*: So they start to trust you.
>
> *Juliet*: Yeah.

Whilst ten commanders who participated in this project were given their positions – and their soldiers – during their time in the ranks, one decided to gather her own group. Bintu, who had been captured by AFL to become a fighter in 1992 at the age of nine, found herself bewildered a few years later when her faction suddenly scattered owing to internal incongruities. Finally, after leaving the bush and not being able to find her family, she decided to set up her own drug business. It was through this business that Bintu was able to gather her forces:

> How I got them? Because at that time I was selling drugs, cocaine and all. So when I was doing my business, I had all my customers. They got used to me. And some of them did not know about the war. So I explained to them how the war is taking place. For most, their parents had died for them. I then started to talk with them how to make war and teach them. So after some time, they started showing interest in fighting the war and so you got more men behind you.

Bintu gathered a force consisting of both males and females, but was unable to give the exact number of her soldiers. She explained that since she had never gone to school, she did not have the ability to count how many soldiers were under her command. When I asked

Bintu if her soldiers would fit into the house that we were in at the moment (a huge property in Monrovia), she assertively stated that it would be impossible. Thus, there must have been at least seventy soldiers under her command, and she herself proudly stated that she was a 'brigade commander'.[34] Concerning gender balance, Bintu stated that 'the men were more than the women' and that 'women were many, maybe about twenty'. After persuading people to join her group, she then approached a male general whom she had got to know in her ULIMO years and asked for material support since she wanted to 'fight for her country'. The general agreed to supply her group with essentials, such as arms, bullets and drugs. Bintu trained her forces for three days, and after this, the group was ready to head to the frontline.

In Bintu's group, five girls took turns cooking the mostly looted food items. When it was not a girl's turn to cook, she took off with the others to the battlefield. Sexual relationships between soldiers were common in the brigade; Bintu herself delivered three babies during her time as commander. Bintu saw only one difference between male and female soldiers: boys and men were capable of rape. She noted that ordering her male soldiers to rape enemies and civilians was indeed a wicked thing to do, but she did it nonetheless. She explained: 'They were under me, I was a WAC commander and what I would tell them to do, they did it.' When the second Liberian civil war finally ceased in 2003, Bintu had lost all but ten of her soldiers to bullets, sickness and hunger.

All the interviewed commanders estimated that they were successful in their duties. When I asked the women how they would define a good commander, three broad themes came up: a good commander should provide her soldiers with proper training, protection and counselling. Mariama, who took up her position as a LURD commander at the age of fourteen, explains why she was successful in her duties:

> I protected them. If we were going on the frontline to fight, I supplied them with arms and advised them. I told them that if you go there, you should take time to do things; don't put yourself in rush. Take your own time. Of course the war we were fighting, we weren't fighting to get rich-o, but we were fighting for our country for us to get peace. And you were not going to fight to become a hero. So when you're fighting, you should take your own time to fight, don't put yourself in rush. The way you fight will tell me what kind of a soldier you are and it is the supportive

fire I can give then. Just how they are firing, that's how I'm firing too with them. It's not to say that you should go and run in front of them, if you do that, a straight bullet will pick you up. So you need to take your own time on how to fire, ain't seeing it? If we were ready to go sometimes, I advised them first and then we would go and come back safely.

### The reality: multitasking

It must be emphasized that the statistics provided at the beginning of this section (women performing combat service support tasks: 55 percent, fighters: 37 percent, commanders: 8 percent) were based on the interviewees' *primary duties*. The majority of Liberia's girl and women fighters were multitaskers with duties including tasks ranging from combat service support to frontline fighting. In this section, I provide examples of young women whose duties were constantly overlapping and changing; women who could indeed be defined as multitaskers.

After joining the fighting forces either willingly or unwillingly, it was typical that a woman's character was 'tested' for a certain amount of time. During this period, severe sexual, physical and psychological violence (among others) were used to create an atmosphere of fear. If a commander considered someone trustworthy and otherwise capable, she was given additional duties, from spying or bodyguarding to commanding. The stereotype of vulnerable and inherently peaceful women was successfully exploited, for instance, with women spies.[35] Watta, a multitasker in NPFL before it split in two, regularly undertook reconnaissance tasks in 1990 at the age of nineteen. During that time, NPFL was searching for people from the Krahn ethnic group and trying to assassinate its most prominent member, President Samuel Doe. Watta explained that besides being in charge of the women responsible for cooking and cleaning services (combat service support) in her group, her duties included camouflaging herself as a friend of the Krahns. She would then go to places where the Krahn were known to gather and convince them that a certain area was safe or packed with food items. Once the Krahns arrived at this area, instead of safety, they found a group of NPFL fighters. As was common among spies, Watta also managed to exploit her commander's trust and escaped the forces during one of her reconnaissance missions after having developed enough courage for this risky attempt.

Lisa began her soldiering career at the age of sixteen by performing combat service support tasks in LURD. She cooked, cleaned and was forced to provide sexual services to the male fighters of her faction. When she had proved resilient and trustworthy, she was first 'promoted' to spy, and then to fighter. After four months of fighting, Lisa and her friends got separated from the other LURD soldiers following a very intense battle. Lisa and her friends accidentally bumped into a well-known AFL general, who abducted the girls. Lisa knew that one of her brothers was also an AFL commander, and asked to be given a chance to meet him. The general apparently pitied Lisa and agreed on the arrangement. Lisa went to meet her brother, who decided to take the gun away from his sister and told Lisa that instead of entering the frontline, she was now to restart her duties in combat service support. During lulls in the fighting, she was also given additional tasks, such as looting or heading to Guinea to buy small commodities for her faction. Hence, all in all, Lisa was a true multitasker, as was Veral (Box 2.2), who assumed the roles of cook, porter, sexual servant and fighter in the first Liberian civil war.

---

**Box 2.2 Veral: bush wife, fighter, cook and carrier**

*Veral*: I was fourteen years old in 1994 and we were captured from Bong mines. They used to call it greater Liberia. So we were captured from that side to this side. We came here, it was not in Gbarnga itself but in a bush in Bong County. Soldiers took us and at the time the commander was in the area. He said his name was Bullet Bounce, and that I should be accepted as his wife. I said that I was small. I never knew about life. He told me that if I would not agree, he was going to kill me. The first time we talked about it I said no, I will not do it. I was too small. So after two days we were with them, they were feeding us and everything in the base, he decided that this day he will call for palm wine. He started to drink. He announced that it was his birthday and he called all the soldiers from around for a celebration. So they danced from the morning until night. He also told that he had decided a certain thing. He had two wives at the time, and he told that if any one of the soldiers would go against his will, he would destroy the person. He would kill the person. But I was not thinking that it was for my sake or anything.

So in the night – there were eight of us girls in that room – he told that he had decided a certain thing. And if anyone would go against his will, he would kill the soldier. So we went to bed.

---

We used to go to bed soon, my friends and I, our parents were not around. When we were in the room lecturing, he came and asked all the girls out. When we were going out, he grabbed me, he told me that he was not talking to me but to the others. So he came and said that I should have sex with him. I said no, and so he jumped on me. We fought, we were wrestling for some time. And he had his ring, he said it was for his protection. And the ring got broken that night. So he left soon after and he said that something was wrong with him.

*Leena*: But he didn't rape you that night?

*Veral*: No, he didn't do it that night. It was because he was thinking about his ring. So the next day, he came into the room and he called again the soldiers and said that I had destroyed his life. Since he had started fighting, a bullet had never entered him. But because I had broken his ring now, anytime he would go on the frontline he would be either killed or wounded. So he was going to kill me that night if I was not going to accept to have sex with him. That is how he came, he surrounded the house and told the soldiers to guard the place. And he came, he jumped on me in the room and he raped me. That is how I was raped. I was raped and I had nowhere to go to; I was his third wife. We were three now. Anywhere he went, I should now go with him. If he went on the frontline, I would go as well.

*Glorious (research assistant)*: What was the name of the group?

*Veral*: NPFL, Charles Taylor. So everywhere he went, I would be with him. If he went on the frontline, I would follow. If he went to the bush, I would follow. When they went to fight, I needed to be there when he came back. This was because he had to have sex and he needed for me to be there as a sex organ for him.

*Leena*: Was it only him that you were with?

*Veral*: Yes, it was only him that I was with.

## Systematic inequalities inside the armed forces

Intersectional discrimination, also known as intersectionality, refers to the reinforcing nature and interaction of multiple categories of social discrimination.[36] The categories of sex/gender, age and class that upheld different types of overlapping inequalities in pre-war and post-war Liberia applied only partially *inside* Liberia's various fighting factions. Whereas social class, for example, definitely played a role in distinguishing the young women (and men) who were most likely to be abducted from those upper-class Liberians who were often able to flee the country, inside the forces it was rank, not social class, that determined an individual's relative status within the group. Rank was not, however, determined only on grounds of interpersonal relations, preferences and capabilities, but also on the grounds of a person's sex. Furthermore, while 'wealth in people' was a discriminatory category (some individuals had a lot of 'human wealth' whereas others were very 'poor'), human relations were also a way to boost personal status by acquiring relationships with people possessing plenty of social capital.

For this third main section of the chapter, I have drawn a distinction between three main categories of exclusion operating within the Liberian fighting forces: discrimination based on rank, sex/gender and social relations. I argue that as a minimum all three categories need to be considered if one wishes to understand the relative status of an individual soldier inside a specific faction. For example, being a girl soldier performing combat service support tasks without any direct personal contacts with higher-ranking soldiers often meant that this person virtually became a slave. At the other end of the spectrum were the highest-ranking males with innumerable contacts – and immeasurable power. When detailing these complexities, I simultaneously consider two common strategies the research participants used to boost their status inside the fighting forces: attempting to advance in rank, and acquiring (sexual) relationships with powerful individuals.

### Rank as a foundational category

> They were treating those girls well because they were fighting; they had equal rights. We the others were the slaves. No water, no small beating.
> *Mary, Gbarnga*

Rank/duty was without a doubt the most determinant feature of one's relative status inside the forces. As explained in previous sections of this chapter, instead of utilising the typical military ranking systems such as a 'private,' 'sergeant' or 'captain,' however, my interviewees described ranks in Liberia on highly general terms. Forming the basis for individual rank were sex, personal preferences, practical skills and acquired human relations. Since girls and women performed most of the combat support service duties, the intensity of their non-armed roles meant that receiving a weapon was not a routine procedure. Several girls also expressed from the very beginning their unwillingness to become fighters, and were therefore directly assigned to combat service support tasks.

In addition to the lower ranks, the patriarchal nature of Liberian society was reflected in the nomination procedures for the highest ranks. In order to become a commander in this type of a system, a girl or woman soldier needed to prove her capabilities both to individuals in higher ranks and to fellow fighters who might be under her command in the future. In practice, a female fighter needed to prove that she was at least as 'wicked' and fierce as her male peers. The majority of the interviewees nevertheless did not see any difference between genders once girls and women had acquired status as either fighters or commanders. The interviewed men war veterans also followed this reasoning. For example, one elderly man who took part in the first civil war as a general burst out laughing when I asked him about the differences between women and men commanders. 'There is no difference: a commander is a commander and that's it,' he stated, still laughing at the apparent stupidity of my question. There were not, however, any woman chiefs of staff in Liberia's fighting factions.

It might be surprising to learn that I consider rank, and not sex/gender, to be the foundational category of intersectional analysis in this research setting. All the research data nevertheless suggest that if one excludes gender biases in achieving certain ranks at the outset, rank determined one's status vertically, whereas gender was mainly relevant horizontally *within* different ranks. For instance, girl and women fighters were in principle equal with their peers, but because of their sex, were more susceptible to sexual abuse than boys and men. Like females in combat service support tasks, many girl and women fighters also figured that this risk could be reduced by forming a relationship with as prestigious a male soldier as possible. In this manner, rank, gender and human relations intersected and reinforced one another in different categories of discrimination.

Whereas female and male fighters were, at least up to a certain point, equal to one another, they had a considerable amount of power over soldiers of lower rank. It was the commander of the force who determined how this power was used. Whereas some commanders allowed and even initiated the sexual abuse of girls performing combat services support tasks in his/her unit, others had strict rules regulating fighters' behaviour. Angela, who held a gun in INPFL, ULIMO-J and AFL, was convinced that there were also variances between different factions in terms of brutality. According to her, Prince Johnson's INPFL was the most 'humane' of these three factions; Johnson apparently declared that all rapists would be killed. In addition, during Angela's time in INPFL, Johnson also forbade the slaughtering of innocent civilians. Angela's opinion was that Taylor's AFL was the most brutal of these three forces, since fighters who were not ready to follow the order to kill would be immediately executed themselves. However, my data do not provide me with the necessary information to compare the brutality of different forces. It seems that a factor more important than the name of the faction itself was the personality of the commander under whom an individual was assigned – more evidence of the effects of personal relationships and luck for survival.[37]

## Gender and sex-based discrimination in the ranks

> This time now, you cannot be raped by any person. So if you don't want someone, nobody will put a gun behind you. But during the war, they put a gun behind you and told you to do it or otherwise they would kill you. Or sometimes they put a gun behind you and told you to go over your brother. So if you didn't do it, they would kill you.
> *Magdalena, Ganta*

Gender and sex-based discrimination inside the fighting forces normally began when a person was assigned a certain rank. There were few males performing 'domestic' combat service support tasks, such as cooking, cleaning or 'comfort services', albeit some male fighters preferred, for instance, to wash their own clothes. Both females and males acted as spies and bodyguards, and the majority of fighters, and indeed commanders, were males.

Interestingly, Zoe Marks (2014) has investigated gender dynamics within the Revolutionary United Front (RUF) in Liberia's neighboring country, Sierra Leone. Marks (ibid.: 68–9) maintains that by examining women's wartime actualities and patterns of sexual violence in *the specific social and military contexts* where the violent acts occur, it is possible to move towards a third phase in the analysis of women's wartime realities. Maria Eriksson Baaz and

Maria Stern (2014: 166, emphasis in original) present similar reasoning by arguing that 'further inquiries into the *context-specific* workings of gender in particular warscapes are sorely needed'.[38]

In her analysis, Marks (2014: 80–86) has identified four social categories of women within RUF determined by an individual's age, military ability, pre-war social status (education) and relationships with men. 'Non-wives' were typically young girls who had either been abducted or rescued by a commander. The majority of non-wives undertook combat service support tasks – referred to by Marks as laborers and domestic servants – but some were also fighters. Sexual abuse of non-wives was prevalent. 'Unprotected wives', on the other hand, were married to RUF fighters holding junior positions in the faction. Although unprotected wives were better protected than non-wives, they were also vulnerable to sexual and other forms of abuse while their husbands were on missions. The third category, which Marks describes as 'protected wives', had the advantage of being married to RUF commanders. Therefore, these women had improved access to food and other resources, as well as better protection in the military barracks. Finally, 'senior women' held the highest social status of females present in RUF. These individuals were typically granted a formal rank, and they had a considerable amount of power within the specific fighting force. Altogether, senior women were 'less than two dozen' (ibid.: 84).

Marks' analysis is highly intersectional and entails many similarities with the views presented in this chapter. However, whereas the classification of Marks is derived from women's relationships to men within RUF, the categorization I suggest here is primarily based on the duties/ranks of women within the fighting factions of Liberia. In this manner, sex/gender and social relations are considered as an 'axis' of possible discrimination that must always be reflected against the individual rank of a female soldier. The differences in our starting premises, being derived from the empirical data, can in this manner be considered as yet more proof that the workings of gender in different conflicts around the world are always context-specific (e.g. Eriksson Baaz and Stern 2014: 166).

As in Sierra Leone, girls and women in the lower ranks were most vulnerable to sexual abuse in the Liberian context. Simply put, having a gun also meant increased sexual autonomy. Sexually transmitted diseases were common, as was physical damage to women's and girls' reproductive organs. Many of the respondents still suffered from these issues at the time of their interviews – more than ten years after the last civil war – and were in need of acute medical care. Psychological traumas were even more widespread. For example, Veral (see Box 2.2) had told her current boyfriend and the father of her children about her brutal experiences in the fighting forces; about the repeated rapes she endured and the consequences this abuse still had on her mental and physical well-being. Although Veral's boyfriend did not abandon her because of these experiences, the situation remained complex at the time of her exploratory interview in 2012, as the interview excerpt below illuminates.

> I told him. And it was not easy for him to accept me. Sometimes he does not feel fine about us, especially when it comes to sex. Because I really don't have sexual feelings in me. That's a problem. I don't have such feelings and sex can be painful to me. So this one time he took my complaints to the people and they said that I've got another sex partner out. But he is not considering the situation. Up to this day we are still disputing on sex. Sometimes when I take a bath touching my [silence], it's painful. Sometimes when he comes to [silence] for having sex, if I'm not responding properly [silence]. So that's the problem for us. He even called my brother and told him about these difficulties. I told my brother that I don't want to tell you about my problem. But because he brought it up, I had to do it. So I told him that I don't have such feelings [silence]. That's how we decided to go to hospitals now.

Owing to the numerous forced and voluntary relationships, a great number of babies were delivered within the fighting forces. Births often occurred in the bush without any medical care, and a few of the interviewees delivered their babies alone. Some forced abortions also took place since babies were an additional burden to fighting forces. During the years of conflict, many of the respondents managed to find relatives or other acquaintances to care for the newborns. Many of these children are nowadays called war children or rebel babies, and this may sometimes have devastating effects on the well-being of these children in the long run (see Carpenter 2007). If relatives or other acquaintances were not available for some reason, and if there was nobody at the base who could take care of the small children, babies had to be taken along to the warfront. Instead of mothers carrying their babies on their backs with a *lappa* cloth, as is typically done in Liberia, the babies were now toted in front. In this manner, the mother-combatant could better protect her baby from the approaching bullets since the baby was situated between her arms.

Rape as 'a weapon of war' is a controversial and multifaceted topic. Sexual violence in wars can be both strategic and non-strategic in the same conflict zone depending on the context, as Maria Eriksson Baaz and Maria Stern (2013: 70) remark. Rape was rampant throughout Liberia's civil wars, but to claim that rape was used systematically as a weapon of war still seems to require further proof. What can be concluded, however, is that some commanders ordered their soldiers to commit sexual atrocities.[39] For example, two of the interviewed women commanders explained that they actually needed boys and men under their command for raping purposes. However, I do not know whether their willingness to command soldiers to rape was personal and/or circumstantial, or whether these orders were given by the chiefs of staff.

When discussing sexual and gendered violence in war, male victims are often neglected.[40] According to Charli Carpenter (2006: 94–7), it is, however, possible to find at least three general categories of sexual violence committed against boys and men in war zones: being a victim of rape and sexual mutilation; being forced to rape; and being a secondary victim when the raping of girls and women is used as a means of psychological torture. I have no evidence of males being raped in the Liberian civil wars, but the absence of evidence does not mean that it did not occur. Nonetheless, boys and men were sometimes forced to rape even their family members and made to witness the sexual abuse of their loved ones. All in all, more empirical case studies of sexual violence against males in violent conflicts are urgently needed – including from the Liberian war zone.

### The importance of social relations

I used to lay down with anybody who could give me power.
*Hoatha, Monrovia*

My commander's wife used to like my business when I was with them, and that is how they treated me well. She said that she likes me because I was so active.
*Annie, Monrovia*

Mats Utas' (2005b) article 'Victimcy, girlfriending, soldiering: tactic agency in a young woman's social navigation of the Liberian war zone' is an illuminating description of one young woman soldier's struggles and survival strategies in the first Liberian civil war. Utas writes an 'ethnography of social tactics' in which he aims to counter 'reductionist portrayals of women in war zones as merely the passive victims of conflict' (p. 403; see also Chapter 1).[41] While Utas' goal in the article is indeed worthwhile, I find the generalizing tone he seems to adopt disturbing since he analyses only singular cases. This extreme level of rationality and calculating cunning might be accurate in the case of Bintu – just as it was present in a few of the individual life stories gathered for this project. However, for most young women soldiers in Liberia the windows of opportunity opened and closed extremely quickly, as the cases presented in this chapter often demonstrate. As is explained in detail in Chapter 1, I therefore prefer to call the agency of girls and women in these rapidly altering situations *social rafting*, rather than social navigation (as Utas does).

Having said that, it must be kept in mind that social networks are an essential ingredient of any *raft of survival* (see Chapter 1). As discussed in different parts of this book, human relations seem to form a complex system in Liberia, a system which Caroline H. Bledsoe (1980: 46–80) has described as 'wealth in people' in her study among the Kpelle.[42] Building on previous ethnographies of social processes, especially the work of Jaap van Velsen (1964) among the Tonga people, Bledsoe (1980: 47) remarked that:

> Van Velsen sees social action as the manipulation of formal roles and statuses in the pursuit of specific goals. The present study adopts this approach, but focuses as well on the importance of social fictions for particular ends [...] kin ties to powerful leaders are often fictionalized, and kin ties that are ambiguous, such as fatherhood, can be claimed or denied as the occasion warrants.

Bledsoe (ibid.) argued that social institutions among the Kpelle should therefore be simultaneously observed from at least two overlapping perspectives. On the one hand, curiosity should be directed at the ideal formal rules (e.g. 'patriliny'). On the other hand, these formal rules should be contrasted with the behavioural actualities. Bledsoe (ibid.) maintained that these two realities 'may or may not resemble each other'. Therefore, in a 'wealth in people' system, social institutions and relations are a way to control and maintain the allegiance of people: powerful individuals *need* followers since 'wealth, status, and security lie in people' (ibid.: 53; Berry 1993: 15).

The novelty of the concept of wealth in people, first introduced in the late 1970s (see note 42), lies in its shift away from structures towards processes (Guyer and Belinga 1995: 106), and its less theoretical and more descriptive (Guyer 1995: 86) way of analysing African societies. As Jennifer Johnson-Hanks (2006: 30) maintains, wealth in people is a dynamic 'system of social inequality, whereby power and prestige are monopolized by certain senior men' – or women.

Although Bledsoe's study concentrated specifically on the Kpelle and the institution of marriage, many of her remarks remain pertinent in the context of this project. Indeed, the status of an individual in today's Liberia is highly dependent on her acquired social networks. Such was the case even on the warfront, where the best security guarantee for a young woman soldier was often to begin a relationship with as high-ranking a male soldier as possible. 'Loving to' a respected commander not only prevented frequent sexual abuse by random male soldiers, but also had the potential to provide access to higher positions within the ranks. In addition, different kinds of goods, ranging from food and clothes to narcotics, were typically acquired through personal relationships. Nevertheless, these relationships were often forced and entailed very severe sexual and other forms of abuse.[43]

In addition to protection and benefits, sometimes even esoteric beliefs played a role in the forming of social relations. This finding is well in line with the arguments of Guyer and Eno Belinga (1995), who maintain that 'wealth in knowledge' remains an under-appreciated aspect within the body of work on wealth in people. The scholars remark (ibid.: 113) that no 'leader could succeed without powers that derived from specialist knowledge, and the ultimate leaders, the ancestors, were considered the embodiment of knowledge itself'. Therefore 'social mobilization was in part based on mobilization of different bodies of knowledge, and leadership was the capacity to bring them together effectively, even if for a short time and specific purpose' (ibid.: 120). On the Liberian warfront, for example, it was commonly believed that certain relationships had *juju* in them – a supernatural force that could protect the intimate partners from bullets and other dangers. For instance, Mariama, the former girl commander whose wartime experiences were detailed in the previous section, explained that having multiple boyfriends was not an option for her because of *juju*. As someone who had managed to find a partner with whom her 'luck matched', she was destined to stay with her wartime boyfriend throughout her years on the warfront.

Intimate relationships were the most important channel for sturdier rafts of survival if one did not possess a weapon. Sometimes, however, protection was provided by random individuals. A few elderly women acting as cooks took young girls under their wing, and the bush wife of Annie's commander offered to protect Annie owing to her resilient and active nature. Juliet also described how she befriended a group of Liberian boy soldiers within LURD whilst there was a huge number of Guinean mercenaries present in her faction. She stated that: 'They were always coming around me, comforting me. They told me that I shouldn't feel sad, and, you know, you can be around us. So they came to me and we walked around. Sometimes we looked for food to eat [...] they were my brothers.' Even today, Juliet meets regularly with these 'street brothers' of hers.

Although female and male commanders were described as equally cruel and wicked on the battlefield, there were some cases in which a female commander clearly provided protection to girls and women in the midst of the conflicts and their aftermath. Princess, for example, described how at the time of her capture some boy soldiers acting under a woman commander were impatiently wanting to cut her six-month-old-fetus out of her body. This extreme cruelty was prevented by the commander of the faction, who told the boys to stop their stupid games and instead capture Princess and bring her along. A few months later, when Princess had already delivered the baby and suddenly began to bleed, the same commander released the two and helped them find their lost family members. After the wars, many former commanders (both female and male) continued to perform such acts of empathy, sometimes in the interests of maintaining their 'social wealth', and sometimes out of humanity. As described in the following chapters, wartime networks did certainly not vanish in peacetime. Instead, former war comrades often became 'street sisters' and 'street brothers' – a type of street family – and would form extensive rafts of survival by each supporting the others in cases of emergencies.

## Conclusion

In this chapter, I have tried to unwind the complex realities of Liberia's girl and women soldiers within the ranks. According to Chris Coulter (2009: 10), 'women's choices in times of conflict and war are at best circumscribed, at worst nonexistent'. This was indeed the case with many of the interviewees, most of whom were abducted and sexually abused. Nevertheless, simply placing these young women in the category of victims would deeply undermine their agency in the war zone and render them readily as second-class soldiers. The unsatisfactory terms 'WAFF', 'CAFF' and 'camp follower' are primary examples of this type of underestimation, as is labelling Liberia's young women soldiers as 'modern African Lara Crofts' on the basis of their wartime attires.

What is needed instead is a curiously contrapuntal awareness of the complexities of the warscapes in which girl and women soldiers try to steer their rafts of survival. In Liberia and elsewhere, some abducted girls and women turned into ruthless female fighters who not only took commands from male generals but also, as commanders, ordered their fighters to loot, kill and rape. Conversely, however, the same commanders protected and counselled their soldiers and sometimes performed sincere acts of kindness towards enemy forces and civilians. Other young women soldiers provided essential combat service support for their factions, bonded with their fellow soldiers, formed sexual relationships with male fighters, gave birth to 'war babies' and tried their best to stay afloat in these uncertain rivers of insecurities. For most of Liberia's young women soldiers, the everyday realities of warfare proved to be far from glamorous, regardless of their initial reasons for joining the ranks.

Intersectional discrimination within Liberia's warring factions was rampant. Rank, sex/gender and social relations formed a complex network of social discrimination in which survival required luck, intelligence and persistence among other things. Acquiring a gun or beginning a relationship with a high-ranking male soldier were extremely useful means of survival, and many opted for a combination of both strategies. Graham's Stockholm Syndrome Theory appears to offer at least a partial explanation for why some girl and women soldiers developed warm feelings for and sometimes even fell in love with their abusers; it seems that human beings under extreme conditions must use all possibilities to find comfort and hope for their own psychological survival. Moreover, this tendency can partly explain the lure of the magic, *juju*, that was considered an effective way of bringing physical 'protection' to fighters on the frontline.

After experiencing the harsh realities of war, reintegration into post-war Liberian society proved to be anything but easy for most young women soldiers. The changes in social environments also brought about changes in the networks of discrimination experienced by individual girls and women. For example, high rank in wartime did not directly translate into power in the post-war era as many had expected to happen. Social class was once again the main determining factor in an individual's relative status in Liberian society. As we will come to learn in Chapter 4, numerous girl and women war veterans ended up on the streets of Monrovia, where the practice of 'loving' for protection is still very common among destitute girls and women whose living environments are in many ways risky. These unfortunate realities reveal the fact that the Disarmament, Demobilization and Reintegration (DDR) programs implemented in Liberia did not fulfil their promises to women war veterans, even though the official reports often paint a rather different picture. In the following chapter, we will turn to this inconsistency, as well as to other controversies concerning the Liberian DDR(R) programs.

# 3
# DDR: Disarmament, Disillusionment and Remarginalization

In December 2003, Development Alternatives Inc. (DAI) prepared a report for USAID entitled 'Assessment of the Situation of Women and Children Combatants in the Liberian Post-Conflict Period and Recommendations for Successful Integration'. Reading the assessment is like looking into a crystal ball, since most of the details 'forecast' in the report did indeed take place in the years following its publication. Among other things it was stated that if

> the recommended reintegration program does not stimulate the identification and treatment of these victimized women and girls [females without guns], they will be ignored. By default, the proposed program will end up largely focusing on ex-combatants (mostly boys) and missing the opportunity to identify and help many abused women and girls. (Bernard et al. 2003: 94)

The research team behind the report was both exceptionally visionary and exceptionally thorough in its work. In this instance, effort was placed on assembling a team that included both researchers and area specialists rather than the routine process of hiring a consultant or two to conduct a rapid analysis in a very short timeframe. The final report is terrific and terrifying: it aptly demonstrates that, with careful planning, it is undeniably possible to provide recommendations that have the potential to make all the difference in post-conflict societies. But it is also haunting that *none* of the recommendations seems to have been taken *seriously* (Enloe 2013) by the parties responsible for implementing the reintegration activities in Liberia. What makes this neglect especially sad in this case is that the United Nations Mission in Liberia (UNMIL) was the first peacekeeping mission ever with an explicit mandate to mainstream United Nations Security Council Resolution (UNSCR) 1325[1] (Njoki Wamai 2011: 53; Basini 2013: 71) – combined with the well-known fact that most female (child) soldiers in African conflicts do not demobilize if specific efforts are not taken to include them in the programs (Coulter et al. 2008: 20).

This chapter takes a curiously contrapuntal look at the chain of events leading up to the unfortunate developments presented above. To do this, it weaves together and contrasts three vast narratives on the insights and realizations of the Liberian Disarmament, Demobilization and Reintegration (DDR) programs: the 'official' institutional point of departure, the 'user-based' experiences of women war veterans themselves, and, lastly, the 'external' views of NGOs, external evaluators and independent researchers. By examining these overlapping yet rather autonomous narratives concurrently, a contrapuntal take on 'what really happened and why' in the context of these programs for Liberian girl and women soldiers is produced.

At first glance, the premises and goals of this chapter might thus appear very similar to Helen Basini's (2013) PhD thesis 'An imperfect reality: gender mainstreaming and Disarmament, Demobilisation, Rehabilitation and Reintegration (DDRR) in Liberia'. In her research, Basini investigates the success/failure of gender mainstreaming in the second Liberian DDR(R) program 'from above' and 'from below' by analysing, among other things, the interviews she conducted with 59 Liberian women war veterans and 31 experts associated with the DDR process(es) in the country. There is, however, a peculiar difference in our research participant selection criteria. Whereas Basini concentrates especially on women who signed up for the program (42 out of 56 individuals), the majority of my interviewees (84 out of 128[2]) did not take part in the DDR process(es) or only went through the disarmament phase (25 out of 128), leaving a very low number of real participants (19 out of 128 individuals). In addition, Basini (ibid.: 89) found her research participants through the help of a local NGO called NEPI, whereas the majority of interviewees for this project were located independent of any organization, largely with a method that could be labelled 'multidimensional snowballing'. Nevertheless, and despite these methodological differences, it is of huge interest that our results point in the same direction: reintegration was largely a failure in Liberia, and especially so for those women and girls who did not participate in the DDR efforts for one reason or another.

The conceptual and ideological basis for the DDR programs in Liberia and beyond was created at the end of the Cold War, when the UN was searching for novel ways to respond to violent conflicts around the world. In 1992, the UN Security Council (UNSC 1992: 3) requested the Secretary-General to prepare an 'analysis and recommendations on ways of strengthening and making more efficient [...] the capacity of the United Nations for preventive diplomacy, for peacemaking and for peace-keeping'. The following June, the newly-elected Secretary-General, Boutros Boutros-Ghali, responded to this request with a report entitled 'An Agenda for Peace: Preventive Diplomacy, Peacemaking and Peace-keeping' (United Nations 1992). This report laid the groundwork for peacebuilding measures undertaken by the UN in the ensuing years, and is commonly considered as the 'genesis of the DDR process' (e.g. Knight 2008: 25). Today, a DDR program is typically envisioned as a multifaceted process that aims to reintegrate former soldiers into civilian life. Normally, a DDR program begins after a peace agreement has been signed. According to the United Nations (2005: 1):

> Disarmament, demobilization and reintegration of ex-combatants form a continuum that is itself a part of the entire peace process: Where disarmament ends demobilization must begin and must eventually lead to reintegration, if sustainable peace and development are to be secured in countries emerging from conflict.[3]

Sometimes additional letters such as R for Rehabilitation in Liberia are added to the acronym DDR. Thus, when referring specifically to the Liberian DDR programs, I will use the acronym DDRR from this point forward instead of the 'general' concept I refer to as DDR.[4]

The first part of the chapter presents the transition processes of Liberia's girl and women soldiers as civilians, and the formal insights of the two DDRR programs implemented in the country after the civil wars. The ensuing section is dedicated to the views of women war veterans themselves. In this analysis, it becomes evident that not only did some serious misconduct take place during the Liberian DDRR processes, but the programs were also planned without adequate contextual understanding and were implemented in a poor and rushed manner. Throughout the chapter, special emphasis is given to the views of Veral, Esther and Anna. Veral 'multitasked' in the first civil war, Esther undertook combat service support tasks in the second civil war, and Anna fought all the way through both wars.

In the final section of the chapter, I try to find some explanations for the disparity between different types of narrators (program designers; end-users; external evaluators), especially by observing the indicators of success chosen by the program designers. By drawing from Cynthia Enloe's views on the process of militarization on the one hand, and Amartya Sen's notions of justice on the other hand, I argue that institutions – such as DDR programs in Liberia and elsewhere – have a tendency to treat institutions *themselves* as manifestations of justice, whereas, for the end-users, it is more important to seek institutions that *are able to deliver* justice on the ground. An apt comparison here would be with an authoritarian country that holds regular free elections (a correct institution is in place), but where it is possible to vote only for candidates supporting the regime in power (there is no real alternative in the elections). It is concluded that by beginning to understand institutions as *instruments* of justice rather than *manifestations* of justice, and by critically examining perceptions of justice within these institutions, both war veterans and post-war societies in general could benefit greatly.

### Exit battlefield, enter civilian life

For many of the research participants, leaving the frontlines behind meant risking one's life. This section begins with a description of the range of ways in which girl and women soldiers in Liberia managed to leave the battlefield behind. Most of the respondents escaped (48 percent) and some fought until the war ceased (33 percent). Others were either convinced to leave the forces by their family members or other loved ones (8 percent), allowed to return home by their commanders (7 percent), wounded (2 percent), or left the forces for some other reason (2 percent).[5] Unexpectedly many of these women veterans explained how a stranger had, in one way or another, eased her path back into civilian life without requiring anything in return. Sometimes a successful escape attempt ended tragically and all too soon with an encounter with yet another rebel group willing to capture the unfortunate escapee.

In addition to describing how these brave young women managed to leave the frontlines behind, I will also detail Liberian DDRR program guidelines in this section. In the program taking place after the first civil war, children under eighteen years of age were allowed to disarm without a serviceable weapon. When war broke loose again on the threshold of the new millennium, it was understood that many mistakes had been made in the planning and implementation phases of the first program. Hence, when it was time to plan and put in place a new program after the second civil war in 2003, it was claimed that lessons had been learnt from the first DDRR effort, and this time around women, regardless of age, would be allowed to disarm without a weapon. Unfortunately, as we will see in the second section of this chapter, it was all too little, too late.

## Leaving the frontlines

A large percentage of the research participants (48 percent) managed to run away from the forces. Often, escape attempts were carefully planned but implemented spontaneously when the opportunity presented itself, such as after an intense battle. Night-time offered protection for many runaways, as did hiding one's plans from everyone. Many spies exploited their special positions after having convinced their commanders of their reliability through successful missions; it was very convenient, albeit risky, for a spy not to return to base after an operation. Oral, who performed combat service support tasks in AFL under Charles Taylor, explained that her decision to escape the troops developed little by little in the course of the second civil war. She explained that the commander of the group was never satisfied with her performance even though she worked as hard as she could, and not only gave Oral some severe beatings, but also demanded constant sexual favours from her. 'The tension was too hard for me,' as Oral described it, and she decided therefore to run away from the base one night with one of her wartime comrades.

Veral, a multitasker in NPFL in the first civil war, also stated that the pressures grew to be too much and she decided to escape from her commander during the lull between the two wars. She explained that the very severe sexual abuse in particular (see Chapter 2) was too much for her:

> Sometimes I started bleeding for months. Once, I bled for three good months. I went to a hospital and they told me that I will never have a child if I don't stop having sex with whoever I was doing it with. That is what made me to leave. Maybe if I continued to stay with him, I would never have children.

Many families did whatever they could to find their missing sons and daughters. Family members were sent out on journeys in search of them, children's names were announced on the radio, and some parents even tried to negotiate directly with the captors of their daughters. A way to bring the girl back home could often be found if the family succeeded in establishing direct contact with her. However, some young women were reluctant to return home and wished to continue living the exhilarating life of a soldier. All the interviewees who described having a willingness to 'fight until the end' were either fighters or commanders with a higher position in the forces than women performing combat service support tasks (see Chapter 2).

Although established relationships and thus Graham's Stockholm Syndrome Theory (see Chapter 2) can partly explain the continuing lure of the fighting forces, sometimes wartime relationships also offered a way for a young woman soldier to return to civilian life. This was the case with Anna, for instance, who joined the first Liberian civil war at the age of ten upon encountering 'the rebels' with her father on a highway in Lofa County. Anna's father panicked and fled without his daughter, who was subsequently captured and made to perform combat service support tasks for the troops. Having become accustomed to life on the frontlines, Anna decided to volunteer in the second civil war for AFL with her 'short AK', but finally decided to leave the forces upon the request of her boyfriend, who was fighting alongside her. Anna (interview 2012) explained:

> I left the forces because I was loving to one ATU boy and he told me that I should come to town for me to be safer. So, I turned my weapon over to my commander and came to town. That's how my boyfriend was living in the bush until the day he died.

In a social system that can be described as *wealth in people* (Bledsoe 1980; see also Chapter 1), human relations are not only important for an individual's psychological well-being, but are also resources to enhance one's societal status. Indeed, with a thick network of social relations, one's *raft of survival* can be significantly improved (see Chapter 1). Hence, favours are not 'just favours', but ways to create mutual bondages through the construction of endless chains of debt that can only be paid back by yet another favour (Bledsoe 1980). In this kind of social environment, one could assume that sincere acts of kindness, especially in times of war, would be extremely rare. Nonetheless, many of the interviewees described being helped by total strangers in their attempts to leave the fighting forces behind. For example, Patience, a former LURD fighter, described how she came across some Guinean 'market women' in the Guinean capital of Conakry while running some errands for her troops in the latter part of the second civil war. The market women convinced Patience that she did not need to return to her commander, hid her, and took her along to Freetown the next day. These women demanded no money for their services, and indeed offered Patience some food and clothes to ease her path back home.

In the midst of the conflicts, the endless chains of debt typical of a wealth in people system also benefited some individuals. For instance, Esther, undertaking combat service support tasks in AFL in the second civil war, managed to leave the forces behind thanks to a favour her grandmother had once done for a certain general with a reputation for cruelty:

> I was cooking at that time. They were coming from a fight. So after we were through the cooking, I saw, what is the name of that man again, General Peanut Butter's group. I went to him because my grandma helped Peanut Butter in the World War 2 [a famous battle that took place in the second Liberian civil war]. She was a midwife. So during that time Peanut Butter's wife was not used to giving births so he brought her to my grandma. She helped her, she did medicine for her. Through that relation now, when he saw me, I started crying on him. And so he put me in his car, put me down in a certain place, and I started to look for my people.

### Program guidelines after the first civil war

The guidelines for the first Liberian DDRR program were set in the Cotonou Agreement (1993) signed between the Interim Government of National Unity of Liberia (IGNU), NPFL and ULIMO. The United Nations Observer Mission in Liberia (UNOMIL) was established with Security Council Resolution 866 (UNSC 1993) to support and monitor the peace agreement. However, when it became evident that the ceasefire would not hold, the program was suspended (Jaye 2009: 20). Two years later, following the Akosombo Agreement of 1994, the Abuja II Agreement was signed, and the new DDRR undertaking was scheduled to start in November 1996. As is typical with DDR programs, the implementation responsibilities were divided between numerous actors: coordination of the disarmament processes was given to ECOMOG forces, the monitoring and verification of faction compliance would be supervised by UNOMIL, and the United Nations Humanitarian Assistance Coordination Office (HACO) was given responsibility for the coordination of demobilization, bridging (rehabilitation) and reintegration activities (UNSC 1997: para. 12). Before these plans were carried out in practice, however, violence erupted in Monrovia, leading to a massive amount of looting on the UNOMIL premises on 6 April 1996. According to a report by Kofi Annan to the Security Council, 'my predecessor [Boutros Boutros-Ghali] was compelled to reduce the strength of UNOMIL drastically and to adjust the Mission's budget to a minimum level' (ibid.: para. 12). Altogether, more than

US$18 million worth of property was looted from UNOMIL in the incident (UNSC 1996: para. 37).

In a report to the Security Council, Boutros Boutros-Ghali explains what kinds of adjustments would have to be made to the DDRR plans because of the looting. Small assistance packages would not be given to former combatants in the demobilization phase as was earlier planned. Instead, those resources would be diverted to bridging (rehabilitation) activities and reintegration assistance. Furthermore, former combatants would stay in the rehabilitation centres for a maximum of twenty-four hours instead of one week as previously planned (ibid.: paras 44, 48). In the same report, the Secretary-General also addresses the situation of child soldiers (under the age of seventeen) in the country, the estimated number of whom was between 15,000 and 20,000. The Secretary-General notes that after the 6 April incident, a special program for former child soldiers coordinated by UNICEF was once again under way. Among other things, the program plans included support 'for the establishment of community centres for vocational and literacy training and shelters, transit-homes and trauma counselling for children'. Plans were also drafted for special reintegration programs for former child soldiers (ibid.: para. 35).

In practice, children and adults were sent to the same disarmament sites. There were ideally seven stages in the disarmament process carried out by ECOMOG soldiers. After arrival and lining up (phase one), former soldiers met ECOMOG soldiers and handed over their weapons (phase two). Children were not obliged to present a serviceable weapon in order to receive demobilization benefits. In the next phase, former soldiers were disarmed and registered. Photographs were taken and basic information was gathered for identity cards. Interviews took place in phase four; at this stage children were separated from adults and their interviews (a maximum of five minutes) were performed by UNICEF staff. Another interview was then conducted by social workers in order to facilitate family reunification. During the fifth stage, a quick medical check was performed and after that (phase six) former soldiers were given a maximum of five coupons in order to gain food and other benefits. Nevertheless, many of the promised benefits were never made available to ex-soldiers. In the final phase, disarmed soldiers were supposed to go home in UNOMIL trucks. There was, however, a lack of vehicles and many individuals were exempted from this service. Passing through all seven phases was supposed to take about forty-five minutes, but actually took a whole day (Peters and Laws 2003: 22-4). According to Peters and Laws (ibid.: 93-5), the children who went through the official DDRR program were given many options for their future – they could stay in transit centres, live by themselves or with friends, go home, or start working, for example on plantations.

The DD phase of DDRR ended on 7 February 1997, and by then approximately 24,500 soldiers had officially been disarmed and demobilized. This included 4,200 children, 250 women and 78 girls, whose number was alarmingly low (Adebajo 2002: 208-9; David 1998; Peters and Laws 2003: 17) – especially if one remembers that young women composed about 30 to 40 percent of all the 'youth' soldiers in the war (see Chapter 2). As is shown in the upcoming sections of this chapter, the reality was that many young women soldiers did not go through the official DDRR process, but instead demobilized themselves.

Hence, the first Liberian DDRR program evidently did not succeed in addressing the needs of girl and women soldiers. This failure is illustrated in a Conference Report on DDR and Stability in Africa, in which it is stated that 'the DDR process focused mainly on gun-carrying combatants, thus vulnerable groups, including women and children and followers of warring factions, were not considered' (UNOSAA 2007: 18).

When the next Liberian DDRR program was designed after the second civil war, it seemed that the lessons learnt from the missteps of the first program were being applied. Indeed, UNMIL was the first peacekeeping mission ever with an explicit mandate to mainstream UNSCR 1325 (Njoki Wamai 2011: 53; Basini 2013: 71). As we will soon come to learn, however, gender mainstreaming happened in the second DDRR program almost exclusively on a blueprint level.

### DDRR plans after the second civil war

The Comprehensive Peace Agreement (CPA) was signed in Accra on 18 August 2003. Not only did it set the guidelines for the new DDRR program, but a supplementary C, cantonment, was also added to the beginning of the DDRR acronym. In the CPA, ECOWAS was given the mandate to create sufficient institutional conditions for the first stages of the DDRR activities. After this initial phase, the International Stabilization Force (ISF) would assume this responsibility and supervise the disarmament process, among other things. A National Commission for Disarmament, Demobilization, Rehabilitation and Reintegration (NCDDRR) would be formed to coordinate the DDRR activities (Government of Liberia 2003).

Article XXXI of the CPA was dedicated to vulnerable groups, including children and women. In the article, it is mentioned that the National Transitional Government of Liberia (NTGL) will, with the support of the international community, plan and implement a program for these groups and 'accord special attention to the issue of child combatants'.[6] An Independent National Commission on Human Rights (INCHR) would be formed (Article XII) to oversee the basic human rights agreed upon in the CPA, and a Truth and Reconciliation Commission (TRC) would be established, e.g. to handle questions of impunity (Article XIII) (ibid.).

Resolution 1509 of the Security Council addresses the practical arrangements of the DDRR program. It was declared that UNMIL should develop, as soon as possible and in cooperation with the relevant parties, 'an action plan for the overall implementation of a disarmament, demobilization, reintegration, and repatriation (DDRR) programme for all armed parties; with particular attention to the special needs of child combatants and women'.[7] UNICEF was given the leadership role in the DDRR activities for children (United Nations 2005), and it was agreed that child combatants, CAFF, WAFF, as well as disabled and wounded combatants would not need to present a serviceable weapon or certain rounds of ammunition in order to gain access to DDRR benefits (United Nations 2011: 2–3).

Disarmament and Demobilization activities after the second civil war were launched with a pilot phase on 7 December 2003 next to Monrovia in Camp Scheiffelin. However, owing to many problems, former soldiers began to riot and took over the disarmament site (Nichols 2005). Modifications to the arrangements were made, the programme restarted in April 2004, and it was concluded by November of that year (Gawler et al. 2009: 20). By the end of the DD component, 103,019 former fighters had been disarmed and 101,495 demobilized; thus, the estimate of about 38,000 participating combatants made prior to the commencement of the DD activities was highly inaccurate.

When looking at these numbers, it might be tempting to argue that the DD processes after the war were highly successful. But the situation was in fact quite the opposite, as Kathleen Jennings remarks: the high participation rate is actually evidence of the programme's failure. Jennings clarifies that despite the high number of disarmed soldiers, only 27,800 guns – one per every four fighters – were collected, when the anticipated amount had been three guns per fighter (Jennings 2007: 208–9; see also Nichols 2005; Paes 2005). Also, in an 'Internal Audit Report' for the United Nations about the

DDRR process in Liberia, it is stated that the 'figures cited cannot be considered reliable, because the targets set are not justified (they were based on unreliable figures) and even the reported accomplishments are questionable'.[8]

As Nichols (2005) remarks, these types of technical failure were, however, only a modest challenge when compared to the problems with the overall design of the program. Rather than creating a *warscape-specific* DDRR program and learning from previous shortcomings, the Liberian program repeated old mistakes and was based on similar programs implemented abroad (Gawler et al. 2009: 23). Consequently, girl and women soldiers/war veterans were once again overlooked in these processes.

## Women veterans' views on Liberian DDRR activities

The majority of those Liberian women veterans who survived the horrors of war as soldiers did not take part in the DDRR activities. This section scrutinizes the Liberian DDRR programs specifically from the viewpoint of women veterans themselves. First, the paucity of institutional structures is examined, followed by an analysis of individual experiences of homecoming. The section ends by detailing some of the survival strategies my interviewees have undertaken to overcome the shame and stigma attached to being a woman war veteran in Liberia today.

The main reason for the low subscription rate of girl and women soldiers in both Liberian DDRR programs was misinformation about the process. 'I didn't have a gun' was the most common reason given by the interviewees for not signing up for the program, followed by 'I was afraid that they would take my picture', indicating the fear of stigmatization and rumors of travel restrictions in the future. In addition, some other reasons were given, such as the misapprehension that the program was only for the government soldiers; inability to travel to the disarmament site; sickness; or responsibilities at home (see also Basini 2013: 182–3; Specht 2006: 83 –92).

Adult women had the same entry criteria as adult men for the first DDRR program – certain rounds of ammunition or a serviceable weapon – but children under eighteen years of age were allowed to subscribe without a weapon. These, in many cases confusing, entry regulations partly explain the low participation rate of girls and women in the first DDRR program. Since the regulations were altered for the second DDRR undertaking, and also women were allowed to subscribe without a weapon, the reason 'I didn't have a gun' can, in this case, partly be explained by poor information chains. For example, Anna, who gave her 'short AK' to her commander when leaving the forces upon the request of her ATU boyfriend, had no idea that she could have signed up for the second DDRR program without a weapon. When I asked about her possible disarmament, Anna (interview 2012) looked at me as if I was fool and stated 'but how could I have disarmed since I didn't have a gun?'

These motives are in line with the findings of Dyan Mazurana and Linda Eckerbom Cole (2013: 204–6), who have found a number of reasons for the low participation rates of girls and women in the DD phases of DDR programs around the world. Firstly, the question of identification causes constant challenges: it is often unclear who counts as a 'combatant' or as a 'WAFF', and guidelines for inclusion vary substantially. For instance, it is extremely common that participation is available only to those soldiers who can present a serviceable weapon or certain rounds of ammunition upon entering the program – as was the procedure with adults in the first DDRR program in Liberia. Secondly, the communication and logistics of DDR processes often create massive challenges, especially in war-devastated environments. Related to this, only male commanders and senior members of fighting forces are typically given the power to draft lists of combatants, lists that tend to favor males. Thirdly, DDR officials themselves sometimes hold gendered assumptions about the roles of women and men in the fighting forces that can further marginalize females of all ages. And finally, long travelling distances to cantonment sites, as well as their deficient healthcare facilities, can be a challenging prospect for women owing to their everyday care-taking duties and other family responsibilities (ibid.).

## Lessons on how to misuse poor institutions

> I disarmed three times after the war. When I received the first money, I was getting high in a ghetto and the police were chasing us. And so my [first] disarmament ID card dropped. But after that I also disarmed with other people's guns. This is how I disarmed three times in different different camps. After, I gave all the money to this certain woman to keep. But she ate all of it and I went to live in a ghetto. At that time I never knew about money business because I never went to school.
> *Catherine, Monrovia*

Of the forty-four interviewees who managed to subscribe to a DDRR program after the wars, the majority reported misconduct of some sort within the program. Many girl and women combatants were exploited by their commanders or fellow fighters, who told them that now that the war had ceased they needed to give guns and ammunition to their commanders, who would take care of disarmament on their behalf. It was also easy to misuse the poor institutional structures for one's own benefit: as described in Catherine's quotation above, some disarmed (and got all the associated benefits) up to three times, whereas others asked their friends to disarm on their behalf.

In 1991, in the midst of the first civil war, Angela decided to return home after having fought for INPFL for a little over a year (see Chapter 2). Her mother was happy to receive her and for a while things went smoothly. When it soon became apparent that there was a constant lack of the basic necessities of life, such as food, Angela decided that it would be best for her to return to the warfront. Hence, in 1993, she volunteered in ULIMO-J and finally ended up in NPFL in 1995. However, after only a few months, Angela was badly injured in a car accident of which she was the only survivor. Passers-by immediately took Angela – the driver and commander of the car – to Monrovia, where she woke up in a hospital with her mother sitting beside her bed, terrified by the deep wound on Angela's face and the fact that she only had a slip on. Angela's mother once again welcomed her daughter home, but this time Angela had decided to live on her own. Nevertheless, her mother succeeded in convincing both Angela and her twin sister Angeline not to take part in the second civil war that would soon erupt. Between the wars, both sisters knew about the newly established DDRR program, but had heard the false rumors that in the disarmament process a photograph would be taken in order to prevent the subscribers from traveling abroad (photos were indeed taken, but for the purpose of ID cards). To gain at least some modest benefits from the program, the sisters decided to give their guns to some civilian men, who promised to return their arms on their behalf. Angeline received US$100 from the process, whereas Angela was left with no money at all.

Esther, who left AFL with the help of a well-known general, explained that, after she had found her family and settled back in her home, a civilian man approached her and urged her to go and disarm. The man gave Esther a gun, and told her to bring back to him everything she received from the disarmament site. Apparently, neither Esther nor the man knew that women were allowed to 'disarm' without a weapon and that even WAFF could disarm in the second DDRR program. Hence, Esther headed to the disarmament site in Ganta, received an identity card, US$150 ('the first disarmament money'), a bucket, a sack of rice, a blanket and some other small things. The next day she took all these things to the man who had urged her to go to the disarmament site. The man told Esther that he would now take everything acquired from the program into his possession – including her identity card required for the 'second disarmament money' – but, in return, the next US$150 would belong to her. As a small courtesy, he provided Esther with some rice. When Esther later realized that she had been fooled, she urged her brother to go to speak with the man, who made generous promises but soon disappeared with Esther's identity card and all the other disarmament benefits. She never saw him again.

Evelyn, whose experiences of transforming from victim to perpetrator were described in Chapter 2, managed to disarm twice after the second civil war. First, she subscribed to the badly managed camp Scheiffelin in 2003, where she first received US$75 (there was a lack of money owing to the high number of participants) and was told that the next US$75 would be given to her later on. However, Evelyn (interview 2012) explains:

> But they gave the money to our various commanders. So we said to ourselves that we as well suffered in the war and some of us have marks all over our bodies. Some of us are wounded and we need to benefit from this. So we left them and went instead to LURD forces site. And we did re-disarmament. The re-disarmament we did, they gave us all our money which was 150 USD cash. When they gave us the first 150 USD, they also gave us ID cards. And they said that before we could receive the second money, you needed to show your ID card. After all this, I did tailoring in the programme. The people in the programme told us that before we graduated, they would provide us materials. But we were the last people and they never gave us anything. They just put us on a waiting list. They told us to wait. And up to now we are still waiting. We haven't heard anything from them.

Evelyn's frustration is in line with Helen Basini's (2013: 242–3) findings from Liberia; of her interviewees, the majority did not receive the promised toolkits or other materials after the educational components included in the DDRR process and felt deeply betrayed.

## The joy of returning home

After having performed combat service support tasks for five months at the age of thirteen for 'Dissidents',[9] Desire found herself in the area around Ganta when peace was announced in 2003. Her male commander released her, gave her a rocket for disarmament purposes, and urged her to go back to her family. When Desire finally reached home, her parents were overwhelmed with joy since they had been certain that she was already dead. The family organized a celebration for her: they 'cooked rice the whole day', killed a chicken and prayed for the girl. In addition, Desire felt comfortable enough to explain everything she had gone through in the forces to her mother, who cried with Desire and convinced her that what had happened was not her own fault, and now was the time for a new beginning.

Desire's positive experiences in returning home were relatively typical among the research participants – only nine interviewees reported troubles with reintegration if they had managed to trace their families. These findings also correlate with those of Basini (2013: 216) and Pugel (2009), to whom the majority of their interviewees reported no major obstacles in homecoming.

For some war veterans, however, there was no home to return to. The most common reason for such a situation was either a lack of contact with immediate family members or having lost everyone in the war. Bintu and a few others did not even know which family they belonged to since they had been so very young upon entering the war. As is detailed in Chapter 2, Bintu was captured at the age of nine and was able to form her own unit only a few years later. She commanded this unit until the end of the second civil war. After the war ceased, Bintu decided to head for Gbarnga, where she met a woman urging her to go and disarm. The woman took Bintu to the nearby disarmament site, and told her to keep the food ingredients, pot, blanket and other everyday necessities she would receive there. The woman, in turn, would keep the US$150 and use some of it to purchase clothes for Bintu and her three children. Bintu explained to me that she had no idea about the value of money because she was uneducated, and hence she believed the woman's offer to be a very generous one. At the actual disarmament site, the disarmament officers gave Bintu an ID card and told her to come back later for the 'second money' and to choose a trade to learn. When that time came, however, one of Bintu's children was severely ill and she had no one to take care of the child. Therefore, she never returned to the camp and began to support herself by selling 'cold water'[10] and, most likely, her body. Bintu stayed for some time with the woman who had transported her to the disarmament site, but soon grew restless and decided to head to the capital. In Monrovia, she was unable to locate her old acquaintances, settled in a slum with her three children, and began to hustle on the streets.

Mama P, an elderly woman from the same neighborhood, observed Bintu and her behavior for a while, and one day decided to approach the young woman. The following excerpt is taken from an interview situation in 2014, where I and my assistant Jessica learnt about how Bintu and Mama P slowly began to build trust in one another.

*Bintu (B)*: After the war my mind wasn't set.

*Mama P (M)*: Yes. [And that is why] taking this child from the street wasn't an easy thing.

*Jessica (research assistant)*: So you went there and asked her to come so, come so?

M: Yes.

*Leena (L)*: Now why did you decide to do it?

M: What? I love girl children! I myself have given birth to girl children and educated them. And to see a fine little child like this on the street, and she is so beautiful, I decided to call her. I called her and told her 'come on, come here'. So she came. And I asked her but what was she doing on the street. And she told me that she ain't got a ma, she ain't got a pa, so she can do whatever she wants to do. So I said no, come. I am your mother now: I can take care of you. And I talked to her. Every day I talked to her. And I told her to stay here [in my house]. And I took care of her, counselled her ... Now I bless God so much that she could come to me. But to talk with these children on the streets, to tell them how life is looking like, it is not easy! They don't know right from wrong. It can take time!

For this one here, I have told her to go to night school so that she could, at least, learn how to read and write. So at least to write her name down. And you will see, the people there, if you can read small and write your name, people there will see you in the society. So you can become someone. And the business that you are doing now, selling dry fish, if you don't know the figures, you cannot do anything. You have to mark down everything. So she has told me that she will do it. Now she is at the third grade.

L: You are going to school now! That's great.

L: So how did you manage to tell her that street life is not good?

M: I told her that every night you dress and go out, you dress and go out, and nothing there. Just to suffer your body. So I told her that don't go there, I will give you food to eat. Don't go there. Come. Come, I will give you food and we will eat. And she came. And I told her to wash her clothes. So, I believe, this is the least you can do in human life to treat a child.

L: B, do you remember when she called you the first time?

B: When she called me first, I remember it.

L: Do you remember how you were feeling at that time?

B: I was feeling so bad.

L: Why?

B: Because everything was disturbed; my people had died and there was no one to comfort me. I thought about my future and the future of my children. So [finally] I decided to sit down and listen to her as a mother.

Only a few of the research participants experienced challenges in their familial homes upon their return from the warfront. Hawah, whose capture is detailed in Chapter 2, managed to run away from her commander one Saturday morning at the local marketplace when she accidentally bumped into her grandmother. The older woman was horrified after hearing her granddaughter's story, and immediately took her to a local hospital. Hawah met her parents at the hospital, and they were informed that their daughter had suffered severe sexual abuse and needed to be hospitalized for a few weeks. Hawah (interview 2013) explained her father's reaction after learning about everything that had happened:

> My pa said that as it all had happened so that my ma had taken me away from him, and forced me to come with her, then anything that had happened to me is not his business anymore. From that very moment on my father said that I'm not his daughter any longer. Up to now, he doesn't even have time for me anymore.

Fortunately, Hawah's mother decided to stay beside her daughter and got a divorce. After receiving treatment at the hospital, Hawah moved into her mother's new small home and persistently tried to settle things with her father, but to no avail. Hawah explained that as someone belonging to the Mandingo ethnic group, it was of the utmost importance that her father be able to marry her out as a virgin. As this was no longer possible with Hawah, he decided that he no longer had a daughter.

It must be emphasized here, nonetheless, that experiences like Hawah's were very rare among the interviewees. Patience, also a Mandingo and a fighter for LURD in the second civil war, was not certain how her family would react upon her return, so she decided to recuperate at her friend's house for a while before reconnecting with her parents. At the same time, however, Patience's family members had heard rumors about her homecoming and managed to track her down. Patience (interview 2013) explains:

> They came to me so I felt fine. I felt at home and they still accepted me as their daughter. Even though what had happened, they never hold me for it because I was under tension; I was just forced to do it. So my father told my mother and my stepmother that even if my daughter had taken a gun to kill me at that time, and I would now be in my grave, I wouldn't say that it is my daughter who had killed me. She was under tension at that time. I wouldn't blame her. So if anybody will treat my daughter differently [than before], I will treat that person the same. So there really was no segregation after the war.

## Overcoming shame and stigma

Esther was pregnant for the first time when she was captured to join AFL at the age of twenty-two. When she returned from the warfront about a year later, her family was extremely happy to receive her back home. But Esther's mother also asked about the whereabouts of the baby since she knew that Esther had been pregnant at the time of her disappearance. In this manner, Esther was forced to explain everything to her mother: that in addition to cooking and other maintenance services, she and the two other young women handling combat service support tasks in her unit had been constantly sexually abused. As Esther explains: 'At that time anyone who wanted to have you, they could have you. Not even a single person but sometimes many.' Because of the abuse, she had had a miscarriage on the warfront, and this is why she felt very sick even on the day of her return.

After Esther had explained to her everything, her mother took her daughter to a midwife for treatment as soon as she could. However,

Esther's reproductive organs were so badly damaged that she had become infertile – a fact that she is reminded of constantly in her everyday life, even today.

> I can say that life is alright today. But right now, because they spoiled my womb, I cannot [give birth] again. But what to do? I have gone from hospital to hospital, from clinic to clinic and no help. My boyfriend is facing problems with this. He has brought three children to our home already to live with us, but he is still having problems with me. He wants to have our own child. So sometimes we can go to hospital and we can both have check-ups. But the problem is not him, it is me.

Veral, a multitasker who escaped her abusive commander between the wars, was welcomed back home by her family, but ostracized by the members of her community. Veral's parents therefore suggested that she move to a new community – somewhere where people would not know about her past as a soldier. Veral explained that, even today, some members of her parents' community have trouble accepting her.

> There are some people who never wanted to lay eyes on me. But for now, it is not 100 percent, but at least 25 to 50 percent that accept me. Like this one woman, who never used to speak to me before, I begged her. She said that we were rebels. But I begged her. I said: 'please forgive me if there is something wrong that I have done against you'. I told her that I was captured and raped and I was forced to join the forces. At that time I was like a hungry lion – I did anything I could do to get my life back. So I said, I'm sorry if I have ever done wrong to you. But gradually they just have to accept us anyway. Although sometimes it is not easy.

In spite of what she had gone through in the preceding years, Veral is one of the rare interviewees in this study who successfully participated in the DDRR program after the first civil war; another example of her endless resiliency. Veral undertook the actual disarmament in the Bong mines in north-central Liberia in 1996, settled in a new community in 1997, and used the disarmament money to pay for her schooling. She also completed a baking and catering course offered to her in the latter part of the DDRR program. Today she occasionally gains some modest income with these skills.

Like Veral, Oretha also displayed extreme persistence in overcoming stigma and rebuilding her life anew after the first civil war. As detailed in Chapter 2, Oretha joined NPFL in 1994, seeking protection for herself and her small baby. After about two years, the fighting began to quieten down, and at the encouragement of her pastor, Oretha decided to leave her life as a fighter and bodyguard. Since she was afraid of possible travel restrictions in the future, Oretha decided not to subscribe to the DDRR program and returned directly back home. Back in her village everyone was very frightened of her, and no one, including her immediate family, was pleased by her reappearance. Word had circulated that a fearless woman fighter, a true killer, was about to bring 'confusion' to the community. Regardless of the obstacles, Oretha decided to persist. She asked her pastor to come to the village and speak with the inhabitants. This he did, going door to door to explain that 'the more you are afraid of her, the more you keep her away from you'. The pastor's visits had the desired effect, and little by little the residents of the village began to forgive Oretha. The most persistent opponent of Oretha's acceptance back into the community was, surprisingly, her own grandmother, who did not allow Oretha to enter her yard for quite a while. In the end, it took immense persistence on the part of the pastor and numerous members of the village to persuade Oretha's grandmother that her granddaughter had changed and was no longer a soldier.

## *Niti, nyaya* and institutional justice

Andrea Tamagnini, the former director of UNMIL's Reintegration, Rehabilitation, and Recovery component, and Teresa Krafft, associate DDR officer with UNMIL, state that the second 'DDRR program was able to absorb an unexpectedly high number of ex-combatants; it accommodated women and children in greater numbers than other programs had done before; and it convinced the majority of its beneficiaries to return to their communities' (Tamagnini and Kraft 2010: 15). In the same manner, the Secretary-General's Special Representative Jacques Klein argued insistently in 2004 that no civilians were entering the DDRR program. He also maintained that the Liberian DDRR process had thus far been 'fantastic' (IRIN 2004). Whitewashing mismanagement for institutional purposes is one obvious reason for the huge disparity between the views of those implementing the Liberian DDRR programs and those that the programs were intended to benefit. However, the indicators one uses to measure success can partly explain these differences as well. In the concluding section of this chapter, I search for possible explanations for the seemingly opposing views concerning the success of the DDRR programs implemented in Liberia. I also suggest a few modifications that could be made for future DDR undertakings.

During my quest for these explanations, I take a curiously contrapuntal look at the reintegration efforts of young women soldiers after the second DDRR program in Liberia. The reintegration phase in this process began in late 2004, and the whole program officially ended on 21 July 2009. By emphasizing the reintegration component of this program, I try to build an understanding of why different types of narrators – programme designers and implementers, end-users, external evaluators and scholars – have such different views about the relative success of the reintegration efforts in the country. The section begins with the exemplary case of Martha. By investigating her experiences of reintegration from several perspectives simultaneously, it is possible to appreciate how a certain reintegration undertaking can be understood in opposing ways depending on the observer's standpoint and, relatedly, the chosen indicators. After looking at Martha's case, I rely on Amartya Sen's categorizations of institutional justice in further claiming that the inherent notions of justice embedded in the chosen program can partly explain the opposing views. Before concluding the chapter, I argue that the DDRR programs in Liberia were not only gendered, but also militarized. Hence, despite tremendous promises to the contrary, the programs were built around militarized masculinities and the view that it is possible to deliver justice by institutional design alone.

### What you measure is what you'll get

> I used to measure the skies, now I measure the shadows of Earth. Although my mind was sky-bound, the shadow of my body lies here.
> *Johannes Kepler (in an epitaph he wrote for himself)*

The experiences of Martha are in many ways revealing as an example of a reintegration experience that can be understood in highly variant ways depending on the chosen perspective. Through a purely institutional lens her case seems exemplary: Martha became a fighter at the age of nine and fought throughout both wars, enrolled in the most recent DDRR program, disarmed, and studied agriculture within the DDRR framework. In addition, a representative of the

Children's Assistance Program (CAP) held discussions with Martha's family to help ease her way back into the community after more than ten years on the warfront. After finishing her studies, Martha took part in a special graduation ceremony with her proud family members by her side. Thus, if we only follow Martha's trajectory up to the point of her graduation – as is typically done in different types of institutional programs – Martha indeed seems like a poster child for the DDRR process: after all the years as a child soldier she was successfully disarmed, demobilized, and returned safely to her family. However, if we extend our inquiry a few years after the graduation ceremony and look at the reintegration phase, the storyline changes somewhat dramatically.

After graduation, Martha was unable to put her newly acquired skills into practice since she did not possess any land. Idleness soon grew into disappointment, and disappointment into frustration. This was not what Martha, or her family, had expected her future to become. Consequently, Martha began to spend more and more of her time with her wartime comrades and began to treat her frustration with substance abuse, as this was the way that Martha and her friends were accustomed to 'forgetting about everything'. To fund the habit and make at least some 'small money' for her family, prostitution and petty crime entered the picture. Soon after, Martha decided to leave her family home and move to a Monrovian slum, where her circle of wartime friends and customers – a type of raft of survival – were easily available. This is where I got to know Martha in 2012.

It therefore seems that indicators for measuring success can be problematic in this particular case for at least three overlapping reasons. First, the *indicators themselves* and the process behind their selection matters. Are the indicators copied from pre-existing DDR programs or are they drafted on a case-by-case basis? Are they contextualized, i.e. with regard to the specific conflict history; expected gender roles; a job market analysis? Contextualized background research data were, for instance, clearly absent in Liberia when plans were drafted for the second DDRR program – in the 'Strategy and Implementation Framework' for the 2003 DDRR program it is stated: 'The general estimate is [that] between 1,000 to 2,000 women [were] involved in various ways with the armed conflict in the country',[11] when the actual number of women (and girls) in the forces was at least ten times as high.[12] It also matters enormously which people are considered experts in determining the relevant indicators and what their formal insights are. Are women – and with what sorts of backgrounds – included in the process? If they are, can they truly influence its outcomes? Existing research shows that women are systematically excluded from peace processes around the world (Shekhawat and Pathak 2015: 56), and Liberia was no exception. As Leymah Gbowee (Gbowee and Mithers 2011: 19) explains in her memoir about her personal experiences about the second DDRR process in Liberia:

> Another problem was UNMIL's approach to persuading former fighters [...] to turn in their weapons and rejoin society. [...] We [members of Women of Liberia Mass Action for Peace] visited the UNMIL office on Tubman Boulevard to offer our help. 'You should involve people with local knowledge of who and what's involved,' I said. No one was interested. 'Don't worry!' we were told. 'We're bringing in experts with a great deal of experience from Kosovo.'

Secondly, as Martha's case demonstrates, the chosen *timeframe* of any indicator also matters enormously. It is obvious that reintegration is a lengthy process that may take several years. In addition, if young veterans have basically come of age during the conflict and have therefore never known peace, one must ask which reality they are supposed to reintegrate into, or, as, e.g., Jaremey McMullin (2013: 1) inquires: '*reintegration into what*?' Related to this, one must consider *whose reintegration* is being measured and how. Individuals reintegrate with the help of the surrounding communities they are rejoining – and these communities might tremendously ease or challenge an individual's post-war recuperation. Hence, it might sometimes be useful to investigate not only individuals' reintegration possibilities and challenges, but also those of the community (see, e.g., Özerdem 2012).

All in all, it can be concluded that the starting premises of any DDR program have a very substantial effect on the outcomes that the program can finally deliver. And further, as I claim in the following sections by referring to Amartya Sen's views on justice, the presumed and often implicit notions of justice that the program in question is built upon lay the ethical groundwork for the whole process.

### Institutions as manifestations of justice

It is typical for the international community to concentrate solely on institutional and administrative reforms in fragile contexts. Instead of trying to map out existing networks on the ground in order to utilize these linkages in the design stages of the programs, the various (post-)warscapes are treated in a singular manner. The obsession with institutional reforms might actually run against the chosen goals that the institution itself sets out to achieve in the first place (Funaki and Glencorse 2014: 849–50; Reno 2012; Utas 2012).

The division between 'institutional' and 'actual' spheres of justice is anything but new. Following the teachings of classical Indian jurisprudence, Amartya Sen (2009: 40), for instance, divides the concept of justice into two 'rather different, though not unrelated' segments: *niti*, referring to correct institutional procedures, and *nyaya*, referring to the actual deliverance of justice on the ground. Albeit both *niti* and *nyaya* signify justice in classical Sanskrit, the former concentrates mainly on correct rules and regulations, whereas the latter looks at the life-worlds of people themselves.

As the previous sections in this chapter hopefully demonstrate, it is very typical for the international community to create highly gendered DDR programs (and other institutions) based on principles of justice in the sense of *niti*. In these programs, very detailed procedures and structures are defined, and the indicators for measuring 'success' or 'failure' tend to concentrate solely on numbers and statistics in an almost positivist manner. Although there are numerous practical reasons for this kind of approach, there also exists the evident risk of forgetting to look *beyond* numbers (i.e. who gets to define the indicators?). Maybe the contradictory views of the designers and end-users of the Liberian DDRR programs could be explained through concepts such as of *niti* and *nyaya*?

In *The Idea of Justice* (ibid.), Sen presents a story about an unbeatable warrior, Arjuna, to help clarify the nature of *niti* and *nyaya*.[13] According to the tale, Arjuna is having serious reservations about leading a battle in which he would inevitably need to kill many of his kinfolk. Seeking to alleviate his doubts, he turns to Krishna for advice. For Krishna, the situation appears surprisingly clear – Arjuna should not be concerned with the consequences of his actions, but rather do his duty on the battlefield (ibid.: 23–4). According to Sen's reading, the story can be seen as a classical example of a debate between a consequentialist (Arjuna) and a deontologist (Krishna). Sen also remarks that Arjuna is clearly grounding his worries in the *nyaya* approach (on the consequences of his actions and the social processes that lead to these consequences), whereas Krishna's views represent the *niti* approach (the duties of Arjuna go well beyond the consequences of his actions).[14]

Sen argues that, in complex moral choices, a *nyaya*-based approach offers practical guidance, whereas a *niti*-based approach leads the decision-maker down a path of ideal rules, perfect procedures and even utopian goals. Hence, whereas the latter appears to pave the way for the creation of perfectly just institutions and societies (albeit an impossible task), the former seems to move us towards the elimination of injustices (which should be, according to Sen, the main goal of any theory of justice). However, Sen does not seek to abandon institutions altogether, but argues instead that 'we have to seek institutions that *promote* justice, rather than treating the institutions themselves as manifestations of justice' (ibid.: 82, emphasis in original). Sen also maintains that existing institutions and agreements need to be constantly evaluated on the basis of the consequences they have on the actual lives of human beings in reality. If those consequences seem unjust, he reasons, institutions and/or agreements must be altered and again regularly re-evaluated (ibid.: 84–6).

The Liberian DDRR processes seem indeed to have been planned in the sense of *niti*. According to Kathleen M. Jennings (2008: 334–5), for example, in the second Liberian DDRR programme the (temporary) removal of (male) idleness was prioritized over everything else – it was securitized. Jennings continues: 'however, the problem arose because ex-combatants were not aware *that the process had become the reward. For them, the process was still the process*, and the expected outcome was typically employment and improvement in living conditions' (ibid.; emphasis added). The evident consequence of reintegration that 'did not deliver' (ibid.) was disappointment and frustration among program participants – a crucial detail that is also demonstrated in various sections of this book.

When the international aid community thus became obsessed with the temporary removal of male idleness in Liberia (ibid.; Jennings 2009), it was only logical to overlook 'minor' matters such as gender. Other than referring to 'vulnerable groups' that deserve 'special attention', girl and women soldiers were, once again, forgotten in a DDR process that was supposed to pay 'particular attention to the needs of child combatants and women' (UNSC 2003b: para. 3f).

Hence, as Sen so aptly argues in theory, and as the Liberian DDRR processes demonstrate in practice, it is not enough to have correct institutions/programs in place. What really matters are the outcomes these institutions/programs are producing in reality. Indeed, a real danger in trying to aim too high by creating utopian institutional designs that cannot be delivered, an approach I refer to here as *niti*, is to create expectations that cannot be fulfilled.

How would the second Liberian DDRR program have looked had it been based on the *nyaya* approach? As a minimum, the missteps of the first DDRR program would have been analysed, and the recommendations of highly skilled professionals, such as those of DAI presented at the beginning of this chapter, would have been taken *seriously*. Even with these two rather modest steps, the outcome of the second DDRR process would look much different today. Moreover, and especially in a gender-sensitive program, the inclusion of female commanders in identifying soldiers alongside their male counterparts would have made all the difference in the process of estimating the numbers and needs of female and male participants in each faction. Finally, a *nyaya*-based DDR program would have been constantly evaluated on the basis of the actual consequences on the ground. If these consequences had been something other than those intended – as was the case in Liberia – the direction of a *nyaya*-based program would have been altered and again re-evaluated.

## Tracking the depth of militarization

Girl and women soldiers are part of masculinist military structures that also have an effect on their post-war reintegration possibilities (see, e.g., Sjoberg and Via 2010). As Tarja Väyrynen (2010: 150) remarks, it is rather typical that in peacebuilding missions women's 'agency becomes limited and remains within the binary oppositions established by modernity'. In addition to the aid industry in general, security-related efforts such as SSR and DDR programs in particular can very easily become gendered and militarized. Cynthia Enloe (2002: 23–30; 2004b) suggests that the depth of militarization of a given society, government or organization can be tracked through 'feminist monitoring questions'. Enloe (2002) urges us to ask:

1. **Are the words of 'combatants' given extra weight when they are addressing officials or the public in post-conflict societies?** Does this emphasis favour certain types of manliness and exclude most women? Here, curiosity should be directed towards listeners. Whose stories are given extra weight in social gatherings? Whose viewpoints are presented in the chambers of power?
2. **If one wishes to gain ground in public life, to what extent does she have to turn to people with militarized power?** These are people who can, for example, label a certain party as a security threat or an ally, and threaten others with the use of coercive force. In the process, those parties

that are not able or willing to communicate in a masculine and militarized way will be marginalized.

3. **Does 'security' refer to militarized security in official and everyday discussions and to what extent does it do so?** If security is simply being understood as militarized security, then 'women's' or 'soft' security matters are almost always sidestepped and postponed for the unforeseeable future. These can include, for instance, 'private matters' such as high rates of domestic or sexual violence in the given society.
4. **What proportion of the (internationally mentored) institution's budget is allocated to the security sector and especially military and police forces?** How is the gender composition within these institutions? If women are allowed to enter, do they also have posts in the upper ranks?
5. **To what extent do local decision-makers define the statuses obtainable by women in terms of their roles during the war?** Typically, some women are seen as 'heroic mothers', whereas others are labelled 'victims of sexual assault' or even 'enemies of the state'. These types of category, often put forward by decision-makers and journalists [and the international aid industry], can lay the foundation for the post-war roles available to women and men in the given society.
6. **What kinds of patriarchal patterns are embedded in the organizations that participate in the reconstruction of a post-conflict society?** Do some of the more patriarchal organizations and their departments hold the most important roles in the reconstruction efforts?

If the DDRR efforts in Liberia are investigated through the prism of Enloe's monitoring questions, it quickly becomes apparent that although rather substantive gender sensitization was undertaken on the blueprint level (especially in the second DDRR effort), these plans were never implemented in practice (see also Basini 2013). For example, in the second DDRR process:

- No proper needs assessment of girl and women soldiers took place at the preparation phases of the DDRR process; there was no gender advisor at UNMIL when the program was planned; no gender budget was included in the DDRR program (Basini 2013: 11, 177, questions nos 4, 6)

- (Men) generals and commanders were given the right to draft lists of eligible DDRR participants (see, e.g., Jaye 2009: 14, questions nos 1–3)
- Since priority was placed on the DD phases and the weapons-for-cash method was chosen (see, e.g., Knight and Özerdem 2004: 505), the approach of the program can be described as 'guns, camps, and cash' (ibid., questions nos 1, 3, 6)
- Reintegration became securitized, and as such the (temporary) removal of male idleness took precedence in the reintegration phase (see, e.g., Jennings 2008, 2009, questions nos 3, 6)
- Vocational training was highly gendered. Girls and women were offered skills in 'feminine' fields (e.g. baking, hairdressing, sewing, soap-making), whereas boys and men were encouraged to participate in 'masculine' education (e.g. masonry, plumbing, mechanics). It is obvious that in a post-war society undergoing reconstruction the 'masculine' skills are especially valuable and marketable (see also Jennings 2009: 488; Basini 2013: 198–9, question no. 6)
- Since gender concerns were underlined, e.g. in an external mid-term evaluation report of the second DDRR program (Bugnion et al. 2006), but were again sidelined (e.g. Gawler et al. 2009: 21–2), it can be stated that the overall culture within (the participating) UN organizations was both highly masculine and militarized (questions nos 3, 6).

Marjaana Jauhola (2016: 351; see also Jauhola 2013) writes that those 'who are "written out of history" and out of global WPS [Women, Peace and Security] discourse and who are the abjected of its sexual politics should become its true evaluators'. As I have demonstrated in this chapter, women veterans were by and large 'written out' of the DDRR programs in Liberia. If the research participants were given a chance to evaluate the success of the Liberian DDRR efforts today, many would without a doubt agree with a former fighter, Sandy, who joined AFL at the age of fourteen. In her exploratory interview in 2012, Sandy remarked as follows: 'Since the war finished, the people took the guns from us and they are not taking care of us – they are doing nothing for us! So we can go on the streets, men have us before they give us money. Before we can get our own food to eat!'

## Conclusion

Michael Wessells (2006: 161) argues that 'DDR processes are tidy in concept but messy in implementation'. As shown in this chapter, this was indeed the case with both Liberian DDRR efforts. As a consequence, the 'hard' security issues – the temporary halting of male idleness through a guns, camps and cash approach – took precedence over 'minor' matters such as gender. In practice girl and women soldiers, regardless of their individual ranks in the war(s), were pushed back into their traditional societal statuses. Social class was once again the main determinant of an individual's status within Liberian society, just as it had been prior to the conflicts.

These challenges were recognized and underlined within the framework of the United Nations, but nothing was done on an organizational level to ameliorate the situation. As Morten Bøås (2009: 1329) maintains: 'the international community was so busy "making plans for Liberia" that it never actually questioned whether these plans were in accordance with the situation prevailing in the country and the political and economic logic of the peace agreement'. The choice of whether or not to intervene in a conflict is deeply political and mirrors the many levels of militaristic masculinities embedded in the UN system and the aid industry in general. If the DDRR programs in Liberia had worked as laid out in the original plans, or if they had at least been reformulated when problems were detected, these programs would have substantially strengthened the *rafts of survival* of former soldiers regardless of their age, gender or rank in the war. Instead, however, fragments of hope were provided by promises of a better future, promises that were rarely fulfilled in practice. Whereas for the war veterans themselves societal justice would have manifested in a marketable education, actual employment and concrete walls in their houses – in 'being someone' in the post-war society – for the program designers, the on-going DDRR process itself was a sufficient indicator of development and justice. *Niti* took precedence over *nyaya* – institutions were understood as *manifestations* of justice rather than *instruments* for justice – and subsequently numerous individuals and groups in need of special attention were again sidelined.

As shown in the following sections, the future prospects of Liberian girl and women war veterans were again tied to their personal rafts of survival. Staying afloat in the murky waters of post-war Liberia demanded wit, persistence, luck and extremely strong social networks. Some exceptional individuals possessed these capacities, whereas 'for the large part of Liberian excombatants remarginalisation not reintegration' was the reality (Utas 2003: 250).

# 4
# Social rafting in post-war Liberia

> The big big people that we were behind during the war, they have already left us. Some of them have died. And we can't continue to sit here and wait. So we need to manoeuvre on our own.
> *Dorris, Monrovia*

> Sometimes the tension is too hard on me when I think about the past. I just want to smoke drugs and forget. I can do anything to erase my mind. If I am getting high, I can forget about the past. Because in the war everything was too hard. Also in the wartime, when you were getting high, you couldn't even feel the bullets if they hit you. You can do anything when you're high! You can be strong. So after everything, the war business, the war habit can still be inside of me. I can try to stop, but it is hard, it's hard! The drugs are hard to leave. For that, I would need someone to come and counsel me, to talk to me all the time. It is like this is the only way for me to relax my mind. So if my life would be proper, like if I had my own place and small business, then I could forget about everything.
> *Tracy, Monrovia*

Heavy rain has been falling for two long weeks and Massa's house is flooding. Every morning she checks on the condition of her few belongings, ushers her four children outside, drags the soaked mattress from the floor and lifts it onto the twisted benches lying on the shared porch outside. In the evening, the mattress is carried back inside, and the five inhabitants all squeeze onto the drenched bed to repeat the whole process again the following morning. Massa rents one of the eight rooms in a communal house for a monthly price of 500 LD (about US$5.5 at the time of writing), a room that has concrete walls but is still very inexpensive owing to the distance to Monrovia's city centre and the overall living conditions of the neighborhood. In addition to the constant flooding during the rainy season, Massa's house is situated 'inside' the quarter and is therefore rather insecure: it is a widely held opinion that houses located close to the road are often safer since there are constantly people and cars around.

In addition to the practical challenges, the rainy season also has a direct effect on Massa's modest livelihood. As her main source of income is selling soft drinks and small plastic bags of water ('cold water') from a cooler she keeps on the communal porch in the daytime, the business has had to be put on hold until the veranda is no longer flooded. This means a daily loss of revenue of anywhere from 300 to 1,000 LD, which is considerable if compared to the amount she typically uses at the market to buy food – if there is rice in the house, she spends about 300 LD at the market, and if there is not, the expenditure is up to 500 LD. Therefore, Massa now cooks at home only on Sundays and buys cheap 'cold bowls'[1] for the family on the other days.

This chapter unravels and details some of the everyday *rivers of insecurities* in which woman war veterans such as Massa must manoeuvre in their post-war trajectories. With the notion of *social rafting* as a starting point, individual capabilities, skills and available resources can be addressed simultaneously in a contrapuntal manner. The main point of interest with regard to the everyday in post-conflict Liberia is the following: how do these women secure the basic necessities of life such as shelter, food and health?

As briefly mentioned in the Introduction, age is a complicated matter in today's Liberia. For example, whether or not one is considered an adult has more to do with one's ability to support herself – 'to become someone' – than with actual chronological age. As Collison (2016: 127) remarks: 'Youth is a social status in Liberia and one that relies heavily upon adult acceptance and recognition, entrepreneurial skill, acquisition of a home and a family and the ability to sustain such wealth, power and stature.' While there are several studies that detail the struggles of youth in post-war Liberia (e.g. Utas 2003, 2008; Hoffman 2011: loc. 1787; Collison 2016: 127–65), the emphasis is almost exclusively on young males. This is not surprising since the gender perspective 'is often relegated to second place in studies and policies about youth in Africa' (Abbink 2005: 6). One aim of this chapter is therefore to counterbalance the already-existing narrations of the current realities of Liberian youth by bringing forward the perspective of a group of (impoverished) young women.

Although the post-war realities of the interviewees might, at first glance, seem to resemble those of any disenfranchised woman in Liberia, some crucial differences remain. First is the question of trauma. As being a woman veteran still carries a stigma in Liberia, many wartime traumas from the frontline and beyond remain unprocessed. Furthermore, even in circumstances where it would be possible and even encouraged to address battle-related traumas, the 'post'-war everyday seems often to be significantly different to civilians than to former soldiers who have witnessed the battlefield first-hand. Indeed, there is a 'clear association between combat exposure and PTSD, with greater levels of exposure leading to greater prevalence' (Cozza 2005: 3). Second, and related, is the question of guilt, which is 'often the elephant in the room' (Sherman 2010: 95). Typically referred to by professionals more broadly as 'moral injury'– a category including not only guilt but also feelings of grief, remorse, betrayal, anxiety, anger, self-loathing and meaninglessness, for instance – this is a type of psychological anguish that is often ignored (ibid.: 1; see also Sherman 2015; Nakashima Brock and Lettini 2012; Puniewska 2015). Therefore, the veteran may be haunted by the battlefield on a constant basis, even years after the signing of a peace agreement.

The chapter begins with an examination of the occupational statuses of Massa and her fellow research participants. Since my data strongly suggest that individuals residing in the shanty towns of Monrovia face a significantly different set of challenges than those living in the semi-urban or rural Liberia, I will then widen the discussion of Monrovian actualities initiated in Chapter 1 by concentrating on Pa Chea's shop, located in one of the various shanty towns of the capital. After this, I compare the everyday of my Monrovia-based respondents to that of the interviewees residing in the town of Gbarnga. The ensuing section is especially dedicated to the phenomenon of prostitution. This emphasis allows for an investigation of the intertwined nature of poverty, trauma and structural inequalities prevalent in today's Liberia. In addition to the individual interviews with the research participants practicing prostitution as a form of income, two group discussions with women prostitutes, an interview with a male 'gigolo'[2] and a group discussion with three male journalists were conducted in order to form a more in-depth understanding of prostitution as a societal phenomenon in Liberia. Prior to conclusions, I finally touch upon the question of peer pressure, which can be thought of as connecting the flows of global trends, consumer goods and the international media environment to the everyday *rafts of survival* of the interviewees.

## The chicken that digs for food will not sleep hungry[3]

Of my 133 respondents, 128 were willing to reply to the question about their current employment status. A significant proportion (46 percent) explained that they were doing 'small business' such as selling food dishes, household decoration material, different kinds of beverages, or their services (e.g. hair plying, sewing). Depending on the market environment, the quality of their product/service and the customer base, these activities produced a daily income of anywhere between 20 to 2,000 LD (from US$0.2 to around US$24). For the majority of the respondents, however, one form of business is not enough to sustain even a tolerable standard of living. It is therefore typical to be engaged in a combination of various kinds of trades, to bolster the income with economic support from boyfriends or families, or to have 'godfathers' or various simultaneous relationships for financial backup. It is very likely that many individuals under the category of 'small business', especially on the lower income levels, are also forced to resort to occasional prostitution. Indeed, approximately 40 percent of the respondents stated that prostitution was their main source of income, making it the second-most common form of employment among the respondents. Since I find the figure to be rather noteworthy, I have dedicated a special section to the phenomenon in a later part of the chapter and refer to it only briefly here.

All in all, it became evident that running a small business in Liberia demands both organizational skills and resilience, as the interview below with *Temama* (in 2013) aptly exemplifies. The *susu* arrangement that Temama is referring to in her interview is a version of a rotating credit association in which members of the closed club pool together an agreed amount of money on a regular basis. In turn, each of the *susu* members is then given the collected lump sum of money for her to use freely for her current needs (see, e.g., Cruz 2014; Geertz 1962; Ardener 1964).

> *Temama* (T): I buy dry cow skin and soak it in water so it can rise. After that I clean it, I remove the sand inside that can sometimes be plenty. I mix some spices, cook it, and put it in a bucket. After that my sister will carry it around to sell it.
>
> *Leena* (L): How much can you earn a day?
>
> T: I buy 250 LD for one skin, then I use 150 LD for small small things like pepper, chicken soup, bitter ball, pepper, oil. When I fix it, sometimes I can get 450 profit from it, sometimes 300 a

day. Sometimes 200, sometimes 150 because the prices can go up and come down.

L: You sell during the weekends as well?

J: Every day. Only on Sundays we usually don't sell but go to the service. So normally I can wake up early in the morning, like 5 a.m., clean up my place, fix the market and give it to my sister to go and sell. If there is food in the house, I also cook before leaving and go to school.

L: So what about the profit? You share it?

T: We can put most of it in *susu*. So by next year my sister can go to school as well.

L: So no money for you?

T: When we put it to *susu*, the money is for me and for her [depending who needs it more].

L: Is there sometimes confusion with *susu*?

T: No there can't be confusion because before you join *susu*, you will choose the person carefully. It all depends of the person who is keeping the money.

In addition to small business and prostitution, there were several other occupational categories that were mentioned in the interviews: farming (5 percent), studying (3 percent) and 'nothing' (2 percent),[4] as well as regular jobs or temporary work on a daily basis, e.g. as cleaners or waiters ('other', 3 percent). When considering these figures, it must be remembered that 'having a job' in the African context should not be understood as a synonym for waged positions, but rather as 'activities that generate actual or imputed income, monetary or in kind, formal or informal' (World Bank 2012: 49; Filmer and Fox 2014: 28–9). Further, there is evidently an urban bias in my data as only 5 percent of the research participants gained their main income from farming activities, whereas around 70 percent of the Liberian workforce is employed in the agricultural sector (CIA 2016). Therefore, the realities reflected in the following are those of the urban and semi-urban poor rather than those living in rural areas.

Why, then, in a country with huge potential in the agricultural sector do not more deprived city-dwellers move to the countryside and begin farming? African youth in general do not see the agricultural sector as a lucrative and desirable form of income: its financial returns are considered insecure and the job itself is physically demanding (Filmer and Fox 2014: 117). Of the research interviewees, for example, only a handful wished to move to the countryside even if they could have gained some income from farming activities, e.g. in family farms. In addition to the global reasons for the youth to reside in urban environments – dynamism, seemingly endless opportunities, an active and exciting life – many of the respondents raised the question of shame. For example, Tracy (interview 2014), who was quoted at the beginning of this chapter, stated the following while observing a picture she had taken of a very small room in one of Monrovia's shanty towns:

> These are *grona* [street] boys, *grona* girls who live here. There are more than ten of them sleeping in this one room. Many of them are expected to provide help for their families in the interior. Going back there [without money] would be a disgrace. So instead you start your life from there, from the floor.

In addition, 'everyone has problems with land in Liberia', as the representative of Liberia's Land Commission pointed out at the Liberian Studies Association's annual conference in 2012. The complications with landownership in the country are further exacerbated by Liberia's dual legal system consisting of both statutory and customary law. Whereas the Anglo-American common law system was taken as a model when the statutory law structures were defined in the Constitution of Liberia (1847, revised in 1984), unwritten customary law practices form the basis for the system applied primarily in the rural areas.[5] Although the constitution, as the supreme law of the country, recognizes the existence of customary law, the two spheres of justice are often in contradiction. For example, while married women can inherit property and land under the civil law, such rights are not granted to women under the customary law system (Kabbah 2014; OECD 2014).

Since gaining access to land is next to impossible for poor youth in Liberia, an alternative would be to find waged positions (often as day workers) on small-scale or more commercial farms. As Paul Richards (2005: 587) notes, however, many young ex-combatants in Liberia reject farming as a form of income 'because they object to labouring for low wages on plantations and to harassment by corrupt and predatory village elites. They fear being fined of every penny they make. If they had access to land and could keep what they earned for themselves, their interest grows.' Richards (ibid.) goes on to state that this is why rural skills training programs in Liberia and the Mano river region in particular should invest in securing the rights of youth within the farming sector. This is a pertinent remark since even very small-scale farming can produce valuable extra income and enhance food security within families. For instance, Theresa (interview 2013), a former fighter whose experiences from the first civil war were detailed in Chapter 2, stated in her photo interview that:

> I took this picture when I was digging my cassava. This cassava you see, I found the place, I brushed it myself, planted it, and here [in the photograph] I am digging it. So no man brushed it for me. I planted this to help myself because I don't want to fall in sin! The salary [as a teacher in rural Liberia] is very small. So at times I sell some, and me and my children eat some. These are some of the things I can do to help myself. But this work you see here is hard for a woman! It is very hard for a woman.

## Manoeuvring in the storms of life

In the first chapter of this book, I briefly referred to the shopkeeper Pa Chea, who allows local youth to spend time in his tiny and tattered store situated in one of the several shanty towns of Monrovia. In addition – chiefly through the experiences of Amy, Teta and Priscilla – I demonstrated what it means to be a *social rafter* in today's Monrovia, and how 'street sisters' and 'street brothers' support one another when the need arises. In the following, I deepen my analysis of street life in Monrovia by considering Pa Chea's shop as an example of a contemporary Monrovian scene into which streams of social rafters drift, only to be taken aback by yet another surprising rivulet offering endless challenges and opportunities to the occasional rafter.

I was first taken to Pa Chea's 'base' by a former girl commander, who urged me to meet a group of ex-soldiers who frequent the place on a daily basis. First, after sipping Coke for a while with Pa Chea and explaining the basic details of my project to him, I conducted one set of exploratory interviews in the shelter of his noisy shop. It quickly became apparent in the process that all the ex-soldiers who typically loiter in the place, such as Teta and Priscilla from Chapter 1, are among the most deprived war veterans in the country. After a round of exploratory interviews, I then conducted several photo interviews in the same shop, as well as made it a habit to pop into the store every once in a while. The high level of substance abuse problems in the community was well manifested by the fact that no matter what time I entered the neighborhood I would always find a few individuals completely high on *tar-white* (brown heroin that is typically smoked through a metal pipe) or some other form of hard drug, as well as smell the syrupy aroma of marijuana in the immediate surroundings of the base. Pa Chea himself, nevertheless, demanded respectful manners from everyone entering his kingdom – whether one was high or suffering from withdrawal symptoms, hungry or with a hangover, 'correct behaviour' was expected at all times.

Martha, whose experiences of the DDR program after the second civil war were detailed in the previous chapter, was one of the first women veterans I got to know at Pa Chea's base. After entering the room for her exploratory interview, she grabbed hold of my arm, stared at me with her piercing eyes and stated in a loud and raspy voice: 'I'm a rebel, gew!' This was followed by a very complicated explanation of her whereabouts in the two civil wars. She was completely high, and I was on my guard; should we stop the interview and continue on another, more sober occasion? That we did not do, however, since Martha was extremely eager to share her story with me and my research assistant Glorious, and her aggression seemed to wither away with each sentence she shared with us. It has to be added, though, that it was actually the reassuring and calm behavior of Glorious that made me want to continue the interview on that occasion: while gently placing her hand on my arm, she decisively but compassionately asked Martha to speak a little more slowly, so that we could fully comprehend everything she wanted to share with us that day.

The following year (2013), Martha seemed like a changed woman. The aggression was gone, her eyes were clear, and she assured me that she would take extremely good care of the camera I was soon to give her for photographing her daily realities. A few weeks later I developed the twenty-two pictures she had taken with her well-kept camera, and found that more than half of the pictures depicted adults in a school-like surrounding. This was in stark contrast to the photo sets women veterans had previously taken of the same neighborhood. Whereas I had become accustomed to staring at photographs of the manoeuvrings of street sisters and street brothers; of substance abuse; of the deprived living conditions of the inhabitants in general; and of the occasional moments of joy despite constant hardships, I was now looking at pictures of the everyday in a vocational training school with seemingly proud and content students. Martha explained to me that 'her name came up' in an assistance program that the National Oil Company of Liberia had launched in collaboration with the NGO Don Bosco. In the program framework, at-risk youth would be provided with vocational training in a certain centre in Monrovia. First, Martha was assigned to a tailoring course, but after a few weeks she was 'promoted' to masonry because of:

> my activeness and my smartness. You see, tailoring is not considered a very good job but masonry is. They chose to transfer me because at certain time I had a confusion with this one girl in our class who claimed that I was gossiping about her. So she wanted to fight with me. And that is how the teacher took us to the counselling room and told me that throughout the time you've been in this school, you've been very respectful. And we can see that you are strong. So we will transfer you to masonry because of your strengths and your activeness.

Martha's experiences are yet another unfortunate example of the gendered nature of the aid industry in Liberia (Jennings 2009; Basini 2013; Abramowitz and Moran 2012) and beyond (e.g. Kabeer 1994; Coulter 2009: 186–91; Visvanathan et al. 2011; Jauhola 2013). Just as in the nineteenth-century missionary schools in Liberia (Payne 1845, quoted in Moran 1990: 52), and as had happened in the DDRR programs implemented in the country in the immediate post-war period (see Chapter 3), skills training was and is routinely gender-segregated. Even today, the 'temporary removal of male-idleness' (Jennings 2009) constantly takes precedence in the educational opportunities that NGOs and other actors offer to young women and men. Although girls and women are sometimes given a chance to educate themselves in 'masculine' professions such as masonry, plumbing and mechanics – as was the case with Martha's program – it is rarely explained to the female candidates that such 'masculine' professions would, most likely, offer a better chance in the job market of today's Liberia than 'feminine' trades such as sewing or hair plying. Martha's picture set is an apt example of the sex-based segregation of occupational training in Liberia: as she was given the rare chance to study masonry, the overwhelming proportion of individuals in her photographs from her school are young men.

The level of empowerment Martha had gained from her on-going education was nonetheless simply breathtaking.[6] Only a year earlier, she had said in her exploratory interview that 'my sister, I am a small girl but my heart is like a man's', and today she was presenting photographs of her class ballot for choosing the most suitable and trustworthy class monitor. In addition to photographing the voting arrangements in general, Martha had asked someone to photograph her in the process of writing down the name of her preferred candidate in the shelter of a blue voting booth. Further, she had taken numerous pictures of her new 'brothers' from school, and they were in stark contrast with the street brothers and street sisters she had spent her days with in the years before entering the school. Nevertheless, when looking at a picture of herself, Martha explained that 'I am not really feeling fine about my body – I used to be fat with plenty of hair and now I am small like this'. Martha's slimness was a sign of her on-going addiction to crack cocaine, which she approached by stating: 'I'm trying to leave it behind. But it is making me sick in the evening so now I am trying to look for money to get a treatment. Before you come back next time, I will be okay.' Regrettably, however, she was not doing too well during my next visit to Liberia, as we will soon come to learn.

Priscilla's trajectory was unfortunately the opposite of Martha's (see Chapter 1 for Priscilla's background story). In the year following her exploratory interview, Priscilla's 'name did not come up in the program', and the active and stylish young woman from the preceding year had turned into a depressed and tormented war veteran seemingly on the brink of losing the tiny fragments of hope she still tried to cling to. This was also the year when Priscilla had, once again, found herself in jail with the consequence of having been forced to sell her 'bucket of goods' (see Chapter 1) to bribe the police to take the picture of her face off the jail director's office wall.

### 'Ebola in town'[7]

Another year passed by, it was now the summer of 2014, and I was again back to Liberia and at Pa Chea's base for my next field research period. This was to be, for the time being, my last encounter with Priscilla, Martha and the others from Pa Chea's shop, and the rumors and fear of a new round of Ebola virus disease (EVD) were spreading in Monrovia's communities (see, e.g., Front Page Africa 2014a). There had been a small outbreak in the region in the spring of that year, an outbreak that 'was not followed by international mobilization and a consistent communication strategy' (WHO 2015: 12). Hence, when entering Liberia in early June 2014, almost all the interviewees laughed when I inquired about the safety precautions they were currently taking. 'These are just rumors, Leena, there is no Ebola in Liberia' and 'the government is just inventing it all up to receive more UN money to put into their own pockets' were among the most common explanations I was presented with in chuckling voices.[8] A pop song called 'Ebola in Town',[9] composed to educate citizens about the dangers of the virus, was omnipresent, yet it seemed that the only lesson the piece really delivered on the streets concerned a dance one had to master in the Monrovian clubbing scene when the beat hit the floor. The street dwellers – and even many elite members of Liberian society – were in denial.

One week later, however, nurses at the Redemption Hospital in a Monrovian neighborhood called New Kru Town declared a strike since one of their colleagues had just died of EVD and the nurses were scared for their lives (Front Page Africa 2014c). The situation escalated dramatically the following week, and Médecins Sans Frontières (2014) declared that the current Ebola epidemic was now 'out of control' in Liberia. International flights were still arriving and departing on a regular basis, yet the body temperatures of passengers were measured on countless occasions, and pamphlets about the symptoms that the Ebola virus might cause were systematically provided to all passengers at Monrovia's Roberts International Airport.[10] There is a telling entry from July 2014 in my research diary concerning the condition of the women residing in close proximity to Pa Chea's shop: 'I've never seen them in such a weak condition before. This is the highest peak of addiction levels I've witnessed thus far and mosquitoes are everywhere. Now when apparently also Ebola is in town, it might be difficult for the poor to get treatment even for everyday diseases such as malaria, typhoid and diarrhoea. This is bad: very, very bad.'[11]

### The death of Mariama

Later the same year, I received a phone call in Finland from Pa Chea himself. Mariama, the very brave commander we got to know in Chapter 2 and whom everyone had admired so much, had passed away. Frightened by her weak condition and afraid of not being able to receive medical care in the capital owing to hospital closures, she had gone to seek help from a 'bush doctor'[12] close to her home village, but he did not possess the knowhow to cure her 'strange' sickness. Pa Chea and his shop dwellers had now collected some US$20 to give to Mariama's family so that she could at least have a decent memorial service. The death of Mariama was not a modest rivulet, but rather a tsunami that had found its way to the social rafters of Monrovia,[13] a storm whose seriousness can probably be best described by this statement made by Massa when I was talking to her on the phone in Finland that November: 'I would rather be back in the warfront than living with this kind of a fear in my heart. In the war you can at least see your enemy and be prepared. Now we are blind.'

The death of Mariama was utterly devastating to the whole community. In addition to being a personal loss to her family and friends, as well as to Pa Chea and his shop dwellers, the whole research team in Monrovia – myself, Glorious and Jessica – had all respected Mariama enormously for her endless resilience and positive attitude to life despite her constant struggles. After commanding her own WAC unit for four years from the age of twelve onwards (see Chapter 2), she and 'her girls' had signed up for a DDRR program in the town of Buchannan. During her years on the warfront, Mariama had not only developed an addiction to 'brown brown', low-quality crack cocaine, but had also lost a piece of her ear to shrapnel from a rocket. She was deeply ashamed of her ear and was never to be seen in public without some sort of headwear. In 2013, while looking at her own picture in her photo interview containing more than 250 pictures, Mariama explained with a sad expression on her face, so untypical for her, that:

> Sometimes when I think about my problems, mostly my ear, I can really be worried. I have to tie my head anywhere I'm going because people can stare at my ear and take me as a *grona* woman [prostitute]. I can be so ashamed and also embarrassed of this ear! It is only with my family-people and someone I know very well that I don't have to tie my head.

A detailed description of the prior drug habit Mariama had been able to leave behind was also a noteworthy part of her interview. While examining a photograph in which a very slender man is smoking his evening dose of *tar-white* in one of the several slums of Monrovia, we had the following discussion.

*Mariama* (M): When I see this picture, I can be laughing because I can think about my past.

*Leena* (L): You've stopped smoking, right?

M: Yes.

L: How did you do it?

M: I have a strong mind. I was sick when I was carried to a hospital. The doctor asked me what kind of a sickness I had. I said that I can smoke cigarettes and grass. But he said no, you are not only smoking cigarettes and grass but something else as well. And so I told him that I can smoke drugs but I want to leave it all behind. He asked me if I was sure about my decision. I replied yes. That's how he put the medicine in a drip and gave it to me. That is how it went all over my body. That is how I forgot about smoking.

Mariama explained that even before this final decision to leave the drugs behind, she had been prescribed the 'drip' in a hospital in order to stay drug-free. Prior to the treatment, she had spent more than a month in the central prison, where her deteriorating condition and total lack of appetite had alerted the attention of the prison guards. After the doctor had convinced Mariama that it would be in her best interests to take the treatment, she agreed, and was feeling pretty much okay at the time of her release a few weeks later. Nonetheless, as her 'mind was not into it', she soon relapsed. Mariama described her feelings at the time like this: 'Even though the treatment can make you feel bad when you begin to take drugs again, you can just put it in your mouth and feel sick at first, but you will still force it. I smoked until all my teeth were brown in my mouth!' We continued our discussion as follows.

L: Why were you smoking before?

M: Really it was not my mind but the friends I used to go around. Everybody was smoking. When I went to Red Light [a neighborhood in Monrovia considered very dangerous at night], I met a friend who used to smoke so much that she didn't even find us food to eat. But I really, really wanted to be friends with her. So I also started smoking with her. There, I also met one boy I began loving to. He used to have money but carried everything to the ghetto to smoke it all. Like if he gave me small money, he would expect for me to keep it so that he could carry it later for drugs. So I told myself that let me smoke too so all of us can smoke the money together. And that is how I started using, and my friends and I got close. When I wasn't smoking, we were not close.

L: Some of the women I've met have told me that they can still be thinking about the time of the war and that is making them feel bad. And that is one of the main reasons why they continue smoking. What do you think about that?

in an illuminating manner. These are some of the excerpts drawn from her photo interview session (each refers to a different picture):

> I took this picture because my son was crawling on his knees for trying to take the water. So that is why I took this picture here. I was feeling bad. Because he was crawling on his knees.
>
> Here I was begging him to walk. And he is walking here together with his little brother. So I was feeling happy small! The time he was walking, I was feeling happy! That is why I took the picture. But now, he cannot walk again and that is why I came to seek bush medicine from Gbarnga some time ago. I pray for him to start walking again but God says no. That is why we are carrying him around.
>
> I see my mom going to school here, I can see my son standing – I can feel happy small!
>
> In this picture he is really trying to get up. That is why I took the picture here. It was his time to wake up and go to take his bath.
>
> I can feel happy! Because here he is walking by himself. So it can make me feel happy.
>
> I was feeling bad again! That is why I took the picture. Because he burned himself again. His hand. He was walking beside the fire and burnt it. So I was feeling bad for him. I carried him to a doctor and he felt a bit better later on.

Although Sonia's struggles are indeed considerable by any measure, there is a remarkable difference in the available social networks between the interviewees residing in the surroundings of Gbarnga, such as Sonia, and those Monrovia-based respondents who have severe substance abuse problems and many unprocessed traumas. Sonia's picture set revealed that, despite all her hardships, she still had her extended family supporting her in her daily struggles. In addition, Sonia repeatedly referred in her interview to 'Eleanor', a friend with whom she often shared childcare responsibilities and daily meals. Eleanor was looking after Sonia's children at the time of our photo-elicitation interview.

Similar to Sonia's pictures, Hawah's set of photographs revealed the huge importance of family and peer support in her daily life in Gbarnga. As is explained in Chapter 3, Hawah faced difficulties in gaining her father's approval after returning home from the second civil war, having been assigned to combat service support tasks. Although the relationship problems with her father are on-going – he would like Hawah to get married with an old man who already has seven wives, a demand that she determinedly refuses to obey – Hawah's relationship with her mother is extremely warm and caring. In one of her pictures, daughter and mother sit side by side with very sad expressions on their faces. Hawah approached the insights of the photograph by detailing their mother–daughter relationship.

> Here we are thinking – she was visiting us at that time. We were dreaming of the time when God will change my life. So when my mother would visit me, she could be happy. Yeah. We lecture, sometimes we can talk about good things too. Not every day are we worrying like this. And you see, that would be so good if she came to see me one day and I could tell her: 'ah, this day now, things are fine with me'. Yeah! My mother is the one who can sometimes counsel me. Because each time my father goes against my will, I can go to her. She will sometimes tell me to forget about it; he is your father. And she can say that anything you do, he is still your father. If God helped me, the first thing I would do is to invite her to live with me. If I had money. So she would live with me and have a better life.

Besides her mother, Hawah's two brothers are also very supportive of her. The older brother lives in Monrovia for his work but allows the younger brother, Hawah and her four-year-old son to live in his house rent-free. In addition, the Monrovia-based brother has given his siblings a small plot of land to cultivate cassava in order to meet their modest everyday needs. Nevertheless, harvesting and maintaining the cassava patch can only be done during the weekends since both Hawah and her brother are still at school. As a very bright young woman, Hawah had won a scholarship for the on-going school year at the time of our photo interview. While studying a picture of herself in a school uniform, she expressed a shy wish: maybe she could win the approval of his father once more by concentrating very hard on her schooling. Although he does not contribute to his daughter's school fees, he is still in favor of her education. One day Hawah would like to become a bank clerk or even an international businesswoman. Maybe then, Hawah reasoned, she could be a 'proper Mandingo woman' in her father's eyes – a proper woman who would definitely be the total opposite of those 'survival prostitutes' whose everyday challenges are touched upon in what follows.

## Hustling is not stealing[14]

> This prostitution life is getting more and more dangerous. Because in Liberia now, the current system is down. Also the security system. Poor men don't have access to justice in this country. So if you are doing prostitution job and you will be killed by somebody, your poor mother will just walk walk walk [from the police station to court, etc.] and nothing will come out of it. So in this country there is no justice, no rights for the poor. In this country you mind yourself the best way you think you can mind yourself. If you have money, you'll have all the rights. So if you are doing prostitution work, you will schedule yourself and tell God that 'God, today I'm jammed. Let me just go on the street and maybe you will give to me what I want.' But if you take it to be like a working thing from Monday to Sunday it is not good. Because the street is risky nowadays. The street is very risky.
> *Patience, Monrovia*

Following the reasoning of one of her local informants, Kathleen M. Jennings (2010: 232–4) divides girls and women who practice transactional sex in Liberia into 'prostitutes', 'hustlers' and 'homegirls'. In this categorization, *prostitutes* are considered 'high class' individuals who serve well-off clientele and typically work under a pimp or a madam. *Hustlers*, on the other hand, are described as 'survival prostitutes' who practice transactional sex on an irregular basis in order to gain the basic necessities of life such as food, rent money or medicine. According to Jennings, many hustlers are also drug addicts and 'probably do not identify themselves as prostitutes' (p. 234). Individuals in the final category of *homegirls* attempt to form relationships with 'sugar daddies' (also referred to in Liberia as godfathers/mothers). Homegirls do not engage in sexual relationships for survival, but rather try to enhance their standards of living through a special form of transactional sex.

In this section I focus especially on the prostitutes who would fall under the category of hustlers. However, as the overwhelming majority of these individuals (fifty-two) defined themselves as prostitutes, I refer to these individuals in their own terminology. Only two of the respondents stated that they worked under a pimp, and almost everyone relied on prostitution as their main source of revenue. In addition covering for the daily needs of the women themselves, prostitution typically provided income for children and partners as well as the extended family, either through direct cash transfers or by contributing to the everyday needs of the family. The majority of the interviewed prostitutes lived in different shanty towns in Monrovia and many had severe substance abuse problems – a telling reminder of the intertwined nature of disempowerment, trauma, poverty and gender discrimination patterns in today's Liberia. In addition to 'hustlers', the category of 'homegirls' is brought to the fore by comparing my own research findings to the already existing research on sexualities in Africa. In this section, peer pressure, the global market economy and the 'traditional' expectations with regard to womanhood/manhood in Liberia are scrutinized. A complementary perspective is teased out from an interview with a male 'homegirl', referred to in Liberia as a gigolo, playboy, big boy or bluff boy.

### Short time for a cold bowl

Under the category of survival prostitutes, it is possible to identify a few subcategories that are reflected in the pricing, time of service and chosen working environment. The most destitute of the research participants explained that since competition for customers is getting more and more fierce, and as novice teenagers are willing to reduce their prices to a very low level, they have to offer 'short time' under market tables, behind cars, in private houses or other nearby environments with prices ranging from 40 to 100 LD. In practice, therefore, these prostitutes can earn enough money from one or two customers for a single cold bowl. The following interview excerpts (Box 4.1) capture the atmosphere on the streets of Monrovia at the time of the interviews.

---

**Box 3 Street life in Monrovia**

These times now I can smoke grass, I take narcotics. And there is also something you can fry that is called coco. When the night then comes, we will put on our short skirts and men can have us. 150, 100 LD for a short time: under the market tables near Point 4, in Duala market. Sometimes they can also carry me to a motel and they can pay 200 LD for sleeping and 150 LD for a short time. I can do it because the habit is in me now, I am used to it. During the war I got used to narcotics and I am used to it now. If I am not taking narcotics, I cannot feel fine. I take it, and if there are not any narcotics around, I will smoke grass.
*Princess, 2013*

> This time now, if you go on the street, you see plenty of girls who have spoiled the prices. Even small children are all on the street. Before we used to go and stand on a particular area to wait for these men to come. And if they came, they would ask us: how much I am giving to you for a short time? And maybe we would say 200 or 250. But nowadays we are too many in number. So when you see one man coming, everybody will start running after that man. And some of us feel shame because if you go with that man, he will have you for cheap. So it would be good to wait for them to come to you. But it is not happening now.
> T-Girl, 2013
>
> I will go on the street and any man I encounter, I will sleep with him. But you see, these days the women are plenty! So they can give you 50, they can give you 100. When one man gives you 50 LD, it is not enough for you to buy your things and support yourself. And so you have to sleep with five-six men a night. So if I go there eight o'clock and stay there until twelve o'clock, I can sleep with five men and have enough for myself to support myself. Find a place to sleep, do other things.
> OB, 2012

As the excerpts in Box 4.1 reveal, 'short time' is cheaper that 'sleeping', and sex in motels typically provides more income than that in outdoor environments. In both cases, the rafts of survival are made sturdier through peer support systems: street sisters and street brothers watch over one another and come to help their friends if dangerous encounters seem to occur. In addition, motel staff are considered an additional security factor since 'the people are there to monitor the two of you. If you are doing something bad for the man, the people will hold you. If the man does anything bad to you, the people will hold him' (Princess, 2013).

In a few photo sets produced by the research participants, there were small crowds of young men sleeping in the middle of the day under bent zinc roofs with no walls around them. The poorest of the poor – and often those having the most persistent substance abuse problems – took turns sleeping. Young men and boys would rest from the early hours of the morning until afternoon, whereas young women and girls would rest from afternoon until late evening. By sleeping in groups, these street dwellers would protect one another if any kind of unwanted hustle was to occur. 'The street business' began after sunset; whereas the majority of women sought to attract the attention of possible customers from the local street corners and small 'entertainment spots', the others hit the street in search of possible theft opportunities, be it petty theft on the beach or armed intrusions into private homes. We had the following exchange around one of these pictures with Glorious and Chantal, a former commander who took part in both wars and later managed to sign up for a DDRR program.

*Glorious (research assistant)* (G): Oh, what are they doing here?

*Chantal* (C): These are the boys that like sleeping in front of the ghetto.

G: Why are they sleeping there? Don't they have a sleeping place?

C: No, they don't have it. They smoke there, sleep there, eat there. They don't have a home.

*Leena* (L): Why?

C: Because some of the ex-combatants feel that their lives are useless, and some of their parents don't look for them, don't care about them. So they feel that there is no hope for tomorrow.

G: So what do you think when you see this picture?

C: I think about myself, when I was on the street. At that time I was not settled.

L: You also have some women who are living like this? No home, sleeping just like this?

C: Yes. But I was unable to take their picture.

L: They are also ex-combatants?

C: Yes, the majority. But some of them are not ex-combatants.

G: How do you see the future of these people [the most deprived ex-combatants]?

C: They are already damaged. But if some of them decide it, they can have a good future. I believe that they can have another chance. There is still hope.

L: But how?

C: If they try to leave the drugs, put themselves together, go back home and ask for forgiveness. As for their families, I'm sure that they can accept them back.

G: So if they don't have family, what can they do?

C: I'm sure they can make lives better for themselves. If people come in and counsel them, they will take it in if only they are willing.

G: Why you took the picture?

C: I took this picture for other people see it. To show that only you can make yourself to become somebody.

G: So what are they doing for living?

C: They can steal and do armed robberies.

L: Do you think that they would be willing to fight again if somebody would pay them?

C: Yes! Some of them.

All the interviewed prostitutes seemed to agree that the most risky move on their part would be to practice their profession in the homes of their customers. As there are no street sisters or brothers or motel staff to turn to if dangerous situations occur, refusal of payment or the stealing of possessions (money, phone) regularly occur. Descriptions of severe violence in home encounters were often referred to in the interview situations, and some respondents also explained how their friends/colleagues had been killed in suspicious circumstances in the 'shelter' of private homes. In these narrations, very detailed information on the whereabouts of these incidents was provided, as well as the names of the victims. Rumors[15] of the body parts of destitute prostitutes being removed in private homes were widespread, and names, times and detailed descriptions of environments were typically brought up in these narrations as well.

During the peak of the EVD epidemic, the 'high class' prostitutes were able to halt their services for safety reasons since their livelihood was not dependent on this trade. The majority of survival prostitutes, however, had no choice but to continue working despite the massive risks. I interviewed two such women in Monrovia in February 2015 whilst I was conducting a small-scale study for a Finnish NGO about the gendered impacts of the EVD outbreak in Liberia (Vastapuu 2015). These young women explained that they were currently taking additional safety precautions to prevent them catching the deadly virus. In addition to using condoms in all instances, they tried to enact every possible safety measure to avoid their customers' sweaty skin. Therefore, whenever possible, these women and several of their colleagues practiced their profession under fans or in air-conditioned rooms, as well as wearing long-sleeved shirts and tights with an open crotch to protect their skin from the sweat of their customers. While these measures in themselves are obviously ineffective, I still find these types of innovation a telling reminder that human nature is prone to finding original solutions even in the most desperate of conditions. These women tried to strengthen their fragile rafts of survival with extra clothing, for instance.

A curfew was announced in Liberia in the midst of the epidemic. Since a few clubs and restaurants were changing their schedules so that they would be open during the day instead of at night to keep the businesses running, some prostitutes were able to meet their customers during the day within the shelter of these clubs. One interviewee also explained that she had now broken from her usual code of conduct and provided her phone number to a select set of customers so that they could reach her whenever they wished to buy her services. Nonetheless, the customers were willing to pay less than half of the typical prices because of the overall economic downturn and the loss of revenues due to EVD.[16] If compared to taxi drivers, for example (of whom the overwhelming majority are men), who had increased their prices since only four people were allowed to share a car at the peak of the crisis, the survival prostitutes seemed to have no negotiating power over loss of revenues due to the epidemic. Nonetheless, the 'high class' prostitutes surely also felt the economic impacts of EVD on their livelihoods since many had to halt their services for a while and find alternative sources of revenue. Some of their everyday working conditions are described in what follows.

### 'The luck is not the same for all of us'

The release of the so called 'Zeid report' (United Nations 2005) brought large-scale attention to the sexual abuse committed by UN staff in field operations and beyond. Since then, numerous studies and reports about transactional sex practices within and around UN bases have been produced,[17] and the UN itself has recently approved a zero-tolerance policy towards sexual exploitation and abuse by its personnel.[18] The UN explicitly states, for example, that utilizing the services of prostitutes or sexual relations with anyone under eighteen years of age is forbidden for UN staff members (ibid.). Nonetheless, transactional and other sexual relations between UN employees and host country residents regularly occur, although the 'luck is not the same for all of us', as one of the research participants sighed.

Many of the respondents thus generally agreed that 'UNMIL business' or 'white man business' was normally a jackpot for the prostitutes themselves. Whereas a night with a local man could at best produce an income of some US$20 per person, UN employees were reported to pay up to US$100 a night – although prices as low as US$5 a night were reported. Even though I definitely do not want to argue here that transactional sex services purchased by UN staff or other humanitarian employees could ever be justified as a form of 'development aid', for example, I do, however, feel that it is necessary to present the perspective of 'survival' prostitutes themselves. Here are some of their views exemplifying the complexity and underlining structural inequalities behind the matter.

> I've only had one UN man as a customer in Ganta. He asked me why I am doing prostitution for. And I told him that this is my living. Since I'm not working, I'm not selling, so this is what I need to do for survival. That's how he asked me what I would like to do. And I said anything! So he gave me one hundred US dollars. And I was selling in Ganta after that time [with the assistance of the money received], but then my house got burned – everything that I had was destroyed. That is how I came to Monrovia.
> *Mary, 2013*

> UN men are not treating me better than Liberian men. You see, all men are the same. But they can pay me better – sometimes they can give me 70 USD, sometimes 50.
> *Angeline, 2014*

> The luck is not the same for all of us. Even if you will wear your best clothes, if the [UN] men don't want to see you, they will not see you. Liberian men, for me, they are not good. They are only there when I'm jammed. That's the only time I go with the Liberian men because they don't give any good money. Liberian men don't respect Liberian women when it comes to prostitution life. They insult us in all kinds of ways. Sometimes, when we make an agreement and then you sleep together, then in the daybreak they will start insulting you and make the people to

look at you in the whole community. That is why I prefer different men than Liberian men.
*Patience, 2012*

I brothel with the UN men a lot because of my height! They can always tell me that they want to teach me how to drive a car because I have a good height for driving. They can go out with me before they give me money. They can give me good money but still they go over me first.
*Careen, 2012*

If finding a 'UN man' as a 'one-night stand' is considered a very lucky incident among some prostitutes, then having a well-off and respectful 'sugar daddy' as a regular lover and financial supporter can be considered the ultimate jackpot. In their study on transactional sex practices among Liberian youth (all enrolled in schools and therefore rather well off; age range between thirteen and nineteen), Atwood et al. (2011) found that transactional sex was seen among their interviewees as a rather normal way of providing oneself with financial freedom and respect. Transactional sex was defined in this context as 'engaging in sexual intercourse in exchange for cash, goods, services, commodities, or privileges that are perceived as needs or wants by the participant' (p. 114), and both peer and parental pressure to obtain different kinds of consumer goods were typically reported as main motivational factors (pp. 115–16). In this manner, Atwood et al. (ibid.) and several similar studies (e.g. Silberschmidt and Rasch 2001; Nyanzi et al. 2001; Luke 2003; Kaufman and Stavrou 2004) emphasize the active agency of service providers rather than treating them solely as victims of sexual abuse.

However, as Hilary Standing (1992) emphasizes, conceptualizing terms such as 'transactional sex' or 'prostitution' is a rather complex matter. Standing notes that as sexual practices are always socially constructed (ibid.: 475), the chosen concepts must lean on local realities and be carefully contextualized.[19] Of special worry for Standing is that the concept of prostitution should not be transferred from the Western sphere to other parts of the world 'without proper scrutiny' (ibid.: 478).

As explained in the previous sections, prostitutes are understood in this book as individuals who have defined *themselves* as such. I made this decision since sexual relationships in today's Africa often have some kind of monetary component to them (ibid.: 477): indeed, love 'is intertwined with sexual desire, money and prestige', as Nyanzi et al. (2001: 83) describe in their study of Ugandan pupils. Secondly, after having had countless discussions in Liberia about the definition of prostitution with individuals from all kinds of backgrounds, I found no alternative but to settle with the self-definitions of individuals.

Of these discussions, a group interview with three young Liberian male journalists was among the most interesting since it captured eloquently the different kinds of societal pressures (e.g. financial, relationship, peer, familial, educational) in which youth have to raft in today's Liberia. All these young professionals worked on well-known Liberian newspapers.

The definition of prostitution sparked a lively debate among the journalists. Although they generally agreed that prostitution necessarily included the act of exchanging *money*, there was no consensus about whether men could be called prostitutes under any circumstances. They eventually came to the conclusion that although some males could in principle be referred to as prostitutes if they sold their sexual services for money and other benefits, they should instead be referred to as bluff boys, playboys, big boys or gigolos. In addition, the journalists concluded that a certain kind of prestige was attached to a boy/man with several sexual partners, whereas a girl/woman with many sexual partners could easily be given the label of prostitute (see also Silberschmidt and Rasch 2001: 1821; Luke 2003: 68).

To have a 'godfather'/'sugar daddy' or a 'godmother'/'sugar mommy' as a lover and financial backup is very common in Liberia and beyond. As is well proven in the previous research conducted in the African context (e.g. Standing 1992; Hunter 2002, 2010; Luke 2003; Coulter 2009: 201), it would clearly be misleading to refer to such relationships as prostitution. Rather, as Silberschmidt and Rasch (2001: 1821–2) argue, sex is often a type of bargaining tool that allows youth to gain access to small 'luxuries' in life. A telling example of the perceived normality of these types of relationships in today's Liberia is that there is often even parental pressure to form relationships with well-off partners who could bring different kinds of everyday commodities to the shared household (Atwood et al. 2011: 116). In 2014, for instance, I interviewed a young male student from the University of Liberia who had an eminent mature woman as his lover and supporter. After we had had a lengthy discussion about prostitution as a societal phenomenon in Liberia – something that he himself definitely did not relate to – Anthony (interview 2014) explained that his parents expected him to bring income into his family home by 'loving to' an elderly woman:

*Anthony* (A): After the war we are seeing our elderly women loving our little boys. It was not happening before. But this time around it is a normal thing, whereas it used to be something that was hidden from the parents. So it is even like a business now. Your parents know today that you are loving to four-five girls and you bring them home each in turn. You introduce them to your mother and they will accept your behaviour. It is happening! Like for me, I come from a poor background and I don't have money. So I am supposed to love an elderly woman who is supporting me and my family!

*Leena*: Is this escalation because of disadvantage; because of poverty or something?

A: Oh yeah! People don't really have their daily income. Well, some of the boys don't even want to do a normal job and they still wish to wear decent clothes. They want to be sharp, you know. And when you see your friends doing it, you think that you can also do it. Or you are just forced to do it. It is that peer pressure – you just have to be into it.

Alongside parental pressure, peer pressure was one of the constant themes touched upon in our discussions about the everyday challenges of the interviewees. Therefore, the question of peer pressure will be briefly touched upon before we come to the conclusions of this section.

### 'Everybody pot boiling, my pot can't boil'[20]

In her set of pictures, Veral (interview 2013) had a few photographs of her teenage daughter Angelica. She explained that although Angelica was very decent and kind in nature – she regularly helped with housekeeping duties, performed well in school and did not 'associate with people who would lead her to the wrong way' – Veral still needed to be strict with her daughter because peer pressure was 'too much' in Liberia today. Veral (interview 2012) explained:

Nowadays there is a kind of peer pressure already for small children. In this picture she is wearing slippers and these kinds of basic clothes on her. But her friends tomorrow, they want to wear jeans trousers, blouses and chains on their necks that she can't afford. So if her friends have those kinds of things, they will want her to join them. And for that she would need to go to look for men from the streets to give all those things to her because I don't really have it now. Especially taking into consideration her current school fees – some seven thousand and plus.

Wanting to look trendy and fashionable among one's peers is hardly a novel phenomenon anywhere in the world. What may be unique, however, in recent developments in Liberia is the level and extent of that pressure. G-Girl (interview 2013), for example, stated that:

> In the old times people thought differently. Their minds have changed. So today other people are there with those nice things and with all this peer pressure you will do everything you can just to get what that other person has. More especially for women. But now even the men have joined – everybody wants to look decent. Men can even dress up more than the women. So nowadays you have to have a very strong mind to resist all this, or otherwise you will find yourself doing things that you are not supposed to do, you know? The peer pressure is too hard nowadays. The pressure today is on everybody's mind. Really, Leena. On everybody's mind.

The peer pressures of today come not only from friends and family, but also the entertainment industry. The latest fashion trends are absorbed from Western TV series, and increasingly from 'African shows' – predominantly 'Nollywood' soap operas originating in Nigeria. Consumer culture is also promoted through religious TV shows (Ukah 2003), and in this manner the TV itself captures the continuous negotiations and borderlines between tradition and modernity. In various kinds of TV series, *juju* practices are contrasted with demands to trust solely in the Christian God; the traditional *lappa* suits compete with the hottest styles seen worn by international celebrities; and parental authority as well as patriarchal structures are being challenged by strong and independent young women. Indeed, the youth in Liberia are surrounded by various forms of societal expectations, and constantly have to negotiate and reassess their roles in demanding social surroundings.

Hipco music – a Liberian musical genre strongly influenced by Afro-American hip-hop and RnB music with lyrics in colloquial dialect – mesmerizingly captures the constant struggles and demands through which local youth have to steer their rafts of survival in Monrovia and beyond. With pieces typically packed with strong societal messages on poverty, corruption, violence and political misconduct, the artists not only challenge and question the current state of affairs, but also act as a source of inspiration for impoverished youth (e.g. Engebretson 2013; Rahimian 2013; Tucker 2014). The power of hipco music in Liberia as a sensitization and information-sharing tool has also been well recognized by NGOs, which have collaborated with hipco artists in order to disseminate different kinds of messages, from Ebola prevention methods to anti-rape and anti-corruption campaigns; campaigns whose success is obviously rather difficult to measure.

A hipco piece was also pulsing in the background as my assistant Quita and I were having a discussion with Sonia about the peer pressures she encountered in her everyday village life in close proximity to the town of Gbarnga in 2015. In one of the pictures she had taken for the photo interview session, her disabled son was playing on a bed in a tiny room. Sonia explained that the bed dominating the space was meant for her and the children. When I inquired about the other possessions in the room, she specifically mentioned a radio that was unfortunately broken at the moment. The contrast between her belongings and the fact that she had continuously brought up the lack of medicine and even food in our earlier encounters confused me. Why did she not just sell the radio and buy medicine? And how come so many of the respondents had a fancy mobile phone, but 'no money' for school fees? Surely one would, indeed *should*, prefer a good dinner to a TV set; antibiotics to a synthetic wig? Thus, we had the following exchange.

*Leena* (L): So this is something I cannot understand. How can you have a radio if sometimes you don't have enough to eat?

*Sonia* (S): But I was having it before!

L: Okay, okay, I understand.

*Quita (research assistant)* (Q): You know, the issue with the radio is that sometimes these small boys can cut the palm and sell the oil and buy a radio. So it is not that if you have the money or you don't have the money ...

L: Yes, I understand this. But what I don't understand is that when you cut the palm, why not save the money instead of buying the radio?

Q: Aha!

S: You know, when your friends have it, everyone has to have it! Everybody has to have one because the friends are having one.

Q: So it is peer pressure. You know, not too long ago you saw so many young boys with a big towel on their shoulder in the evening. That was a style they learned somewhere.

L: Aaa!

Q: Another lesson [laughter].

L: I was also talking with some women in Monrovia and they told me that there is huge pressure nowadays to have beautiful hair, clothes and all that, and at the same time there is no money. And this combination can make you do all kinds of bad things. So you have to have a strong mind to resist all this. Is it the same here?

S: The same thing is here. But even more in Gbarnga.

L: Even in the village?

S: Yeah! You see the things that your friends have and then you ain't got a hand for it. But you are hoping to get some.

L: Sometimes, if you happen to have money, would you buy slippers instead of food even though you were hungry?

S: Yeah! You can choose like that because you want to have those slippers.

In their award-winning book *Poor Economics: A Radical Rethinking of the Way to Fight Global Poverty*, Abhijit V. Banerjee and Esther Duflo (2011) pose questions similar to those I put to Sonia and her fellow interviewees: why do the poor sometimes seem to place more value on assets other than food in life? Why would anyone choose to be hungry just to buy a pair of slippers? Banerjee and Duflo (ibid.: 35–8) do not offer any clear-cut answers, but reason that the poor typically prioritize things that have the ability to make life a little less boring.

In addition, I would argue, things carrying the potential to elevate one's status within the given social group – be it among village elders, church volunteers, teenage girls, gang members or top-end politicians – are often preferred in a manner that might seem bizarre to an outsider. For instance, when a prostitute decides to invest her previous week's income in a new *lappa* suit instead of a mosquito net, she possibly aspires to earn respect within her congregation while simultaneously trying to capture the attention of a possible groom. Or, in another instance, she might opt for her daily dose of *tar-white* to silence her rambling thoughts for the night instead of using the money to buy a much-needed cooking pot. If her 'pot was boiling', if only her 'life would be proper' and she had her 'own place and small business' (Tracy, interview 2014), maybe then she would choose differently and prefer that which seems rational to an outsider.

## Conclusion

In this chapter, I have touched upon some of the everyday rivers of insecurities in which young women war veterans have to manoeuvre in today's Liberia. To capture some of the complexities and structural constraints behind these movements, I have utilized the concept of social rafting. By taking a close look at these women's everyday survival mechanisms – how to find and secure basic necessities such as food, security and health – I have tried to exemplify that survival in these dangerous rivers requires endless persistence, innovative solutions and robust social networks. By discussing 'survival' prostitution and the related definitional challenges, I have illustrated how structural inequalities, various levels of discrimination and novel forms of peer pressure are reflected in the daily lives of young Liberian women.

To conclude this chapter, however, let us turn back to Massa and her living conditions and consider how things have changed since the rainy season of 2014 – the year in which the description of her on-going challenges at the beginning of this chapter were recorded. I was able to reach Massa by phone in early 2016. The previous year had been extremely hard for her – the father of Massa's children, her long-time partner, had not only announced that he was going to move in with his new girlfriend and leave Massa, but the couple had also lost a baby earlier that year. Somehow, nonetheless, Massa had been able to save some money and move with her children to a better neighborhood close to the centre of Monrovia in December 2015. Although this area is in many ways deprived and often referred to as a slum, her rented room is nevertheless in a good location as it is close to the road (safety), and she also saves a remarkable sum of money in transportation fees. From her current location, she can walk to the city centre in less than twenty minutes. Massa was again filled with positive expectations for the future: she would expand her small business and use the *susu* arrangement to save some money for the forthcoming needs of herself and her children. Thus, the tide had undeniably turned again and things would be 'alright'. These and other tiny scraps of hope[21] are the main topic of the following chapter, in which some of the dreams and aspirations of these courageous and tremendously persistent young women are detailed.

# 5
# Let my children's future be alright

In this picture I'm sitting silently. Worrying how my future will be. Sometimes, if I'm like this, my friends come to me and we share fun. Like when I sat silently one day, my friend whose picture you saw earlier asked me: but why are you sitting silently? I told her that I am thinking and that is why I'm sitting like that in my room. In this picture I'm worrying about my school and my daughter's future. Because now now[1] she doesn't have a father. Since her father is not carrying his responsibilities, she doesn't have one in my eyes. I'm really regretting why I born a child for him. Love is blind.
*Temama, 2013*

Angeline has asked me to sit down on a lonely bench in one of the corners of the room while her twin sister is getting ready for the new day. It is already 1 p.m., yet I have apparently arrived too early since both sisters have been working until the early hours of the morning. On the few posters plastered hastily on the cardboard walls, there are phrases such as 'police is your friend' and 'put an end to sexual violence today'. I feel confused. The air is filled with bursts of laughter and heated sounds of disagreement over an ongoing game of ludo; joints are rolled; and a bottle of palm wine is moving from hand to hand, from mouth to mouth. It is just another ordinary day in this run-down community, and I have nothing else to do than to sip the lukewarm water from the 5 LD plastic bag that someone placed in my hand a moment ago. Minutes pass, tens of minutes, an hour.

Just when I am about to ask if I could join the next round of ludo, two children enter the room in their spotless school uniforms. They are the offspring of some of the residents, I am told, while the pupils themselves adjust their slender legs onto the tiny wooden benches located at the doorway that leads the occasional visitor to individual bedrooms. Maths, the history of the republic, the alphabet – the children seem to have their age-specific homework to complete, a task they eagerly undertake while simultaneously keeping an eye on a small toddler at their feet. Suddenly, the phrase 'I sell my body for the sake of my children so that their future would be alright' seems to materialize before my eyes. Finally the twins arrive, we are soon off, and will leave the children to continue their assignments in the modest shelter of the corridor.

Hope for a better future is the main focus in this final main chapter of the book at hand. Despite coming from positions of extreme feebleness, the majority of the research participants have not lost their ability to dream, to aspire for something better. On the contrary – it seems that hope for a better tomorrow, at least for their children, is the main ingredient, the main source of fuel, allowing individuals to raft and stay afloat in the constant everyday struggles narrated in the different chapters of this book.

The chapter is divided into three main sections based on the nature of the fragments of hope derived from the interview material. First, some of the educational aspirations of the interviewees are outlined. Typically, the respondents hoped for educational opportunities for both parents and children alike. Education was normally seen as a path towards running a small business or gaining improved professional status. Professional dreams are the topic of the second main section of the chapter. Professional status was taken as a viable way of becoming 'someone' in both immaterial and material terms – of acquiring a real bed or a shoe rack, of having decent *lappa* clothes at Sunday service, or perhaps even owning a concrete house or a car. The third main section then explicitly touches upon the material aspirations of the research participants. Finally, in the concluding section, the answers to the question of 'how do you see the future of the person in this photograph' is touched upon as it grasps the overall state of mind of each respondent at the time of her interview. Although the chapter contains excerpts from the interviews of various respondents, a special emphasis is placed on the statements of Juliet and Veral.

## I want to learn book

> When I look at this picture [a photograph of a school building], I can just imagine myself going to school in the future. So I can feel sorry for myself anytime I see a school. My older brothers are all learning book but I don't have the hand for it. You see, my parents are already paying for my children's fees. So I need to do something to generate money for myself, to get myself to school.
> *Juliet, 2013*

The old Ministry of Education of Liberia lies in the centre of Monrovia, on Broad Street. The building itself has seen better days, but the location is perfect for arranging a rendezvous with someone who resides in another district of town. In front of 'Education' there are lines and lines of small stands with traders selling anything from copybooks to Liberian dollars, from dried cow meat to cooked cassava. In between the tables, numerous wheelbarrows are endlessly pushed around – soft drinks, DK clothes[2], coconuts. You name it and you can most likely find it here. Indeed, it seems that Education is constantly on the move: it is bustling.

The hustle and bustle around Education is an apt allegory for the formal education structures of Liberia. Ever since the first settlers began to arrive on the shores of the country we today know as Liberia, the sector has been exposed to frequent alterations. From the start, the immigrants tied educational activities strongly to religious ambitions: 'Liberia was seen not only as a home for American freedmen but as a center for the Christianization and civilization of Africa, as well' (Livingston 1976: 246). Back in the USA, both abolitionists and slaveholders considered the education of colored people to be a path towards something new; either rebellion or emancipation, depending on the status of the person talking. The majority of the settlers who arrived in the area of Liberia prior to independence in 1847, however, had little or no formal schooling. Although only 25 percent of the immigrants over ten years of age could read, the figure was still rather high compared to the USA of the era, where literacy among the black population was as low as 5 percent. Nonetheless, considering the educational background of the arrivals, their task of 'educating and civilizing Africa, in addition to establishing government and commerce to support themselves' (ibid.: 247–8; Huberich 1947) was simply utopian, as will be shown in what follows.

### Liberia's education sector: a 'mess'

During the 1850s, several highs schools were being built in many parts of Liberia by various religious groups. In the same decade, the construction of Liberia's first institution of higher education began, with significant funding and guidance from America. Liberia College opened its doors in 1862, and was renamed the University of Liberia in 1951 to mark a new beginning after a massive fire. The fact that between 1862 and 1903 only eleven students succeeded in graduating from the College is a telling illustration of the constant challenges the institution encountered in its early days (Livingston 1976: 249–251; Lulat 2005: 277–8). As Lulat (2005: 279, emphasis in original) remarks: 'in the absence of state involvement in *systematic* educational planning and provision, from the very beginning, higher education in Liberia developed on a haphazard basis'.

Regrettably, primary and secondary education in Liberia were developed in an equally fragmentary fashion. By 1843, more than five hundred children attended the schools established by numerous church missionary societies. The education of the local population was certainly not a priority for the American Colonization Society, although it was reported that some native children entered the homes of settlers and slowly absorbed 'civilized' manners (Huberich 1947).

Up until 1960, the missionary schools were mainly responsible for the provision of 'modern' education in the interior, whereas government schools dominated in the coastal counties. When the number of public schools rapidly increased, the quality of the education simultaneously plunged. A ten-year development program for the education sector was initiated in 1960, and the ambitious goal was set to achieve universal elementary education by the end of the program period (Gormuyor 1992: 340). That goal was never reached. Interestingly, Nagel and Snyder (1989) analysed the educational development of Liberia from 1972 to 1985, hence shortly after the aforementioned development program, and only four years prior to the first civil war. They concentrated specifically (ibid.: 9) on the roles played by international funding agencies and came into the conclusion that:

> While no system, education or otherwise, whether in a developing or developed state, operates completely smoothly or works exactly as planned, the extent of fragmentation, conflict, and drift in Liberian education was so great that it was difficult to view the state of affairs as accidental. Ironically, the chaos seemed ordered, organized in a way that suggested that systematic forces were at work, forces that were pulling the education sector apart.

Following organization theory, Nagel and Snyder (ibid., emphasis in original) then went on to describe the education sector of Liberia as a 'mess', a '*system* of problems' with its internal logic. As a combining feature within these problematics, they saw the direct or indirect involvement of numerous international funding agencies – each with their particular competition patterns and logics. With new units and institutions constantly established as a response to emerging problems, the consequence was evidently worsening fragmentation and chaos (ibid.: 17); indeed, a 'mess'.[3]

Even though formal education is highly appreciated in today's Liberia, it unfortunately remains 'significantly behind most other countries in the African region in nearly all education statistics' (USAID 2016). This reality is also recognized in 'Liberia Demographic and Health Survey 2013'. In the survey, it is remarked, for instance, that 33 percent of women and 13 percent of men in Liberia have no education at all, and about one third of Liberians have only attended primary school. In addition, more than half of the country's female population is illiterate (Government of Liberia 2014: 35–7).

In early 2016, in response to haphazard conditions, Minister of Education George Werner announced that a radical reform would soon take place in early childhood and primary education. Werner's original plan was to outsource these for a duration of five years to a private enterprise called Bridge Academies, a company whose teaching practices rely on education materials stored on phones and tablets. Bridge International Academies (2013) contends that this method 'enables us to monitor teacher and student performance in real time, constantly reviewing and revising to ensure that we are offering a world class education that will prepare our students for the 21st century'. The company claims that with its approach even very poorly educated teachers can deliver high-quality lessons with a price tag of US$6 per month per pupil (Front Page Africa 2016; Bridge International Academies 2013). After an outraged response – for example, from Kishore Singh, the UN Special Rapporteur on the right to education (OHCHR 2016) – Werner backtracked and clarified that in the first stage only 120 public schools, 3 percent of the whole, would be piloted under multiple operators. The first stage of the project, entitled Partnership Schools for Liberia, was launched in September 2016, yet civil society's response towards the initiative has remained highly critical.

The higher education sector in Liberia also remains unstable. For instance, during the 2013 entrance exam for the University of Liberia, all 25,000 candidates failed the exam. The reason for this 'epic fail', as it was soon labelled, was, on the one hand, the decision of the university to hire an outside consultant to oversee that year's examination process in order to restore confidence in administration practices. On the other hand, the university had also decided that in order to pass the 2013 exam, a candidate would need to achieve at least 60 percent in mathematics and 70 percent in English, with no scales being utilized in the grading process. As a consequence, not a single examinee fulfilled the initial requirements. In the aftermath of the scandal, the university finally agreed to accept 1,800 students under the orders of the president (Butty 2013; Smith 2013).

To summarize, the education system of Liberia is certainly a 'mess', as President Ellen Johnson Sirleaf herself declared after the 2013 fiasco (Reuters 2013). The miserable state of the sector, however, does not prevent individuals from having educational goals in their lives. Indeed, very strong aspirations related to 'learning book' were detailed in most interviews with the research participants, as is exemplified in the photo interview session with Ariana in the ensuing section.

### Buying a future with 'contributions'

Ariana lives in a town called Kakata, some ninety minutes' drive from the capital in the north-east. After being a fighter for AFL in the second civil war starting at the age of thirteen, she registered in a DDRR program and got back to school. With the help of the DDRR funding, Ariana was able to finish her high school studies but lacked the resources to go farther on her educational path. At the time of our first interview in 2012, three months after her high school graduation, Ariana sustained herself with the help of her older sister and boyfriend. As she was definitely very smart and attentive, someone with a potentially bright future ahead of her, I was eager to get hold of Ariana's photo set from the photo studio, which I did about a week after our initial meeting.

To my complete surprise, almost all the photographs in the set were portraits of Ariana herself, posing for the camera with a very proud expression on her face. I quickly got angry and frustrated. Why had this bright young woman not followed the instructions we had previously settled upon for photographing her daily realities and aspirations, but instead used the opportunity to take selfies? Had she not told me that she both understood the instructions and was completely fine with them? One can even hear my frustration during the first few minutes of the recording of the photo interview session. 'But why did you do this?' I ask on the tape, and seem to be quite agitated. Ariana (interview 2013) replies in a soft voice: 'Leena, the reason is that I'm really focusing on this. I really want to be a medical doctor one day.' To exemplify this craving, she had traveled for more than an hour by motorbike taxi to borrow a nurse's uniform from her friend for the photo shoot. Thus, in her pictures, Ariana poses for the camera in a nursing gown comprised of pale blue pants, a multicolored yet very simple top and a pair of professional white sandals. In addition to using her weekend food budget to cover travel expenses, she had given her friend around US$5 as a 'thank you gift' for allowing her to borrow the uniform. Not knowing any medical doctors personally, Ariana had figured that with a borrowed nursing gown she could, at least, exemplify her stubborn desire somewhat appropriately in the forthcoming photo interview session. I felt utterly stupid.

As was the case with Ariana, the majority of the research participants lacked the resources to pay the school fees and/or the subscription costs for possible entrance examinations. It was generally agreed that with the right kind of 'contribution', the doors to almost any institution would open, but they would remain closed if no bribe was provided. I witnessed this process in practice with a member of my friend's family when the desperate father finally gave up and paid both the stated subscription fee and the US$50 'contribution for late attendance' directly to the trade school's headmaster.

Although many Liberians seem to reason that corruption should not exist in principle, it is still approved when teachers, policemen and other low-paid public servants ask for offerings of various kinds (see also Reno 2012: 129). Their salaries simply remain too low when compared with the ever-increasing cost of living in the country. Furthermore, as Funaki and Glencorse (2014: 849) remark, even the whole concept of corruption is far from clear in the everyday vernacular of Liberians. In the current anti-corruption work being implemented in the country, the nuances are rarely recognized, however, a belief that 'corruption is universally understood' often determines the insights of these undertakings (ibid.).

The following anecdote provides an example of the everyday understanding of the term in today's Liberia. I was once taking a public taxi in Monrovia when the driver kindly remarked to us passengers that a small 'contribution' for selected traffic officers could significantly ease the daily hassle of getting around the city during rush hour. 'Hey, man, that is corruption,' I commented in an ironic tone. 'But don't you know the difference between corruption and contribution, white woman?' a passenger sitting next to me asked in the same tone of voice, with wrinkles of laughter around his eyes. 'In corruption, you are *forced* to provide money or other things in order for you to achieve a certain thing, but if you give someone a contribution, it is like a gift you are giving *voluntarily*. So while the first one is obligatory, the second one is completely up to you.' When all the other three passengers and the driver then nodded their heads after hearing this explanation, I had no choice but to agree with them that my understanding of corruption was somewhat different from theirs.

Taking a step back from the definitional challenges of corruption to pedagogical matters, how does the education sector appear from the viewpoint of a teacher herself? That is, of someone who is occasionally 'forced' to ask for 'contributions' of all sorts? The photo-elicitation session with Theresa, whose wartime experiences are elucidated in Chapter 2, provides the perspective of a rural primary school teacher.

In the aftermath of the second civil war, Theresa was accepted into a nine-month-long teacher training program organized by the Liberian government. There were more than two hundred primary school teacher candidates in her training group, and the courses provided varied from language studies to psychology; from history to the social sciences. For the first six years of their teaching careers, Theresa and the majority of her fellow course participants practiced their profession without any official salary. By asking the pupils to pay for the course material, the tests and some other minor matters, and by practicing small-scale cassava farming outside teaching hours, Theresa was able to earn enough money to cover the basic needs of herself and her children. At the time of our photo interview in 2012, Theresa had been receiving a monthly salary of 9,000 LD (around US$125) for the last two years from her teaching job in a rural village in Margibi County. She had been assigned to this village school only a few months earlier and told that there was no room for negotiation –either she took on this new position or she would find herself jobless. Hence, on weekdays Theresa was forced to leave her youngest children under the care of her teenage daughter, who was to be the head of the household when she herself could not be around owing to the distance between her home and the village school.

In her photo-elicitation session, it became evident that Theresa truly enjoyed her position as a teacher. While examining a photograph of a group of children in one of her several classes, Theresa (interview 2012) explained: 'Especially the small small children, I love to teach them! Everything that you say is registered in their minds.' Then again, while still staring at the same photograph, she whispered that this place would not be suitable for her own children since 'the country devil was very active', especially in the Margibi region. For the same reason, I had experienced great difficulty in finding a motorbike taxi to the same village earlier that morning. After the majority of the young men had given peculiar excuses such as claiming that the one-hour ride would be too long and bumpy for their bikes, one adult motorbike driver volunteered to take me to my destination and proudly explained that he himself was not afraid of the 'bush devil'. Apparently, it was the peak of the Poro society's[4] recruiting period in the area, and young men were convinced that there was a real risk of abduction on the route on which we were about to embark. I did not give too much thought to the issue at the time since rumors are omnipresent in Liberia. Nevertheless, when Theresa stated that at the moment there was a real lack of boy pupils in her school since the 'country devil' had recently paid a visit to the neighborhood and 'carried all the boy children into the bush', I began to think that maybe the apprehension of the motorbike drivers had not been ill placed after all.[5] In addition to practical matters such as tuition fees, the distance between home and school, and constant illnesses, matters of 'the bush' might in this manner also occasionally have an effect on the everyday scholastic lives of students and teachers, especially in certain areas of the country.

By way of conclusion, it can be summarized that it is certainly a very complicated task to receive proper or even decent schooling as a poor person in Liberia. The challenges vary from the numerous kinds of fees associated with education, such as exam costs and school uniforms, to the quality and accessibility of the school building itself. In spite of these and many other hardships, aspirations related to educational goals were extremely strong among the interviewees. Having a decent education was seen as one of the only viable ways to improve one's living conditions and achieve a better occupation in the future; a way to move from the hazardous rafting circumstances towards something a bit more organized and stable. The interviewees seemed to reason that it was indeed through educational achievements that the primary aim of improving one's living conditions with a decent job or bigger business could be achieved – a goal to which we will turn in the next section.

## I would like to become a big business woman

> My dream? I want to find a job so that I could help my children to have their own future.
> *Rhoda, 2013*[6]

> I'm a legal hustler now. But my first dream is to sit down and complete my career in cosmetology. If I could afterwards find work in any of these beauty salons, that would be alright for me.
> *Anna, 2013*

As explained in Chapter 4, only a few of the respondents currently have waged positions, but many do have tiny businesses that they would like to develop and expand. Whereas prostitutes were typically dreaming of being able to leave their current profession behind and begin some form of small business, modest business owners were hoping to find means of making their businesses grow. At the other end of the spectrum were the few high school or university students who had the goal of one day becoming 'big business women', doctors, NGO employees or the like. Thus, the better the initial position of the interviewee, the more ambitious she was in her aspirations.

To launch a 'small business' as a woman in Liberia is fairly straightforward: the most important thing is to have a small lump sum of money to get the business going. In this regard, not much has changed since Mary Moran's (1990: 129) field research in the 1980s: at the lower end of initial costs – and profit – are various kinds of sweet and savoury snacks, whereas 'the more serious civilized businesswoman is usually involved in sewing, baking, or producing some rarer type of finger food'. As in the 1980s, having access to a freezer in today's Liberia can significantly improve business opportunities, as it makes it possible to produce small plastic bags of frozen soft drinks, ice for coolers owned by other small-scale entrepreneurs, or simply very cold sodas, beers and water bags for consumers.

In the years following the second civil war, the former commander Juliet was able to put together a modest hair salon in one of the shanty towns of Monrovia. Her customer base quickly grew since Juliet possessed a huge network of friends and other acquaintances around the capital. Soon she was able to support herself, her partner and her children with the salon. The initial costs, such as the money necessary for the 'seven pieces of zinc, four mats, ply woods, a door, all that', Juliet (interview 2012) had gathered a penny at a time with the help of a nearby *susu* club. For a few years, things seemed relatively bright for Juliet and her family: income was modest but stable, the children were healthy, and Juliet was even able to save a small amount of money for the future needs of the family. Then, one morning in 2009, a storm entered the salon in the form of a visit by the newly elected city mayor, Mary Broh, who declared that the salon was scheduled to be demolished in the early hours of the following morning. She added that there would be no room for negotiation. This was part of a wider purge by the mayor, whose aim was to clean the slums, street corners and beaches of Monrovia of waste, litter and illegal businesses or other random settlements (Carter 2013). Since Juliet's makeshift salon had no official permit, it was therefore destroyed the next morning alongside several other modest businesses located in the same narrow alley.

The purges of Monrovia are a typical example of the 'violence of urban development', as Ayona Datta (2012: 31) describes it in her ethnography on Delhi. Violence certainly has its consequences, and the trauma resulting from the annihilated enterprise was still so prevalent at the time of my latest encounter with Juliet that she could not imagine herself trying to restart the business in the near future. To begin with, there was no money for the initial costs, nor any guarantees that the mayor would not order yet another purge in the future. For these reasons, Juliet was thinking of either restarting her educational endeavor or launching a door-to-door business selling soaps, creams and other beauty products to her former customers and beyond. Maybe, 'small small', she could then set aside enough funding to reopen her beauty salon in an official manner, satisfying also the city mayor. Nevertheless, since Juliet's parents were already paying her children's school fees, they could not offer financial support for her personal schooling, and thus her educational aspirations would need to be put on hold for the time being. As Juliet's boyfriend, her children's father, was also suffering from frequent setbacks in his business of selling DK shoes on Monrovia's street corners – the police had confiscated his selection of shoes several times and demanded an ever-increasing amount in bribes to have them returned – the family budget was very tight at the time of our photo interview.

A study by Sirleaf Market Women's Fund (2012: 1) identifies four types of business category run by market women in today's Liberia. The most successful of these women possess growing businesses that fully meet the needs of the whole household. In the second category are modest but stable businesses that can support a small household, whereas on the following level the commercial activity can only partially fulfil the household demands. Finally, in the fourth category, are those minor or declining businesses that bring some (unreliable) income to the family unit. With a few exceptions, all the interviewees were in the last of these four categories. Many of the research participants, however, explained in a proud tone that either their mothers or other women relatives had been successful 'big business women' prior to the wars (the first category in the above-mentioned study). These women had typically had some form of fashion business and a sustainable customer base: the trendiest *lappa* clothes were purchased from countries such as Nigeria and Ghana, whereas Western outfits were typically acquired through contacts in the USA. Years of warfare had bankrupted most of these businesses, but since the memories lingered on, they were persistently mentioned in the interview situations. For instance, aspirations such as these were brought up by some respondents (excerpts from different interviewees):

> I want to be a big business woman but not in Monrovia. I want to be going out of the country and coming back.

> So if I had money, I would like to open up a big business. Now I'm selling small small myself but I would like to have other people selling for me. By next year, I want to do out of town business.

> I really want to go to school. But I have no hand. So after school I would like to sell, and if I go to school, I could do even bigger business afterwards. In the future I'd like both my boyfriend and myself to work. That is my dream.

The Sirleaf Market Women's Fund study (ibid.: 4) also found that peer-managed *susu* associations were the preferred mechanisms for saving money for future business needs (see Chapter 4). Since the microcredit schemes and low-interest loans typically offered by NGOs were considered administratively too complex (ibid.), it is surprising that NGOs do not seem to utilize the well-known *susu* system or its variations in their work, but rather opt for locally unpopular systems such as microloans. Possibly these kinds of messages from the grass roots could be better recognized and delivered to the administrative meetings if more local staff were hired to leading positions in the numerous NGOs operating in the country.

Veral, for example, whose wartime experiences are detailed in several sections of this book, had in her photo set a picture of herself in office surroundings. In the photograph, Veral poses behind a table covered with piles of papers and notebooks, a calendar and a shining laptop that she is studying with a very concentrated look on her face. A huge umbrella is leaning against the wall in the right-hand corner, indicating that this is the rainy season. The final touch is provided by a poster on the wall that reminds the occasional visitor to 'talk to your children about STIs, HIV and AIDS'. The room is probably the office space of an international NGO, a detail not explicit in Veral's interview material. According to Veral's (interview 2013) explanation, the photograph was in any case a projection of the life ahead of her.

*Veral* (V): This is about my future. For now, I'm in school [university]. So I think that after my graduation, I should have an office like this with my own computer. I will be working there and submitting reports to my bosses, or people are submitting their reports to me.

*Leena* (L): Is it NGO work? Or some other kind of work?

V: Yes, NGO work. At the moment I'm doing agriculture as my major. This is my first year at the university and I have three more years to go. So after my studies, I want to produce food for my country and that is why I decided to do agriculture. This is my future because after my graduation I'm educated and will be working with my computer. But at the same token, I will be working in the field. I have to calculate everything that I must put into the fields that year and how many dollars I have generated so far. So I want to work for an NGO but have my own fields as well, to produce food also for my own needs.

L: Is it very expensive to study at the university?

V: Sure, very expensive. Like for this semester I'm paying US$650. I don't have a scholarship. But my boyfriend is paying for it. He sells by the road and helps me with the fees. But in the future he won't be able to help me because he himself is also going to school. Now we are trying to look for scholarships: they've got county scholarships and such. So maybe for next semester I could find one. It is not easy, especially with the condition of my eyes.

The condition that Veral is referring to in her interview is glaucoma, a permanent eye disease causing vision loss and sensitivity to direct sunlight. Although it has nothing to do with it, Veral remained convinced that her sickness was caused by her brutal former commander, described in detail in Chapter 2. One day, Veral had decided to run away from the forces owing to the continuous abuse but was caught by the commander himself. As a 'lesson', he had tied Veral to a tree, told his soldiers to force her eyes wide open, and urinated in her eyes. Veral explained that soon after this incident the problems with her eyes began. In this way not only do her painful eyes remind Veral on an everyday basis of the horrible things she had gone through in the past, they also have an impact on her university studies and her future opportunities. Given that this is such a huge factor in her life today, the very first picture in her photo set was a close-up photograph of her eyes. Veral (interview 2012) explained:

> *Veral* (V): I took this picture because of my eyes, especially to show the infection in my eyes. What happened to me, how my eyes are red. I took it so you can see the main problem I face in my life.
>
> *Leena* (L): How do you survive with this pain and all this suffering?
>
> V: Well, the doctors only put me on drugs. They have given me some medicine to drop in my eyes so that at least the pain could go away for a little while. But it can't finish altogether. So this is just life. I just have to accept the common life. What are good or bad things, I'm living with them. I can't cut my eyes, I can't take them and throw them away. But it is also not easy. Even when I go to classes, I have to sit right in front of the board before I can see. Too much light is not good for my eyes, so I don't really play a lot with computers. Also sunlight is too much, I must go under the shade and wait after the sun has set before getting under it.
>
> L: You've got dark glasses? Sunglasses?
>
> V: Yes, I've got them. But I bought them from the market so they were not prescribed to me by any doctor. But actually I feel shame about this condition.
>
> L: Why?
>
> V: Well, that is one of the main reasons why I even bought the shades. Because when the people see that my eyes are getting red, they will say that 'Oh, but you're eyes are red!', or 'What have you done to your eyes?' So sometimes this condition makes me feel rejected even among my friends.

## Let me have a concrete house

Despite the breakdown of Juliet's business described above, and all the other challenges she had endured in her prior life, Juliet (interview 2012) still had in her mind a clear image of her future 'dream house':

> I want to have a house like this [house in the picture], this is my dream house. Because in Liberia now, if you build a house you'll

have a fortune. Like if your children need a hand or anything else, they can be there. It should be a concrete house, a very strong house that my children and even grandchildren could stay in. There should be three bedrooms in my house: one for me and my husband, one for my children, and another one for my parents or other visitors. The two bathrooms and kitchen should be inside the house, and in the garden I would grow greens, cassava leaves and other food stuff.

Juliet's description captures many of the features present in several interview situations with the research participants. Indeed, there were only a few photo sets without pictures of either ideal houses and/or the interviewees' current living conditions, of which the latter were typically deemed very modest and insufficient. Possessing one's own concrete house some time in the future was the ultimate signifier of progress and accomplishment. For that goal to be achieved, however, it was typically argued that one would need to acquire a proper education and decent business skills, as a minimum. On the other hand, a concrete building would satisfy the aspirations of those interviewees whose living environments were currently the most precarious ones.

A few months after our initial photo interview session in 2012, Juliet was able to rent a modest place with her boyfriend in which the whole family could reside. This achievement was significant, as the couple had been forced to live in their family homes before – Juliet and the children in her parents' house, and Juliet's partner in his own family home. As is typical in Liberia, the couple had paid one year's rent in advance for their own place, and, with the assistance of their families, acquired all the necessary things a new household needs in Liberia: pots, buckets and other kitchenware, a flask, a tablecloth, two chairs, a mattress, some sheets, a few pictures and teddy bears, and even some plastic flowers. Unfortunately, the couple's happiness was once more short lived. A few months after they had moved in, their next-door neighbor left a candle burning on going to bed and the house was in ashes the following morning. Juliet and her family had luckily been away that night, and were spared the flames, but everything they had so tediously gathered just a while ago was now gone. The only human victim of the incident was the 'guilty person', who could no longer be hold responsible for the accident. When the landlord then stated that he would not return any of the rental money paid in advance, Juliet and her partner had, once again, no alternative but to begin to strengthen their raft of survival from scratch. They contacted all possible family members and friends in Liberia, got in touch with some relatives who had established lives in the USA, begged for money from their parents, and tried to set aside a few dollars from the shoe business of Juliet's boyfriend for their basic everyday needs.

Soon after, however, the couple began to witness streams of help pouring through their parents' front door. Someone brought in an extra bucket, another donated rice and a plate. Many of Juliet's street sisters brought her some pieces of clothing, even whole *lappa* suits, handbags, sandals and jewellery. A TV set was donated to the couple, as was an old table and a mattress. It seemed that everyone wanted to participate in one way or another. For me as an outside observer this experience was a perfect example of how social capital – wealth in people (Bledsoe 1980) – can work among the urban poor in today's Liberia. If an appreciated member of the community is found to be in extreme need of a helping hand to sustain or strengthen her raft of survival, these hands are most often available for the socially capable.

In her book *Civilized Women: Gender and Prestige in Southeastern Liberia*, Mary Moran (1990) draws a distinction between 'civilized' and 'country'/'native' people among the Glebo in Cape Palmas in the early 1980s. Although Moran's point of departure is area-specific, and the research material was gathered more than thirty years ago, some of her remarks remain pertinent in my research setting. Moran (ibid.: 3) maintains that the majority of the Glebo hope to attain a civilized status 'if not for oneself, then for one's children'. She discovered that, among the Glebo, the level of civilization of an individual was determined by her occupation (office work was seen as civilized whereas farming was not), education level, residence, type of religious congregation and family background (ibid.: 12). Although a 'civilized woman' ideally resembled a Western-style housewife, these women actually both managed their households (ibid.: 4) and undertook different types of small business, making them economically independent (ibid.: 128–9). This finding is well in line with the statements of my research participants, of whom many stated: 'I want to be a housewife but work as well'.

The word civilized was occasionally utilized by the respondents in a manner that resembles the variations that Moran presented in her research. In addition to differences in clothing, a topic that deserves such a detailed approach that it must be left to some future piece of research, household decoration was also at times referred to with such terminology. According to the respondents, as a marker of civilization, a concrete house should at least be furnished with a 'real bed, dresser, shoe rack, tissue cover, all that', as Olive (interview 2013) detailed in her photo interview session. In addition, a TV was typically mentioned, as well as a separate sitting room with photographs on the walls, plastic flowers, tablecloths, curtains and decorative pillows. Photographs of 'dream houses' or 'dream rooms' reflected these aspirations in practical terms. In addition to the details specified above, all kinds of beauty products – shampoos, creams, soaps, perfumes – seemed to be taken as 'markers' of civilization. Finally, a carefully cleaned toilet and a sufficient stockpile of toilet paper inside the master bedroom would signify to the occasional visitor that the owner of that room was to be respected.

A clean yard with flowers, fruit trees and a grass mat would provide the final touch to the civilized household (compare to Moran 1990: 64). Furthermore, small-scale vegetable gardens were often found among the interviewee's aspirations (ibid.). Veral (interview 2013), for instance, explained that even if she was to find herself in the 'most civilized house' in the future, she would still have her 'backyard garden with greens'. In this way, she could utilize her agricultural skills and save herself the daily trouble of going to the market to buy food. 'If I'm saying to the people that I have studied agriculture, then I also must practice it in my community,' Veral (ibid.) reasoned, with a determined look in her eyes.

## Conclusion: 'So I decided that life ahead of me will be better tomorrow'

> I want to be like this in the picture. I don't want to be dry [thin]. In this picture I am looking clean like that. Look at me! [laughter]
> *Sonia, 2013*

This chapter has looked to the future instead of the present, and examined the lives that the interviewees of this project hope to achieve in the future. By concentrating on three aspects of their stated aspirations – education, professional dreams and housing – I have shown how these goals are manifested in the everyday lives of the research participants. Prior to concluding the chapter, however, let us take a quick look at some of the self-portraits that were to be found in some form or another in all the photo sets taken for this project.

Photographing oneself either alone, with family or with friends in a photo studio is a very popular free-time activity in Liberia.

Therefore, I was not surprised to find countless 'selfies' in the photo sets of the interviewees. These pictures were typically taken by a friend, a family member or someone who just happened to be around. As the research participants seemed to interrogate their own pictures in such a detailed manner, I quickly assumed the habit of asking 'How do you see the future of the person in this photograph?' or 'What do you think about when you see this picture?' when either self-portraits or photographs of the interviewee's children were under discussion. These questions had a tendency to provoke rather thorough deliberation on the current living conditions of the respondents and their children, as well as provide a reflection on their mental well-being at the time of the interview.

For instance, while looking at a picture of herself, Priscilla (interview 2013), one of the destitute main characters of Chapter 1, explained that 'I'm thinking that when I will be in my own house, I will prepare my husband's and children's food. As a mother. That is the reason I took the picture to remember it.' Then again, many of those prostitutes who had ended up in similarly devastating surroundings did not feel a comparable sense of empowerment while viewing their personal portraits. Rather, many of these women took notice of their exhausted and shabby condition and expressed a desire to be 'decent', 'civilized' or 'fat' again. Anna (interview 2013), for instance, analysed her own picture, presenting a very slender woman with big, sad eyes, in the following manner.

> *Anna* (A): When I see my picture, I can feel bad because of the life I'm living.
>
> *Leena* (L): How do you see the future of this woman?
>
> A: When I see this picture, I can only think about the past, not the future. When I see this, it makes me think about how to get money, make business and live a good life.
>
> L: What can make it happen that you'll have a good life?
>
> A: Money can make you happy. By stopping my smoking habit, by going to church and thinking hard about everything [I can become happy]. It all depends on my seriousness.

Even though personal photographs sometimes sparked negative feelings about the current life of an interviewee, almost everyone still possessed some hope for the future. As stated previously in this chapter, hope for a better tomorrow seemed to be among the strongest forces pushing the respondents to stay afloat and continue to overcome their everyday struggles, despite the never-ending hardships. If worldly life did not seem to fulfil personal aspirations, however, then final solace would be provided by religion, and phrases such as 'if God is willing' or 'it is in His hands' were extremely typical in the interview situations.

Among the most persistent wishes of both Angela and Angeline, the twins whose living conditions are described in the introduction of this chapter, was that their children should 'become someone' in the future. For example, in her photo interview session, Angeline (interview 2013) stated with a twinkle in her eye that 'this will be the engineer and this the doctor' whilst pointing to a picture of her two boys. The eldest sister of the twins was aware that her little sisters were prostitutes and took care of Angela's son, Jason. He had been told that since his mother is working very long days in a beauty salon, he cannot live with her any longer. In a picture taken on previous Sunday – the day Angela normally puts on her nicest *lappa* suit and heads first to church and then to her sister's house to meet Jason – his eyes seem to pierce through the camera lens. Proudly regarding the picture in her hand, Angela (interview 2013) explained:

> This is a very lovely and smart boy. He is in the fifth grade now, but I don't know what he wants to do as his work. We have never spent enough time together. But I would like him to become a lawyer, I see his future very bright. I want him to be a good man, a very respectable person. He should be very good to his wife. And kind to other people as well.

Similar kinds of thoughts were also brought up by Mariama (interview 2013), who passionately argued that:

> Our children shouldn't be like us in the future. We saw all types of things in the war that we were not supposed to see. So I want my children's future to be bright. Let them do something reasonable in the future.

How, then, did the main characters of this chapter – Juliet and Veral – react to questions about their personal future? After the numerous hardships presented throughout this book, Juliet asked me in 2013 if she could take another round of pictures for a second photo elicitation interview. Since I found it very interesting to observe whether there would be any differences between the two sessions, I gladly agreed to her request. The only remarkable change between the two compilations was the huge number of former generals and fighters – both male and female – in her second photo set. Juliet explained that with this picture set she wished to demonstrate the everlasting bond shared by many war veterans in Liberia – how they shared good times together and supported each other if needed. Indeed, many of the street sisters and brothers present in her pictures had personally helped Juliet and her partner in their struggles when their first shared home had burnt down the previous year. In one of the pictures in the second photo set, Juliet is posing for the camera in a *lappa* suit she had received as a donation. After complimenting her on her style and appearance in the picture, I ask Juliet how she believes the future of 'this woman' will be. Juliet (interview 2013) replies with a smile in her voice: 'When I'm looking at myself here, I can say thank you God. Because now I feel that I can take care of myself and be a responsible mother to my children. And my living area is fine too.'

If I were forced to choose only one quotation to describe the endless resiliency and relentlessly persistent nature of the interviewees in this project, I would, without hesitation, turn again to Veral's interview material. After having detailed her horrific experiences in the war and her struggles in its aftermath, Veral began to consider her life prospects for the future. Before answering my question, she took time to observe the deep purple evening horizon behind the lonely mango tree. When she spoke again, Veral (interview 2012) stated in a decisive tone that:

> *Hope is not gone altogether.* I feel that as long as I'm young, I still have a positive life ahead of me. So that is the reason I decided to go to school. No matter if the conditions will be hard and what have you – I must go to school. The world we now live [in] is filled with competition. So I decided that life ahead of me will be better tomorrow, and for that reason I should go to school. At least to help my child.

# Conclusion

A little rain each day will fill the rivers to overflowing[1]

While gathering evidence that it ought to be possible to traverse the Pacific Ocean with a simple handmade raft, Thor Heyerdahl came across ancient sketches of rafts assembled from massive logs of balsa wood. 'They had a square sail and centerboard and a long steering oar astern. So they could be maneuvered,' Heyerdahl (1984: 24–5) delightedly reasoned, but was soon taken aback when his friend, a former sea captain, warned Heyerdahl that: 'The Incas navigated in the open sea with whole flotillas of these balsa rafts. Then, if anything went wrong, they could be picked up by the nearest raft. [...] In a storm you can be washed off the raft and drowned many times before anyone gets to you.'

Through examining and redeveloping the popular concept of social navigation (Honwana 2000; Utas 2005a, 2005b; Vigh 2006a, 2006b), the agency of Liberia's women war veterans has been understood in this book through the concept of social rafting. I have demonstrated that in the Liberian civil wars and their aftermath, the *rafts of survival* of the research participants were often hastily thrown together using some random pieces of odd junk lying in the immediate surroundings of the individual rafter. As with the balsa rafts of the ancient Incas, I have in this way shown how the rafts of Liberia's women veterans sometimes formed 'flotillas of rafts' in which individual rafters supported one another in emergencies. Unlike those of the Incas, however, the rafts of these women could hardly be manoeuvred, let alone navigated, as they often had neither sails nor a helm to steer the vessel at hand. In this manner, these rafts of survival were often exposed to unpredictable winds that sometimes pushed these simple vessels towards the desired destination, but, at other times, forced them astray.

In this book, I have examined the life trajectories of the research participants largely in chronological order. After the methodological deliberations of Chapter 1, which also marks the only break in the linear narrative of the book, the following main chapter was dedicated to analysing the patterns of girl and women soldiering within Liberia's civil wars. By moving from recruitment tactics to actual wartime roles and duties, I argued that military rank was the main determinant of the treatment received by an individual soldier on the frontline: rank designated the position of a soldier vertically, whereas gender was mainly relevant horizontally within different ranks. The decision to emphasize rank instead of gender in the chapter was grounded on the empirical material and provides a fresh alternative with which to analyse the experiences of girl and women soldiers within fighting forces in Africa and beyond.

Chapter 3 investigated the Liberian DDR programs from three intersecting perspectives. By considering the views of women war veterans as a kind of *soggetto*, and by contrasting these narrations with (and comparing them to) the official guidelines of the programs on the one hand, and the 'external' views of independent evaluators and researchers on the other hand, a *curiously contrapuntal* account of these programs was composed. The implications of these efforts were then analysed in the subsequent chapter, in which I studied the rafts of survival of women war veterans in the Liberian post-war environment. Building partly on the empirical material previously presented in Chapter 1, the main area of interest in this chapter was how the research participants succeed in finding their daily bread in the post-war environment despite the constant instability in their everyday lives.

Finally, the last chapter of the book was dedicated to the future objectives of the respondents. The dreams and aspirations of the interviewees were approached from three overlapping perspectives: first, from the viewpoint of educational goals, second, from the perspective of professional dreams, and third, from the standpoint of aspirations related to housing. As important as personal objectives were, the most persistent wish among the interviewees was to find a way to guarantee at least a 'decent' future for their children.

To understand the agency of the research participants as rafting rather than navigating was not only a conceptual choice, but it also involves historical and theoretical rationales. When observing Liberia's past through the lens of *curious contrapuntalism*, one is quickly reminded that Liberia was founded in the heart of the nineteenth-century scramble for Africa. For a country whose independence was declared under the auspices of the inherently racist American Colonization Society in 1847 (e.g. Sherwood 1917; Wander 1971), and whose political and financial power has been in the hands of the Americo-Liberian elite ever since, the word navigation would have appeared rather vulgar in terms of this particular research project. Indeed, the word choices of an 'intellectual' can be thought of as actions in themselves, as Edward Said (1996: 20, emphasis in original) reminds us:

The intellectual's representations, his or her articulations of a cause or idea to society, are not meant primarily to fortify ego or celebrate status. Nor are they principally intended for service within powerful bureaucracies and with generous employers. Intellectual representations are the *activity itself*, dependent on a kind of consciousness that is sceptical, engaged, unremittingly devoted to rational investigation and moral judgement; and this puts the individual on record and on the line. Knowing how to use language well and knowing when to intervene in language are two essential features of intellectual action.

'Speak a new language so that the world will be a new world,' declared Rumi (Iqbal et al. 2015) as early as the thirteenth century. But what if the words, the languages, the written and the spoken are simply not enough? What if the life-worlds of the 'Others' seem almost unfathomable to the outside observer? If such an instance such is occurring in a research project, one is tempted to turn to methodological deliberation, as I did in Chapter 1.

In this research setting, an epistemological choice was made to reach, indeed to *look*, beyond words. By trying to make sense of the everyday realities and aspirations of the research participants through a visual participatory methodology, namely *the auto-photographic research approach*, a rather unconventional contrapuntal understanding of these realities comprised of both verbal and visual material was constructed. The problematic task of representation was approached by including visual demonstrations alongside the written research material. Nonetheless, since the interpretation of these data are always limited by the life-worlds (Husserl 1970) and the points of location (Rich 1985) of the exponents themselves, another set of composers would most likely have produced a 'different kind of war story' (Nordstrom 1997). What was remarkable in this research setting, however, was the level of intimacy that the auto-photographic research approach seemed to facilitate. Observing the everyday life of anyone in a visual form is a moving experience, but especially so if the everyday of the 'Other' is detailed both orally and visually by the narrator herself. On occasions, it seemed that both the photographer/interviewee and I myself almost forgot about our own presence while concentrating on the on-going story. Therefore, I would warmly recommend the research approach to anyone, with the reservation that it proved to be not only time-consuming, but also laborious and rather expensive.

## Warscapes as contrapuntal environments

Although this book draws upon disciplines such as postcolonial theory, feminist scholarship, visual security studies and anthropology, it is probably most at home in the (emerging) discipline of *feminist peace research*, and more specifically in a subfield that can be defined as feminist narrative approach to security (Wibben 2011). Feminist peace researchers[2] understand sites of conflicts as necessarily gendered environments and share the understanding that wars do not end with the formal signing of peace agreements (see, e.g., Lorentzen and Turpin 1998; Giles and Hyndman 2004; Wibben 2016). Without a doubt, the warscapes (Nordstrom 1997) of our world extend far beyond the actual conflict sites and stretch from the homes of individuals to the care work undertaken in hospital wards and beyond (see, e.g., Robinson 2016; Vaittinen 2017).

This book has contributed to this body of literature by suggesting that *curious contrapuntalism* might offer an 'imaginary map', a theoretical signpost, for observing the world's phenomena in a novel and stimulating manner. Curious contrapuntalism draws upon the pre-existing theoretical perceptions of Cynthia Enloe and Edward Said, and in this way combines the feminist curiosity of Enloe with the postcolonial sensibility of Said. In practice, this imaginary map hopefully allows the observer to remain constantly alert to the workings of power within warscapes and beyond: it is certainly not a coincidence that the Global South, feminists and 'soft' security matters, for example, are still seen as insignificant in the various map rooms of power, such as those in academia. Nevertheless, I must emphasize here that this book is not primarily a theoretical one, and a great deal of work remains to be done in order to polish and redevelop curious contrapuntalism in the years to come.

The main empirical contribution of this book was to develop an understanding of the warscape(s) of Liberia from the perspective of women war veterans themselves. In doing so, it has added another layer to the pre-existing research on the Liberian wars and their aftermath in the region. Furthermore, it has confirmed the notion that each warscape must be understood in the specific conflict context, each having its own logic, as well as its own inherent gender roles (e.g. Eriksson Baaz and Stern 2014: 166). Through the interplay of the theoretical background and the empirical material, I have demonstrated that one way to build a deep understanding of a specific conflict environment is to *read the conflict contrapuntally*. This means the process of comparing and contrasting various sources of information while extending the senses in multiple directions simultaneously. By observing, for instance, the oral, written and visual strands of information concurrently, and by being sensitive to the inherent notions of gender and the workings of colonialism within these documents, it is possible to create a contrapuntal composition of a certain conflict that takes the multiple narrators and their variegated stories of war and its aftermath *seriously*. Thus, instead of settling for the 'official truth', or for the stories narrated to us by prominent individuals or organizations, we must also remain vigilant and open to 'other kinds of war stories' and conflict histories.

In the introductory chapter, I expressed a hope that the reader/spectator of this project could become a kind of *vulnerable observer* (Behar 1996) with a curious attitude whilst browsing the pages of this book. First, this means the sort of reading/observing in which the spectator forces herself to become aware of her own privileges and subject positions in relation to the narrations provided. Doing so entails a critical observation process that asks, for instance: 'Why have I been provided with these particular stories here?' or 'Whose narrations are left untold and why?' I have no doubt that if the reader has managed to become a vulnerable observer, he/she has yearned to find in the pages of this book the views of boy and men soldiers; those of civilian women and men; and the statements of the Liberian elites. Here, I cannot say more than that at this time, in this particular project, it is not their turn to talk. This book is about *women war veterans in Liberia*, about their views, their narrations, and our written and visual interpretations of these life trajectories. The rather rare excerpts from other societal groups have been included here only when it was deemed absolutely necessary to do so. Nonetheless, the vulnerable observer, the curiously contrapuntal reader, definitely understands that one must also familiarize oneself with other narrations of the Liberian civil wars and their aftermath if she wishes to acquire a holistic understanding of the warscape in question.

# Epilogue: 'When I sing, I can forget about my problems'

In late 2016, I had the opportunity to visit Liberia once more and talk to some of the main research participants of this project either in person or by phone. Unfortunately, too many of the interviewees had passed away during the Ebola epidemic – not only from the virus itself, but owing also to treatable illnesses such as tuberculosis. Among the victims of Ebola was the fiancé of Theresa, a partner whom she had finally been able to find after all her lonely years as a single mother.

Juliet had continued to experience turbulent years. After having taken care of her children's father for many months whilst he was temporarily paralysed for unknown reasons in the midst of the Ebola epidemic of 2014, the couple had found it increasingly hard to manoeuvre through daily life when he was finally well again. Soon after, Juliet had been hospitalized because of a deep burn in her leg that resulted in a severe infection. Although she only barely survived, her boyfriend did not even visit her in the hospital. 'He had nothing to give, and that is why he was embarrassed to show his face to my parents,' Juliet explained. When the couple was finally healthy and back at home, disputes began to grow more and more severe, with both parties suspecting the other of having outside relationships. During one of these quarrels, Juliet's partner hit her so fiercely that her cornea was damaged, and a priest was consulted as a counsellor. No solution was found. As a consequence, the relationship that had begun on the warfront during the second Liberian civil war was soon to be over. As the months passed, however, some kind of reconciliation was beginning to emerge. At the moment of our encounter in late 2016, Juliet was living happily together with a 'serious' and 'kind' boyfriend, whereas her ex-partner was sharing a room with his girlfriend and their one-year-old baby boy. Juliet earned her living selling sugar cane sticks at the market six days a week, and was seemingly deeply in love.

The situation of Veral remained demanding. As she had not been able to win a scholarship to continue her university education, and as all the family savings had been 'eaten' during the Ebola crisis, Veral had been forced to put her studies on hold. She was still waiting to get an operation for her stomach problems and some proper treatment for her glaucoma. Veral was able to find some solace by singing in the church choir. 'When I sing, I can forget about my problems,' she explained, seeming as courageous and persistent as she had always been.

The rays of hope that Massa had felt at the beginning of 2016 shed light on her future until the last days of April. In the first months of the year, she and her two friends had pooled together their modest savings and set up a small business by one of the main roads in the capital. As expected, the items they sold comprised soft drinks, cold water and the occasional beer or liqueur bottle. Soon, however, City Mayor Mary Broh ordered another wave of purges, and the modest business was demolished without a day's notice. Massa's misfortune unfortunately continued, as the following month her father passed away in the 'interior', and she was obliged to provide all her available dollars for his funeral arrangements. And so, on the brink of the rainy season, Massa found herself once more selling 'cold water' in her new yard. Maybe in this community, the rain would not enter the house as badly as before, she said, sighing.

The twins Angela and Angeline had rafted in rather opposing directions. Whereas Angela had suffered from an unknown 'African sickness' for a considerable amount of time with no cure in sight, Angeline had moved into a new house with her fiancé and children. The couple's home was located in a safe and stable environment, and Angeline had finally been able to leave 'prostitution life' behind. Currently, she was 'resting' as a housewife. With the income of her fiancé, Angeline continued to try to help her dear sister, but the sickness that caused weight loss and a rash all over Angela's body prevailed. During our latest encounter in 2016, we spent a whole day at JFK hospital in Monrovia waiting for a proper diagnosis and treatment. Regrettably, Angela's 'weird' sickness turned out to be HIV.

Pa Chea's base was no longer there, although Pa Chea and his children still resided in the house where the small shop had been situated for several years. During the worst months of the Ebola epidemic, Pa Chea had been forced to turn everything available into cash, and therefore 'the business died, and that's it'. Since then, he had been working 'in the security sector', and was now trying to find a way to release his own daughter from the central prison. The majority of the young women who used to loiter in the area were, nevertheless, still around: some of them were sharing a room together, whereas others' whereabouts were unknown. According to Pa Chea, none of the women had been able to find a stable occupation and their substance abuse problems prevailed. The only exception was Priscilla, who was not around when I was visiting the remains of the 'base'. Everybody seemed to be extremely happy for her since Priscilla had 'taken the drip' offered by a local church trying to encourage the youth to leave street life behind. Teta had originally also signed up for the program, but soon ran away with the small amount of cash provided by the organizers for daily expenses. 'Instead of the drip I treated myself with drugs,' Teta explained, followed by raspy laughter and a wink of an eye.

The last time I was able to reach Amy by phone was in January 2017. Everything was fine now, she explained, since her small business had reclaimed its rightful place as the 'official' gathering spot for the local youth. Even during the phone call that took place around 9 p.m. Liberian time, I was able to hear a concert of 'lectures' about the daily hustles and struggles around downtown Monrovia. As always, Amy's boombox was on, spreading endless hipco beats into another promising night in the allegedly rainiest capital city in the world.

# Notes

## Preface

1 For more on the roles of women in the peace process, see, e.g., Moran and Pitcher (2004).
2 This is not meant to be a comprehensive overview of Liberia's civil wars. For a deeper understanding of these wars and their background, it is worth examining the volumes by Mats Utas (2003), Mary Moran (2006), Stephen Ellis (2007), Danny Hoffman (2011) and Colin M. Waugh (2011), for example.

## Introduction

1 *Johnny Mad Dog* (2008) draws inspiration from the novel *Johnny Chien Méchant* (2002) by Emmanuel Dongala. The main actors in the film are Liberian children and youth, of whom some took part in the second Liberian civil war as child soldiers.
2 This quote is often attributed to Union Army general William Tecumseh Sherman, although its origin has often been disputed (Keyes 2006: 240–41).
3 According to a widely endorsed definition, a child soldier is 'any person under 18 years of age who is part of any kind of regular or irregular armed force or armed group in any capacity, including but not limited to cooks, porters, messengers and anyone accompanying such groups, other than family members. The definition includes girls recruited for sexual purposes and for forced marriage. It does not, therefore, only refer to a child who is carrying or has carried arms' (UNICEF 1997).
4 Balomenou and Garrod (2015) provide a profound introduction to the various strands of participant-generated photographic methods. Interestingly, Denov et al. (2012) utilized *Photovoice*, a version of this methodological genre, with former Sierra Leonean child soldiers in 2012. However, their approach differs both methodologically and theoretically from the one presented here.
5 Emmi Nieminen's artwork can be found at mobile-emmi.tumblr.com.
6 'Western art music' is a widely endorsed concept that also Said frequently utilizes. The concept is, however, highly contentious since it firstly elevates only itself as 'art' with regards to other genres of music. Furthermore, and especially when examined through the lens of curious contrapuntalism, the whole canon of 'Western art music' can be seen as both masculine and colonial. 'Western art music' was, indeed, a blind spot for the great postcolonial thinker Edward Said, who adopted, praised and in this manner strengthened the canon without hesitation.
7 Geeta Chowdhry's comparison between African-American women's traditional quilting techniques and Said's contrapuntal method is another possible visualization of contrapuntalism. Also, the method and 'philosophy' of art collage fits in perfectly here (Sylvester 2005; Särmä 2014).
8 Sachs (2001: 551). Contrapuntally organized music is most common in classical music, but can also be found in pieces composed by popular music artists from the Beach Boys to Massive Attack and from the Fugees to Sufjan Stevens.
9 Gayatri Spivak (2005: 525), a personal friend of Edward Said,

has described Mufti as Said's 'beloved student'.
10 This article sparked a lively debate within the (postcolonial) feminist community. Sixteen years after 'Under Western eyes' was published, Mohanty (2003) wrote an explanatory, updated version of the article entitled '"Under Western Eyes" Revisited: Feminist Solidarity through Anticapitalist Struggles'.
11 The bibliography on both intersectionality and feminist postcolonial theory is colossal and, for this reason, the references provided here are necessarily inadequate. For a more comprehensive introduction to feminist postcolonialism see, for example, Lewis and Mills (2003). For intersectionality see, e.g., Grzanka (2014).
12 Taking street knowledge and 'popular art' seriously would have most likely horrified Edward Said. In her memoir about her father, Najla Said (2005: 23) writes that when she was introduced to Batman comic books in a class on postmodernism in Princeton, his reaction was of the most passionate kind. Edward Said apparently stated: 'No daughter of mine is going to Princeton to read comic books; my daughter reads Shakespeare and Virgil. That class is a waste of time; it's utter rubbish. I will not allow it!'

## 1 Auto-photographing rivers of insecurities

1 E.g. Andersen et al. (2014); Andersen and Möller (2013); Aradau and Hill (2013); Bleiker (2009); Campbell and Shapiro (2007); Hansen (2011, 2014); Heck and Schlag (2013); Shapiro (2009); Särmä (2014); Vuori (2010).
2 'The BBC' is an umbrella term used in Liberia for international media, so the reference to this broadcasting company does not mean that 'the BBC' had actually published the picture.
3 The 'Congo People' refers to the descendants of freed American blacks, many of them former slaves, who began to arrive to the area of today's Liberia in the 1820s. Earlier, many slave ships had sailed through the Congo River, hence all the newcomers were named as 'Congo People'. In turn, the newcomers began calling the native residents as 'Country People'.
4 See, e.g., Adelekan (1996); Akyeampong (2005); Ellis (2009); Carrier and Klantschnig (2012: 41); UNODC (2014); WACD (2014).
5 Communication with Monrovian drug users and the Deputy Chief of Investigation from the Drug Enforcement Agency (DEA) of Liberia in July 2014. To put these prices into perspective, in 2007 the average retail price of a gram of brown heroin in the UK was US$90 (EMCDDA 2014).
6 I did not have a chance to ask Priscilla in private if she had drugs among the items she was selling on that particular day, and I wanted to respect her right to deny it. However, since Priscilla was a substance abuser and had previously spoken about her small-scale drug business, it is likely that she had drugs in her bucket on this occasion as well.
7 Thank you, Juha Vuori, for the inspiration for this idea.

## 2 Girl and women soldiers in Liberia's civil wars

1 It is of course impossible for a civilian to accurately grasp the true nature and horrors of warfare. Nonetheless, maybe a fraction of understanding can be achieved through art, such as poems written by frontline soldiers themselves.

Even though the most celebrated war poets are typically educated white men, and can therefore be neglected as suitable candidates for describing the realities of young women soldiers of Liberia, these poems seem to grasp something universal: they narrate realities and emotions that may seem almost inexplicable (see, e.g., Reilly 1981; Sassoon 1983; Stallworthy 2008).

2 Compare to Ellis (2003: 462); Ellis (2007).

3 See, e.g., Mazurana et al. (2002: 100); Coulter et al. (2008); MacKenzie (2010: loc. 4529).

4 In her research, Zoe Marks (2014: 80) found that the statuses of females within the Revolutionary United Front (RUF) in Sierra Leone were determined by their age, military ability, pre-war social status (education) and wartime relationships.

5 See also Honwana (2006); Mazurana et al. (2002); Rosen (2005); Wessells (2006).

6 It has to be noted, however, that some interviewees might have calculated it to be in their best interest to claim that they were abducted even if they were not. This type of behaviour seems to have taken place both in Liberia (Utas 2011: 218) and neighboring Sierra Leone (Brett and Specht 2004: 85; Coulter 2009: 99). Nonetheless, since numerous women (30 percent) stated that they joined the forces willingly, I do not see a consistent pattern of 'victimcy talk' in my data in this regard.

7 On single-sex versus dual-sex systems in Liberia, see Moran (1989, 2006).

8 See also Basini (2013).

9 One can find an excellent description of the pre-war lives, struggles and naivieties of the privileged Liberian elite in Helene Cooper's (2008) memoir *The House at Sugar Beach*.

10 See the Introduction. See also BBC News (2011a); Gbowee and Mithers (2011); Johnson-Sirleaf (2009); Solomon (2009).

11 Sjoberg (2010: 32–3). Julie Rajan (2011: 1–2) has shown that women suicide bombers have been portrayed by the Western media as special cases whose physicality, mental well-being, sexuality and victimization have been given enormous emphasis. At the same time, however, women bombers' motivations and perceptions of their missions have been almost completely neglected.

12 Mary H. Moran (2010) provides an excellent overview of the body of literature on gender, militarism and peacebuilding, whereas the literature review by Maria Eriksson Baaz and Maria Stern (2014) details gender and violence in the African context. See also Tickner (1992); Turshen and Twagiramariya (1998); Enloe (2000a, 2000b); Goldstein (2001); Mazurana et al. (2002); Sjoberg and Gentry (2007); Coulter (2009); Sjoberg (2010).

13 In autumn 2013, for example, Samantha Lewthwaite, popularly known as the 'White Widow', was seen day after day on the front pages of the world's leading newspapers (e.g. BBC News 2011b; see also Sjoberg and Gentry 2007).

14 Wessells (2006: 23, 110) remarks that in some situations child soldiers might indeed have better living conditions than civilian children (e.g. medication, protection, food), and thus the decision to enlist is completely rational.

15 See also Utas (2005a) on the looting economy in the first Liberian civil war.

16 See, e.g., Sheriff (2008).

17 For more on the history of 'camp followers' in the global North, see, e.g., Enloe (2000b); Vining and Hacker (2001).

18 The exportation of the concept of post-traumatic stress disorder (PTSD) to non-Western populations, for example, has faced this kind of criticism (see, e.g., Johnson and Thompson 2008: 43; Kienzler 2008).
19 Graham et al. (1994). For more on the ambiguities surrounding the concept, please see Namnyak et al. (2008) and Adorjan et al. (2012).
20 Compare to Coulter (2008).
21 See also Singer (2006: 81); Wessells (2006: 76–7).
22 See also Hoffman (2011); Wessells (2006: 77).
23 See also Ellis (2000).
24 See also Ellis (1995, 2001, 2007); Hoffman (2011); Utas (2003).
25 See, e.g., Käihkö (2016) on military cohesion within LURD, MODEL and Taylor's GoL.
26 See Morgan (2007) on individualization of uniforms and the persistent masculine ideals among the United States Corps of Cadets at West Point, NY.
27 See also Enloe 2000b; Wheelwright 1989.
28 Lara Croft is a fictional character in a highly popular video game, *Tomb Raider*, released in 1996. For more information, see, e.g., Mikula (2003).
29 Chris Coulter (2008: 88) has described a similar unwillingness of former girl and women soldiers to discuss their violent acts in Sierra Leone.
30 Several of the interviewees had witnessed acts of horrific violence such as that described by Evelyn. I do not wish to provide a 'pornography of violence' by detailing all these atrocities here, but in providing this one example, I hope to make the reader aware of the scale of brutalities these women had to witness and commit.
31 WAC = Women's Artillery Commandos. Please see below for a detailed description.
32 See also Specht (2006: 23).
33 Compare to Hoffman (2011: loc. 1797).
34 Usually, the terms brigade and unit were used synonymously in the interview situations. The size of a brigade/unit could range from ten to several hundreds of soldiers.
35 The stereotype of vulnerable women has been used all over the world. For example, between 1909 and 1919 there were more than six thousand women serving as members of the British intelligence community (Proctor 2003: 1). Not surprisingly, similar tactics were used in Liberia's neighboring country, Sierra Leone (Coulter 2009: 15).
36 See the Introduction.
37 Compare to Marks (2014: 74).
38 Building on the concept of ethnoscape, which was coined by Arjun Appadurai, Carolyn Nordstrom (1997: 37–8) developed the term war-scape (often referred as 'warscape') to describe the multifaceted and complex environments where violent conflicts occur. In these environments, warring factions as well as a vast array of national and international actors form a mesh of counteracting and contrasting interests that 'link solider and civilian, violator and peacemaker, for none make sense in isolation from the other'.
39 There were also commanders who very clearly protected soldiers and civilians from sexual violence (see also Eriksson Baaz and Stern 2013: 71).
40 See, e.g., Carpenter (2006); Sivakumaran (2007); Gorris (2015); Féron (2015, 2017).
41 For more on the three typical stereotypes attached to child soldiers in Liberia and Sierra Leone, see Murphy (2003).
42 The concept of wealth in people, or wealth-in-people, was first used by Suzanne Miers and Igor Kopytoff in *Slavery of Africa: Historical and Anthropological*

*Perspectives* (1977). See also Guyer and Belinga (1995: 91, fn 1).
43 Compare to Marks (2014).

## 3 DDR: Disarmament, Disillusionment and Remarginalization

1 UN Security Council Resolution 1325 (UNSC 1325) was approved unanimously on 31 October 2000. The resolution stresses the importance of adopting a gender perspective on all stages of conflict and its aftermath. Since the passing of Resolution 1325, six complementary Security Council Resolutions have been adopted.
2 Data based on 128 cases. Five interviewees either did not want to discuss their DDRR experiences or the data were inconsistent.
3 A detailed summary of each stage of the process can be found in the same document on page 15. Please note that the word combatant is utilized in this context (see, e.g., Enloe 2004b: 96).
4 According to James Pugel (2009: endnote 10), who interviewed various UNMIL and UNDP employees on the matter, rehabilitation 'was essentially a "non-component" (never realized) for the Liberian DDRR programme'.
5 Data based on 123 cases.
6 Please note that the word combatant is used here (see note 3).
7 UNSC (2003: para. 3f). Once again, notice the choice of the word combatant.
8 UN internal report on DDRR (United Nations 2006: 7, note 23).
9 A very small faction under one of the main fighting forces.
10 In Liberia and elsewhere in the Global South, it is possible to gain some modest income by purchasing a huge sack of small plastic bags of mineral water ('cold water' – sometimes stored with ice in a cooler) and sell those individually, e.g. on streets, in marketplaces, or at coach stations.
11 The Draft Interim Secretariat (2003: 64). It is clarified in the Foreword for the Strategy (p. 2) that the 'draft interim secretariat was constituted to formulate the DDR programme – with the co-ordination responsibility vested in the UNDP. The secretariat was composed of the UNDP, UNMIL, OCHA, USAID, UNICEF and World Vision. […] This document represents the concerted effort of various organizations and expertise. It envisages an implementation arrangement that brings together the strong political leadership of the UN mission and the programmatic capacities of the various UN agencies to ensure an effective and comprehensive implementation process – as well as local ownership. As a result, all contributors of this document will collectively identify with the success of the programme.'
12 See Chapter 2.
13 The original version of the story can be found in the Indian epic Mahabharata under the section called Bhagavadgita.
14 *The Idea of Justice* is indeed a sophisticated, multilayered argument for a move towards a *nyaya*-based elaboration, both in theories of justice and the practical world. In this context, it must be noted that Sen (2009: 40) divides theories of justice into 'transcendental institutionalist' (Hobbes, Locke, Rousseau, Kant, Rawls) and 'comparative' (Smith, Condorcet, Wollstonecraft, Bentham, Mill) clusters. Sen maintains that whereas the former hope to achieve perfectly just societies and institutions through social contracts, the latter compare people's lives and social realities, and, through these comparisons, try to enhance justice and diminish injustices in the given circumstances. Amartya Sen is

thus clearly speaking on, or rather subscribing to, the second school of thought.

## 4 Social rafting in post-war Liberia

1. In Liberian English, 'cold bowl' can mean leftover food that is stored for later use in a covered 'bowl'. It can also refer to a plate of food that is being sold individually in modest restaurants for a price starting somewhere around 100 LD.
2. In this context, 'gigolo' refers to a young male who has a 'sugar mother' as a lover and financial supporter. For a more thorough discussion of the definition, please see the discussion later in the chapter.
3. African proverb.
4. Again, many individuals who find themselves under the 'nothing' category are likely to resort to occasional prostitution.
5. In 2015, a charity called Lawyers Without Borders finalized an index of antiquated court reports from Liberia. The aim of compiling old court cases was to help to restore the country's legal system (Bowcott 2015).
6. On the links between education, empowerment and substance abuse, see, e.g., Perkins and Zimmerman (1995); Kim et al. (1998); Peterson and Reid (2003); Beckerleg and Lewando Hundt (2005); Bourgois and Schonberg (2009).
7. Starting in March 2014, West Africa was hit by the largest outbreak of Ebola virus disease (EVD) ever recorded. EVD belongs to a group of diseases called viral haemorrhagic fevers and is often fatal: in human infections, the case fatality has varied from 25 to 90 percent depending on the species of the virus and the available supportive care. Human-to-human transmission happens when infected bodily fluids such as blood, faeces, vomit, semen, genital secretions and breast milk come into contact with breaks in the skin or mucosa. At the start of the epidemic in particular, there were warnings that Ebola could also be spread by sweat, but the evidence with regard to sweat and some other bodily fluids is still unclear. Indeed, EVD is still rather poorly studied if compared to other viral diseases such as influenza (Chughtai et al. 2016). As of March 2016, the epidemic had claimed 11,323 lives, with 4,809 dying in Liberia alone (WHO 2016).
8. Such speculation was not only heard on the streets, but also at the highest levels of power (see, e.g., Front Page Africa 2014b).
9. For more on the song's background and purposes, see, e.g., Pflanz (2014).
10. For the international response to the Ebola epidemic, see Richards (2016).
11. Without proper diagnostics, it is almost impossible to tell the difference between the early symptoms of EVD and, e.g., malaria and typhoid, both of which are pervasive in the region (see, e.g., Bernstein 2014). According to one study (Walker et al. 2015), the number of untreated malaria cases may have increased by 140 percent in Liberia in 2014 alone.
12. For more on the overlapping roles of the formal and informal healthcare providers in Liberia, see, e.g., Kruk et al. (2011a, 2011b).
13. I have argued elsewhere that the EVD outbreak in Liberia reinforced intersectional discrimination patterns in the country (Vastapuu 2015).
14. Subtitle borrowed from the superb book entitled *Hustling Is Not Stealing: Stories of an African*

*Bar Girl* (2003) by John M. Chernoff.
15 Rumors should not be neglected in these types of interview situations but should instead be carefully listened to. Often in Liberian slums and elsewhere, rumors are not 'just rumors' but are treated by many as actual reality. Therefore, rumors not only affect the behaviour patterns of individuals and groups, but also shape and narrate important aspects of the social environment in which they are produced and situated (see, e.g., Scheper-Hughes 1992; White 1997; Musila 2015).
16 According to the World Bank Group (2015), the economic impact of EVD in 2015 in the three worst-affected countries (Liberia, Sierra Leone, Guinea) alone was expected to be more than US$1.6 billion. In Liberia itself, GDP growth for 2014 fell from the expected 5.9 percent prior to the crisis to 2.2 percent in the midst of the epidemic.
17 E.g. Murphy (2006); Higate and Henry (2009); Simić (2010, 2012); Karim and Beardsley (2016). See also the special issue of the *Journal of Intervention and Statebuilding* (2015).
18 See, for instance: www.un.org/en/peacekeeping/issues/cdu, accessed 11 July 2016.
19 For edited volumes on 'African' sexualities, see e.g. Arnfred (2004); Tamale (2011a).
20 Lyrics from 'Pot Boiling Remix' performed by a group of well-known Liberian hipco artists (Rahimian 2013).
21 'Scraps of Hope' is an inspiring art-based postcolonial feminist research project headed by Dr Marjaana Jauhola. For more information, please visit the project website at scrapsofhope.fi/ (accessed 11 July 2016).

## 5 Let my children's future be alright

1 In Liberian vernacular 'now now' is a manner of emphasizing the present moment.
2 Second-hand clothes typically originating in the USA that are purchased 'blind' in bulk packages costing from US$100 to US$300. Another term used for DK clothes is *dogafleh*, a term that originates from a Kpelle saying for 'bend own market' (Sheppard 2012: loc. 1940). DK clothes are normally sold at a fixed price (US$'2 for 5') from market stalls or wheelbarrows. Considered to be 'good-quality clothes' that are much more durable than 'Chinese clothes', *dogafleh* can be found in almost every Liberian household.
3 Compare to Chapter 3.
4 See next note.
5 According to a report by UNMIL (2015: 19), a man riding a motorbike in Bomi County was 'allegedly abducted and forcibly initiated when he accidentally strayed into Poro territory and interrupted their activities'. Indeed, it has been argued that many indigenous children have learnt their most valuable life lessons far away from 'civilized' institutions – in 'bush schools', ancient cultural, religious and educational organizations that are still in (limited) operation today. The most famous of these 'secret societies' are Poro and Sande, which function among various ethnic groups in Liberia, Sierra Leone, Guinea and Ivory Coast. However, since Poro and Sande require oaths of silence from their members, I decided early on not to encourage the interviewees to discuss 'matters of the bush', thereby possibly placing them in uncomfortable positions, or even danger. For more information, see, e.g., Richards (1975); Bledsoe (1980, 1984); Steady (2006); Ellis

(2007); Government of Liberia (2014); Greenslade (2012); Allen and Werman (2012); Wandia (2016); Azango (2016).

6 A case study by Sirleaf Market Women's Fund (2012: 1) also found that the first priority for the majority of the interviewed market women was to educate their children with the generated income.

## Conclusion

1 Liberian proverb.
2 Some of the researchers indicated here might possibly prefer to be described by some other terminology. Therefore, it is necessary to emphasize that the 'labelling' here is the author's own.

# References

Abbink, J. (2005) 'Introduction', in J. Abbink and I. van Kessel (eds), *Vanguard or Vandals: Youth Politics and Conflict in Africa*, Leiden and Boston, MA: Brill, pp. 1–36.

Abramowitz, S. A. (2014) *Searching for Normal in the Wake of the Liberian War*, Philadelphia: University of Pennsylvania Press.

Abramowitz, S. and M. H. Moran (2012) 'International human rights, gender-based violence, and local discourses of abuse in postconflict Liberia: a problem of "culture"?', *African Studies Review*, 55(2): 119–46.

Adebajo, A. (2002) *Liberia's Civil War: Nigeria, ECOMOG, and Regional Security in West Africa*, Boulder, CO, and London: Lynne Rienner.

Adelekan, M. L. (1996) 'West African subregion: an overview of substance abuse problems', *Drugs: Education, Prevention and Policy*, 3(3): 231–7.

Adorjan, M., T. Christensen, B. Kelly and D. Pawluch (2012) 'Stockholm Syndrome as vernacular resource', *Sociological Quarterly*, 53(3): 454–74.

Akyeampong, E. (2005) 'Diaspora and drug trafficking in West Africa: a case study of Ghana', *African Affairs*, 104(416): 429–47.

Allen, B. and M. Werman (2012) 'Female circumcision temporarily stopped in Liberia', Public Radio International (PRI), www.pri.org/stories/2012-03-29/female-circumcision-temporarily-stopped-liberia, accessed 20 June 2016.

Amos, V. and P. Parmar (1984) 'Challenging imperial feminism', *Feminist Review*, pp. 3–19.

Andersen, R. S. and F. Möller (2013) 'Engaging the limits of visibility: photography, security and surveillance', *Security Dialogue*, 44(3): 203–21.

Andersen, R. S., J. A. Vuori and C. E. Mutlu (2014) 'Visuality', in C. Aradau, J. Huysmans, A. Neal and N. Voelkner (eds), *Critical Security Methods: New Frameworks for Analysis*, Abingdon and New York: Routledge, pp. 85–117.

Aradau, C. and A. Hill (2013) 'The politics of drawing: children, evidence, and the Darfur conflict', *International Political Sociology*, 7(4): 368–87.

Ardener, S. (1964) 'The comparative study of rotating credit associations', *Journal of the Royal Anthropological Institute of Great Britain and Ireland*, 94(2): 201–29.

Aretxaga, B. (1997) *Shattering Silence: Women, Nationalism, and Political Subjectivity in Northern Ireland*, Princeton, NJ: Princeton University Press.

Arnfred, S. (ed.) (2004) *Re-Thinking Sexualities in Africa*, Uppsala: Nordiska Afrikainstitutet.

Atwood, K. et al. (2011) 'Transactional sex among youths in post-conflict Liberia', *Journal of Health, Population and Nutrition*, 29(2): 113–22.

Azango, M. (2016) 'Liberia: Domestic Violence Bill hangs as Liberia celebrates Day of African Child', *Front Page Africa*, 15 June, allafrica.com/stories/201606160689.html, accessed 20 June 2016.

Bakhtin, M, (ed.) (1986) *Speech Genres and Other Late Essays*, ed. M. Holquist and C. Emerson, Austin: University of Texas Press.

Balomenou, N. and B. Garrod (2015) 'A review of participant-generated image methods in the social sciences', *Journal of Mixed Methods Research*, 13 April, online issue, pp. 1–17.

Banerjee, A. V. and E. Duflo (2011) *Poor Economics: A Radical Rethinking of the Way to Fight Global Poverty*, New York: PublicAffairs.

Basini, H. (2013) 'An Imperfect Reality: gender mainstreaming and Disarmament, Demobilisation, Rehabilitation and Reintegration (DDRR) in Liberia', Doctoral dissertation, University of Limerick.

BBC News (2011a) 'Profile: Leymah Gbowee – Liberia's "Peace Warrior"', BBC News Service, 7 October, www.bbc.co.uk/news/world-africa-15215312, accessed 2 March 2016.

—— (2011b) 'Profile: Samantha Lewthwaite', BBC News Service, 26 September, www.bbc.co.uk/news/uk-24204517, accessed 27 February 2016.

Beckerleg, S. and G. Lewando Hundt (2005) 'Women heroin users: exploring the limitations of the structural violence approach', *International Journal of Drug Policy*, 16(3): 183–90.

Behar, R. (1996) *The Vulnerable Observer: Anthropology that Breaks Your Heart*, Boston, MA: Beacon Press.

Benhayoun, J. E. (2006) *Narration, Navigation, and Colonialism: A Critical Account of Seventeenth- and Eighteenth-Century English Narratives of Adventure and Captivity*, Brussels and New York: Peter Lang.

Bernard, B. et al. (2003) 'Assessment of the situation of women and children combatants in the Liberian post-conflict period and recommendations for successful integration', Report prepared for USAID Washington: Development Alternatives, Inc., December, pdf. usaid.gov/pdf_docs/PNACY688.pdf, accessed 3 July 2016.

Bernstein, L. (2014) 'With Ebola crippling the health system, Liberians die of routine medical problems', *Washington Post*, 20 September, www.washingtonpost.com/world/africa/with-ebola-crippling-the-health-system-liberians-die-of-routine-medical-problems/2014/09/20/727dcfbe-400b-11e4-b03f-de718edeb92f_story.html, accessed 6 October 2017.

Berry, S. (1993) *No Condition Is Permanent: The Social Dynamics of Agrarian Change in Sub-Saharan Africa*, Madison: University of Wisconsin Press.

Biswas, S. (2007) 'Empire and global public intellectuals: reading Edward Said as an international relations theorist', *Millennium – Journal of International Studies*, 36(1): 117–33.

Bledsoe, C. (1980) *Women and Marriage in Kpelle Society*, Stanford, CA: Stanford University Press.

—— (1984) 'The political use of Sande ideology and symbolism', *American Ethnologist*, 11(3): 455–72.

Bleiker, R. (2009) *Aesthetics and World Politics*, New York: Palgrave Macmillan.

Bleiker, R. and A. Kay (2007) 'Representing HIV/AIDS in Africa: pluralist photography and local empowerment', *International Studies Quarterly*, 51(1): 139–63.

Bøås, M. (2005) 'The Liberian civil war: new war/old war?', *Global Society: Journal of Interdisciplinary International Relations*, 19(1): 73–88.

—— (2009) 'Making plans for Liberia – a trusteeship approach to good governance?', *Third World Quarterly*, 30(7): 1329–41.

Boretz, B. (2001) 'Music as anti-theater', in J. Rahn (ed.), *Music Inside Out: Going Too Far in Musical Essays*, New York: Taylor & Francis, pp. 161–90.

Bourgois, P. I. and J. Schonberg (2009) *Righteous Dopefiend*, Berkeley: University of California Press.

Bowcott, O. (2015) 'Western lawyers

go back in time to repair Liberia's broken legal system', *Guardian*, 7 May, www.theguardian.com/law/2015/may/07/liberia-legal-system-lawyers-without-borders, accessed 14 June 2016.

Brett, R. and I. Specht (2004) *Young Soldiers: Why They Choose to Fight*, Boulder, CO, and London: Lynne Rienner.

Bridge International Academies (2013) 'Bridge International Academies: About', www.bridgeinternationalacademies.com/company/about/, accessed 20 June 2016.

Brigg, M. and R. Bleiker (2010) 'Autoethnographic international relations: exploring the self as a source of knowledge', *Review of International Studies*, 36(3): 779–98.

Bugnion, C. et al. (2006) 'External mid-term evaluation report of the Disarmament, Demobilisation, Rehabilitation and Reintegration programme in Liberia', Final Report for the UNDP, 2 October, erc.undp.org/evaluation/documents/download/1289, accessed 6 June 2016.

Bullivant, R. (1984) 'Counterpoint', in D. Arnold (ed.), *The New Oxford Companion to Music*, Oxford: Oxford University Press, pp. 501–6.

Burnet, J. E. (2012) *Genocide Lives in Us: Women, Memory, and Silence in Rwanda*, Madison: University of Wisconsin Press.

Butler, J. (2010) *Frames of War: When Is Life Grievable?*, London and New York: Verso.

Butty, J. (2013) 'Admission standards toughened at University of Liberia', Voice of America, www.voanews.com/content/liberia-university-admission-exam-mass-failures/1737581.html, accessed 4 June 2016.

Calain, P. (2013) 'Ethics and images of suffering bodies in humanitarian medicine', *Social Science & Medicine*, 98: 278–85.

Campbell, D. (2004) 'Horrific blindness: images of death in contemporary media', *Journal for Cultural Research*, 8(1): 55–74.

Campbell, D. and M. J. Shapiro (2007) 'Guest editors' introduction in special issue on securitization, militarization and visual culture in the worlds of post-9/11', *Security Dialogue*, 38(2): 131–7.

Carbin, M. and S. Edenheim (2013) 'The intersectional turn in feminist theory: a dream of a common language?', *European Journal of Women's Studies*, 20(3): 233–48.

Carpenter, C. R. (2003) '"Women and children first": gender, norms, and humanitarian evacuation in the Balkans 1991–95', *International Organization*, 57(4): 661–94.

—— (2006) *Innocent Women and Children: Gender, Norms and the Protection of Civilians*, Aldershot: Ashgate.

—— (2007) *Born of War: Protecting Children of Sexual Violence Survivors in Conflict Zones*, Bloomfield, CT, and London: Kumarian Press.

Carrier, N. and G. Klantschnig (2012) *Africa and the War on Drugs*, London: Zed Books.

Carter, K. (2013) 'Liberia's political wildcard: a profile of Mary "General" Broh', Fund for Peace – Global Square blog, library.fundforpeace.org/blog-20131126-marybroh#comments, accessed 15 June 2016.

Chernoff, J. M. (2003) *Hustling Is Not Stealing: Stories of an African Bar Girl*, Chicago, IL, and London: University of Chicago Press.

Chowdhry, G. (2007) 'Edward Said and contrapuntal reading: implications for critical interventions in international relations', *Millennium – Journal of International Studies*, 36(1): 101–16.

Christiansen, C., M. Utas and H. Vigh (2006) 'Introduction', in C.

Christiansen, M. Utas and H. Vigh (eds), *Navigating Youth, Generating Adulthood: Social Becoming in an African Context*, Uppsala: Nordic Africa Institute, pp. 9–30.

Chughtai, A. A., M. Barnes and C. R. Macintyre (2016) 'Persistence of Ebola virus in various body fluids during convalescence: evidence and implications for disease transmission and control', *Epidemiology and Infection*, pp. 1–9.

CIA (2016) 'The World Factbook: Liberia', 12 July, www.cia.gov/library/publications/the-world-factbook/geos/li.html, accessed 22 July 2016.

Clark-Kazak, C. (2009) 'Towards a working definition and application of social age in international development studies', *Journal of Development Studies*, 45(8): 1307–24.

Collier, J., Jr (1957) 'Photography in anthropology: a report on two experiments', *American Anthropologist*, 59(5): 843–59.

—— (1967) *Visual Anthropology: Photography as a Research Method*, New York: Holt, Rinehart and Winston.

Collier, J. and M. Collier (1986) *Visual Anthropology: Photography as a Research Method*, Albuquerque: University of New Mexico Press.

Collison, H. (2016) *Youth and Sport for Development: The Seduction of Football in Liberia*, New York: Macmillan.

Comfort, S. (2011) 'Interview with Cynthia Enloe', *Works and Days*, 29(57/58): 41–7.

Cooper, H. (2008) *The House at Sugar Beach: In Search of a Lost African Childhood*, New York: Simon & Schuster.

Coulter, C. (2008) 'Female fighters in Sierra Leone war: challenging the assumptions?', *Feminist Review*, 88: 54–73.

—— (2009) *Bush Wives and Girl Soldiers: Women's Lives through War and Peace in Sierra Leone*, Ithaca, NY: Cornell University Press.

Coulter, C., M. Persson and M. Utas (2008) *Young Female Fighters in African Wars: Conflict and Its Consequences*, Uppsala: Nordic Africa Institute.

Cozza, S. J. (2005) 'Combat exposure and PTSD.' *PTSD Research Quarterly* 16, 1: 1-8.

Crenshaw, K. (1989) 'Demarginalizing the intersection of race and sex: a black feminist critique of antidiscrimination doctrine, feminist theory and antiracist politics', *University of Chicago Legal Forum*, 140: 139–67.

Cruz, J. (2014) 'Memories of trauma and organizing: market women's susu groups in postconflict Liberia', *Organization*, 21(4): 447–62.

Datta, A. (2012) *The Illegal City: Space, Law and Gender in a Delhi Squatter Settlement*, Farnham: Ashgate.

David, K. (1998) 'The Disarmament, Demobilization & Reintegration of child soldiers in Liberia, 1994–1997: the process and lessons learned', Collaborative report by UNICEF-Liberia and the US National Committee for UNICEF.

Davies, J. (2010) 'Introduction: Emotions in the field', in J. Davies and D. Spencer (eds), *Emotions in the Field: The Psychology and Anthropology of Fieldwork Experience*, Stanford, CA: Stanford University Press, pp. 1–31.

Davis, A. (1983) *Women, Race and Class*, New York: Vintage Books.

De Certeau, M. (1984) *The Practice of Everyday Life*, Berkeley: University of California Press.

De Groot, R. (2005) 'Perspectives of polyphony in Edward Said's writings', *Alif: Journal of Comparative Poetics*, 25: 219–40.

Denov, M., D. Doucet and A. Kamara (2012) 'Engaging war affected youth through photography: photovoice with former child soldiers in Sierra Leone', *Intervention*, 10(2): 117–33.

Didur, J. and T. Heffernan (2003)

'Revisiting the subaltern in the new empire', *Cultural Studies*, 17(1): 1–15.

Dinklage, R. I. and R. C. Ziller (1989) 'Explicating cognitive conflict through photo-communication: the meaning of war and peace in Germany and the United States', *Journal of Conflict Resolution*, 33(2): 309–17.

Draft Interim Secretariat (2003) 'Liberian Disarmament, Demobilisation, Rehabilitation and Reintegration programme: strategy and implementation framework', National Commission on Disarmament, Demobilization, Rehabilitation and Reintegration, 16 January, reliefweb.int/sites/reliefweb.int/files/resources/Full_Report_1258.pdf;;, accessed 9 January 2015.

Drumbl, M. A. (2012) *Reimagining Child Soldiers in International Law and Policy*, Oxford and New York: Oxford University Press.

Duffield, M. (2001) *Global Governance and the New Wars: The Merging of Development and Security*, London and New York: Zed Books.

Ellis, S. (1995) 'Liberia 1989–1994: a study of ethnic and spiritual violence', *African Affairs*, 94(375): 165–97.

―― (2000) 'Armes mystiques: quelques éléments de réflexion à partir de la guerre du Liberia', *Politique Africaine*, 3(79): 66–82.

―― (2001) 'Mystical weapons: some evidence from the Liberian war', *Journal of Religion in Africa*, 31(2): 222–36.

―― (2003) 'Violence and history: a response to Thandika Mkandawire', *Journal of Modern African Studies*, 41(3): 457–75.

―― (2007) *The Mask of Anarchy: The Destruction of Liberia and the Religious Dimension of an African Civil War*, London: Hurst.

―― (2009) 'West Africa's international drug trade', *African Affairs*, 108(431): 171–96.

EMCDDA (2014) 'Price of heroin at retail level', Report of the European Monitoring Centre for Drugs and Drug Addiction, www.emcdda.europa.eu/stats09/ppptab2a, accessed 10 March 2014.

Engebretson, J. (2013) 'Hipco – the living art of Liberia', *Guernica*, 4 January, www.guernicamag.com/daily/jess-engebretson-hipco-the-living-art-of-liberia/, accessed 6 April 2016.

Enloe, C. H. (1983) *Does Khaki Become You? The Militarisation of Women's Lives*, London: Pluto Press.

―― (2000a) *Bananas, Beaches and Bases: Making Feminist Sense of International Politics*, Berkeley and Los Angeles: University of California Press.

―― (2000b) *Maneuvers: The International Politics of Militarizing Women's Lives*, Berkeley, Los Angeles and London: University of California Press.

―― (2002) 'Demilitarization – or more of the same? Feminist questions to ask in the post-war moment', in D. Zarkov and C. Cockburn (eds), *The Postwar Moment: Militaries, Masculinities and International Peacekeeping*, London: Lawrence & Wishart, pp. 22–32.

―― (2004a) *The Curious Feminist: Searching for Women in a New Age of Empire*, Kindle eBook, Berkeley and Los Angeles: University of California Press.

―― (2004b) '"Gender" is not enough: the need for a feminist consciousness', *International Affairs*, 80(1): 95–7.

―― (2013) *Seriously! Investigating Crashes and Crises as if Women Mattered*, Kindle eBook, Berkeley and Los Angeles: University of California Press.

Eriksson Baaz, M. and M. Stern (2013) *Sexual Violence as a Weapon of War? Perceptions, Prescriptions, Problems in the Congo and Beyond*,

London and New York: Zed Books and Nordiska Afrikainstitutet.

—— (2014) 'The gendered subject of violence in African conflicts', in J. J. Hentz (ed.), *Routledge Handbook of African Security*, New York: Routledge, pp. 157–67.

Féron, É. (2015) 'Suffering in silence? The silencing of sexual violence against men in war torn countries', in R. Anderson (ed.), *World Suffering and Quality of Life*, New York: Springer, pp. 31–44.

—— (2017) 'Wartime sexual violence against men: why so oblivious?', *European Review of International Studies*, 4(1).

Ferraro, K. J. and J. M. Johnson (1983) 'How women experience battering: the process of victimization', *Social Problems*, 30: 325–39.

Filmer, D. and L. Fox (2014) *Youth Employment in Sub-Saharan Africa*, Washington, DC: Agence Française de Développement and World Bank.

Front Page Africa (2014a) 'Liberia: deadly Ebola bounces back in Liberia – 10 unconfirmed deaths', *Front Page Africa*, 16 June, allafrica.com/stories/201406160729.html, accessed 10 April 2016.

—— (2014b) 'Ebola extortion? Senator says authorities inflated outbreak', *Front Page Africa*, 28 May, allafrica.com/stories/201405281080.html, accessed 16 April 2016.

—— (2014c) 'Ebola deaths turn Redemption Hospital into ghost town', *Front Page Africa*, 18 June, frontpageafricaonline.com/index.php/health-sci/1987-ebola-deaths-turn-liberia-s-redemption-hospital-into-ghost-town, accessed 16 April 2016.

—— (2016) 'Liberia: education minister negotiates public private partnership deal', *Front Page Africa*, 29 January, allafrica.com/stories/201601291751.html, accessed 20 June 2016.

Funaki, Y. and B. Glencorse (2014) 'Anti-corruption or accountability? International efforts in post-conflict Liberia', *Third World Quarterly*, 35(5): 836–54.

Galtung, J. (1969) *Rauhantutkimus*, Helsinki: Weilin+Göös.

Gates, S. and S. Reich (eds) (2010) *Child Soldiers in the Age of Fractured States*, Pittsburgh, PA: University of Pittsburgh Press.

Gawler, M., V. A. Yengbeh, Jr, and A. Tokpa (2009) 'UNDP Liberia Country Programme 2004–2007: Terminal Evaluation: Final Report', UNDP Liberia, 18 September, erc.undp.org/evaluation/documents/download/4188, accessed 8 July 2016.

Gbowee, L. and C. Lynn Mithers (2011) *Mighty Be Our Powers: How Sisterhood, Prayer, and Sex Changed a Nation at War*, New York and London: Beast Books.

Geertz, C. (1962) 'The Rotating Credit Association: a "middle rung" in development', *Economic Development and Cultural Change*, 10(3): 241–63.

Gershoni, Y. (1997) 'War without end and an end to a war: the prolonged wars in Liberia and Sierra Leone', *African Studies Review*, 40(3): 55–76.

Giles, W. M. and J. Hyndman (eds) (2004) *Sites of Violence: Gender and Conflict Zones*, Berkeley: University of California Press.

Goldstein, J. S. (2001) *War and Gender: How Gender Shapes the War System and Vice Versa*, Cambridge: Cambridge University Press.

Gormuyor, J. N. (1992) 'Early childhood education in Liberia', in G. A. Woodill, J. Bernhard and L. Prochner (eds), *International Handbook of Early Childhood Education*, New York and London: Garland Publishing, pp. 337–41.

Gorris, E. A. P. (2015) 'Invisible victims? Where are male victims of conflict-related sexual violence in international law and policy?',

*European Journal of Women's Studies*, 22(4): 412–27.

Gouse, H. et al. (2016) 'Implementation of cognitive-behavioral substance abuse treatment in sub-Saharan Africa: treatment engagement and abstinence at treatment exit', *PLOS ONE*, 11(1): 1–9.

Government of Liberia (2003) 'Comprehensive Peace Agreement (CPA)', Government of Liberia, 18 August, www.usip.org/sites/default/files/file/.../liberia_08182003.pdf, accessed 2 April 2015.

—— (2008) '2008 National Population and Housing Census: preliminary results', Government of Liberia, June, webcache.googleusercontent.com/search?q=cache:65HhFZf8lwMJ:unstats.un.org/unsd/dnss/docViewer.aspx%3FdocID%3D2075+&cd=1&hl=en&ct=clnk&gl=fi&client=firefox-b-ab, accessed 13 March 2016.

—— (2011) 'An Act to establish the Children's Law of Liberia, September', Government of Liberia, September, www.unicef.org/liberia/Liberia_Childrens_Law2011.pdf, accessed 8 September 2015.

—— (2014) 'Liberia Demographic and Health Survey 2013', Liberia Institute of Statistics and Geo-Information Services (LISGIS), August, dhsprogram.com/pubs/pdf/FR291/FR291.pdf, accessed 9 July 2015.

Graham, D. L. R., E. I. Rawlings and R. K. Rigsby (1994) *Loving to Survive: Sexual Terror, Men's Violence, and Women's Lives*, Kindle eBook, New York: New York University Press.

Greenslade, R. (2012) 'Journalist who revealed genital mutilation in Liberia forced into hiding', *Guardian*, 30 April, www.theguardian.com/media/greenslade/2012/apr/30/journalist-safety-liberia, accessed 14 May 2016.

Grusky, O. (2004) 'Signs of HIV', *Contexts*, 3(1): 52–9.

Grzanka, P. (ed.) (2014) *Intersectionality: a Foundations and Frontiers Reader*, Boulder, CO: Westview Press.

Guyer, J. I. (1995) 'Wealth in people, wealth in things: introduction', *Journal of African History*, 36(1): 83–90.

Guyer, J. I. and S. M. Eno Belinga (1995) 'Wealth in people as wealth in knowledge: accumulation and composition in equatorial Africa', *Journal of African History*, 36(1): 91–120.

Hansen, L. (2011) 'Theorizing the image for security studies: visual securitization and the Muhammad cartoon crisis', *European Journal of International Relations*, 17(1): 51–74.

—— (2014) 'How images make world politics: international icons and the case of Abu Ghraib', *Review of International Studies*, 41(2): 263–88.

Harper, D. (2002) 'Talking about pictures: a case for photo elicitation', *Visual Studies*, 17(1): 13–26.

Heck, A. and G. Schlag (2013) 'Securitizing images: the female body and the war in Afghanistan', *European Journal of International Relations*, 19(4): 891–913 (first published 27 April 2012).

Heidegger, M. (1962) *Being and Time*, Oxford and Cambridge, MA: Blackwell.

Heyerdahl, T. (1984) *Kon-Tiki: Across the Pacific by Raft*, New York: Simon & Schuster.

Higate, P. and M. Henry (2009) *Insecure Spaces: Peacekeeping, Power and Performance in Haiti, Kosovo and Liberia*, London: Zed Books.

Hoffman, D. (2011) *The War Machines: Young Men and Violence in Sierra Leone and Liberia*, Kindle eBook, Durham, NC: Duke University Press.

Honwana, A. (2000) 'Innocents et coupables: les enfants-soldats comme acteurs tactiques', *Politique Africaine*, 4(80): 57–78.

—— (2005) 'Innocent and guilty: child-soldiers as interstitial and tactical agents', in A. M. Honwana and F. de Boeck (eds), *Makers and Breakers: Children and Youth in Postcolonial Africa*, Trenton, NJ, and Dakar: James Currey and Codesria, pp. 31–52.

—— (2006) *Child Soldiers in Africa*, Philadelphia and Bristol: University of Pennsylvania Press.

hooks, b. (1982) *Ain't I a Woman: Black Women and Feminism*, London: Pluto.

—— (1984) *Feminist Theory: From Margin to Center*, Boston, MA: South End Press.

—— (1992) *Black Looks: Race and Representation*, Boston, MA: South End Press.

Huberich, C. H. (1947) *The Political and Legislative History of Liberia*, 2 vols, New York: Central Book Co.

Hunter, M. (2002) 'The materiality of everyday sex: thinking beyond "prostitution"', *African Studies*, 61(1): 99–120.

—— (2010) *Love in the Time of AIDS: Inequality, Gender, and Rights in South Africa*, Bloomington: Indiana University Press.

Husserl, E. (1970) *The Crisis of European Sciences and Transcendental Phenomenology; an Introduction to Phenomenological Philosophy*, Evanston, IL: Northwestern University Press.

Iqbal, F., G. Khawaja and K. M. Rahman (2015) 'Understanding empathy with reference to Rumi', *Asian Journal of Social Sciences & Humanities*, 4(4): 104–12.

IRIN (2004) 'Liberia: where are the weapons? Is disarmament really working?', IRIN News Service, 28 July, www.irinnews.org/report/50857/liberia-where-are-the-weapons-is-disarmament-really-working, accessed 18 May 2015.

Itano, N. (2003) 'The sisters-in-arms of Liberia's war', *Christian Science Monitor*, 26 August, www.csmonitor.com/2003/0826/p07s01-woaf.html, accessed 13 July 2015.

Jackson, M. (1989) *Paths toward a Clearing: Radical Empiricism and Ethnographic Inquiry*, Bloomington: Indiana University Press.

James, W. and R. Barton Perry (1912) *Essays in Radical Empiricism*, New York: Longmans, Green and Co.

Jauhola, M. (2013) *Post-Tsunami Reconstruction in Indonesia: Negotiating Normativity through Gender Mainstreaming Initiatives in Aceh*, Abingdon: Routledge.

—— (2016) 'Decolonizing branded peacebuilding: abjected women talk back to the Finnish Women, Peace and Security Agenda', *International Affairs*, 92(2): 333–51.

Jaye, T. (2009) 'Transitional justice and DDR: the case of Liberia', International Center for Transitional Justice: Research Unit, June, ictj.org/sites/default/files/ICTJ-DDR-Liberia-CaseStudy-2009-English.pdf, accessed 13 November 2016.

Jennings, K. M. (2007) 'The struggle to satisfy: DDR through the eyes of ex-combatants in Liberia', *International Peacekeeping*, 14(2): 204–18.

—— (2008) 'Seeing DDR from below: challenges and dilemmas raised by the experiences of ex-combatants in Liberia', *Fafo Report*, 3: 1–52.

—— (2009) 'The political economy of DDR in Liberia: a gendered critique', *Conflict, Security & Development*, 9(4): 475–94.

—— (2010) 'Unintended consequences of intimacy: political economies of peacekeeping and sex tourism', *International Peacekeeping*, 17(2): 229–43.

Johnson, H. and A. Thompson (2008) 'The development and maintenance of Post-Traumatic Stress Disorder (PTSD) in civilian adult survivors of war trauma and torture: a review', *Clinical Psychology Review*, 28(1): 36–47.

Johnson-Hanks, J. (2006) *Uncertain Honor: Modern Motherhood in an African Crisis*, Chicago, IL: University of Chicago Press.

Johnson-Sirleaf, E. (2009) *This Child Will Be Great: Memoir of a Remarkable Life by Africa's First Woman President*, New York: Harper.

Journal of Intervention and Statebuilding (2015) 'Special Issue: Service, sex, and security: everyday life in the peacekeeping economy', *Journal of Intervention and Statebuilding*, 9(3).

Kabbah, H. (2014) 'A guide to the Liberian legal system and legal research', GlobaLex, February, www.nyulawglobal.org/globalex/Liberia1.html, accessed 13 May 2015.

Kabeer, N. (1994) *Reversed Realities: Gender Hierarchies in Development Thought*, London: Verso.

Karim, S. and K. Beardsley (2016) 'Explaining sexual exploitation and abuse in peacekeeping missions: the role of female peacekeepers and gender equality in contributing countries', *Journal of Peace Research*, 53(1): 100–15.

Kaufman, C. E. and S. E. Stavrou (2004) '"Bus fare please": the economics of sex and gifts among young people in urban South Africa', *Culture, Health & Sexuality*, 6(5): 377–91.

Keyes, R. (2006) *The Quote Verifier: Who Said What, Where, and When*, New York: St Martin's Press.

Kieh, G. K. (2008) *The First Liberian Civil War: The Crises of Underdevelopment*, New York and Oxford: Peter Lang.

Kienzler, H. (2008) 'Debating war-trauma and Post-Traumatic Stress Disorder (PTSD) in an interdisciplinary arena', *Social Science & Medicine*, 67(2): 218–27.

Kim, S., C. Crutchfield, C. Williams and N. Hepler (1998) 'Toward a new paradigm in substance abuse and other problem behavior prevention for youth: youth development and empowerment approach', *Journal of Drug Education*, 28(1): 1–17.

Kleinman, A. and J. Kleinman (1996) 'The appeal of experience; the dismay of images: cultural appropriations of suffering in our times', *Daedalus*, 125(1): 1–23.

Knight, A. W. (2008) 'Disarmament, Demobilization, and Reintegration and post-conflict peacebuilding in Africa: an overview', *African Security*, 1(1): 24–52.

Knight, M. and A. Özerdem (2004) 'Guns, camps and cash: disarmament, demobilization and reinsertion of former combatants in transitions from war to peace', *Journal of Peace Research*, 41(4): 499–516.

Korf, B., M. Engeler and T. Hagmann (2010) 'The geography of warscape', *Third World Quarterly*, 31(3): 385–99.

Kotilainen, N. (2016) 'Visual theaters of suffering: constituting the Western spectator in the age of humanitarian world politics', Doctoral dissertation, Department of Political and Economic Studies, University of Helsinki.

Kruk, M., P. Rockers, T. Varpilah and R. Macauley (2011a) 'Population preferences for health care in Liberia: insights for rebuilding a health system', *Health Services Research*, 46(6): 2057–78.

—— (2011b) 'Which doctor?: determinants of utilization of formal and informal health care in postconflict Liberia', *Medical Care*, 49(6): 585–91.

Käihkö, I. (2016) 'Bush generals and small boy battalions: military cohesion in Liberia and beyond', Doctoral dissertation, Department of Peace and Conflict Research, Uppsala University.

Law, B. (2006) 'Meeting the hard man of Liberia', *BBC News*, 4 November, news.bbc.co.uk/2/hi/programmes/from_our_own_ correspondent/6113682.stm, accessed 15 November 2015.

Legislature of Liberia (2014) 'Senate has passed Controlled Drug and Substances Act', Government of Liberia, April, legislature. gov.lr/senate/news/2014/4/senate-has-passed-controlled-drug-and-substances-act, accessed 10 March 2014.

Lewis, R. and S. Mills (eds) (2003) *Feminist Postcolonial Theory: A Reader*, Edinburgh: Edinburgh University Press.

Livingston, T. W. (1976) 'The exportation of American higher education to West Africa: Liberia College, 1850–1900', *Journal of Negro Education*, 45(3): 246–62.

Lorde, A. (1984) *Sister Outsider: Essays and Speeches*, Trumansburg, NY: Crossing Press.

Lorentzen, L. A. and J. E. Turpin (eds) (1998) *The Women and War Reader*, New York and London: New York University Press.

Luke, N. (2003) 'Age and economic asymmetries in the sexual relationships of adolescent girls in sub-Saharan Africa', *Studies in Family Planning*, 34(2): 67–86.

Lulat, Y. G.-M. (2005) *A History of African Higher Education from Antiquity to the Present: a Critical Synthesis*, Westport, CT: Praeger.

MacKenzie, M. (2010) 'Securitization and de-securitization: female soldiers and the reconstruction of women in post-conflict Sierra Leone', in L. Sjoberg (ed.), *Gender and International Security: Feminist Perspectives*, Kindle eBook, London and New York: Routledge.

Marks, Z. (2014) 'Sexual violence in Sierra Leone's civil war: "virgination", rape, and marriage,' *African Affairs*, 113(450): 67–87.

Mazurana, D. and L. Eckerbom Cole (2013) 'Women, girls, and Disarmament, Demobilization and Reintegration (DDR)', in C. Cohn (ed.), *Women and Wars*, Cambridge and Malden, MA: Polity Press, pp. 194–214.

Mazurana, D. and S. McKay (2001) 'Child soldiers: what about the girls?', *Bulletin of the Atomic Scientists*, 57(5): 30–35.

Mazurana, D., S. McKay, K. Carlson and J. Kasper (2002) 'Girls in fighting forces and groups: their recruitment, participation, demobilization, and reintegration', *Peace & Conflict*, 8(2): 97–123.

McKay, S. and D. E. Mazurana (2004) *Where Are the Girls? Girls in Fighting Forces in Northern Uganda, Sierra Leone and Mozambique: Their Lives during and after War*, Montreal: Rights & Democracy.

McLellan, A. T. et al. (1993) 'The effects of psychosocial services in substance abuse treatment', *Addictions Nursing Network*, 5(2): 38–47.

McMullin, J. R. (2013) *Ex-Combatants and the Post-Conflict State: Challenges of Reintegration*, London: Palgrave Macmillan.

Médecins Sans Frontières (MSF) (2014) 'Ebola in West Africa: "the epidemic is out of control"', *MSF News & Stories*, 23 June, www.msf.ca/en/article/ebola-west-africa-epidemic-out-control, accessed 19 February 2015.

Miers, S. and I. Kopytoff (1977) *Slavery in Africa: Historical and Anthropological Perspectives*, Madison: University of Wisconsin Press.

Mikula, M. (2003) 'Gender and videogames: the political valency of Lara Croft', *Continuum*, 17(1): 79–87.

Mohanty, C. T. (1984) 'Under Western eyes: feminist scholarship and colonial discourses', *Boundary 2*, 12(3): 333–58.

—— (2003) '"Under Western eyes" revisited: feminist solidarity through anticapitalist struggles', *Signs: Journal of Women in Culture & Society*, 28(2): 499–535.

Moraga, C. and G. Anzaldúa (eds) (1981) *This Bridge Called My Back:*

*Writings by Radical Women of Color*, Watertown, MA: Persephone Press.

Moran, M. H. (1989) 'Collective action and the "representation" of African women: a Liberian case study', *Feminist Studies*, 15(3): 443–60.

—— (1990) *Civilized Women: Gender and Prestige in Southeastern Liberia*, Ithaca, NY, and London: Cornell University Press.

—— (1995) 'Warriors or soldiers? Masculinity and ritual transvestism in the Liberian civil war', in C. R. Sutton (ed.), *Feminism, Nationalism, and Militarism*, Arlington, VA: Association for Feminist Anthropology/American Anthropological Association, pp. 73–88.

—— (2006) *Liberia: The Violence of Democracy*, Philadelphia: University of Pennsylvania Press.

—— (2010) 'Gender, militarism, and peace-building: projects of the postconflict moment', *Annual Review of Anthropology*, 39: 261–74.

Moran, M. H. and M. A. Pitcher (2004) 'The "basket case" and the "poster child": explaining the end of civil conflicts in Liberia and Mozambique', *Third World Quarterly*, 25(3): 501–19.

Morgan, E. (2007) 'Masculinity and femininity in the corps', *Race, Gender & Class*, 14(3/4): 117–30.

Mufti, A. R. (2005) 'Global comparativism', *Critical Inquiry*, 31(2): 472–89.

Murphy, R. (2006) 'An assessment of UN efforts to address sexual misconduct by peacekeeping personnel', *International Peacekeeping*, 13(4): 531–46.

Murphy, W. P. (2003) 'Military patrimonialism and child soldier clientalism in the Liberian and Sierra Leonean civil wars', *African Studies Review*, 46(2): 61–87.

Musila, G. A. (2015) *A Death Retold in Truth and Rumour: Kenya, Britain and the Julie Ward Murder*, Woodbridge, Suffolk, and Rochester, NY: James Currey.

Möller, F. (2009) 'The looking/not looking dilemma', *Review of International Studies*, 35(4): 781–94.

—— (2013) *Visual Peace: Images, Spectatorship, and the Politics of Violence*, Basingstoke and New York: Palgrave Macmillan.

Nagel, J. and C. W. Snyder (1989) 'International funding of educational development: external agendas and internal adaptations: the case of Liberia', *Comparative Education Review*, 33(1): 3–20.

Nakashima Brock, R. and G. Lettini (2012) *Soul Repair: Recovering from Moral Injury after War*, Boston, MA: Beacon Press.

Namnyak, M. et al. (2008) '"Stockholm Syndrome": psychiatric diagnosis or urban myth?', *Acta Psychiatrica Scandinavica*, 117(1): 4–11.

Nichols, R. (2005) 'Disarming Liberia: pitfalls and progress', in N. Florquin and E. Berman (eds), *Armed and Aimless: Armed Groups, Guns, and Human Security in the ECOWAS Region*, Geneva: Small Arms Survey, pp. 108–43.

NIH (National Institute of Drug Abuse) (2016) 'Drug facts: treatment approaches for drug addiction [revised]', NIH Publications, January, www.drugabuse.gov/publications/drugfacts/treatment-approaches-drug-addiction, accessed 6 June 2016.

Njoki Wamai, E. (2011) 'Security Council Resolution 1325 implementation in Liberia: dilemmas and challenges', in F. Olonisakin, K. Barnes and E. Ikpe (eds), *Women, Peace and Security: Translating Policy into Practice*, Abingdon and New York: Routledge, pp. 52–65.

Nordstrom, C. (1997) *A Different Kind of War Story*, Philadelphia: University of Pennsylvania Press.

—— (1998) 'Girls behind the

(front) lines', in L. A. Lorentzen and J. Turpin (eds), *The Women and War Reader*, New York and London: New York University Press, pp. 80–89.

Nyanzi, S., R. Pool and J. Kinsman (2001) 'The negotiation of sexual relationships among school pupils in south-western Uganda', *AIDS Care*, 13(1): 83–98.

OECD (2014) 'Liberia', *Social Institutions & Gender Index (SIGI)*, pp. 1–7, genderindex.org/sites/default/files/datasheets/LR.pdf.

OHCHR (2016) 'UN rights expert urges Liberia not to hand public education over to a private company', Press release, Office of the United Nations High Commissioner for Human Rights (OHCHR), 22 March, www.ohchr.org/EN/NewsEvents/Pages/DisplayNews.aspx?NewsID=18506, accessed 17 June 2016.

Paes, W.-C. (2005) 'The challenges of Disarmament, Demobilization and Reintegration in Liberia', *International Peacekeeping*, 12(2): 253–61.

Perkins, D. D. and M. A. Zimmerman (1995) 'Empowerment theory, research, and application', *American Journal of Community Psychology*, 23(5): 569–79.

Permeswaran, Y. (2008) 'The Women's Army Auxiliary Corps: a compromise to overcome the conflict of women serving in the army', *History Teacher*, 42(1): 95–111.

Peters, K. and S. Laws (2003) *When Children Affected by War Go Home: Lessons Learned from Liberia*, London: Save the Children UK.

Peterson, A. and R. Reid (2003) 'Paths to psychological empowerment in an urban community: sense of community and citizen participation in substance abuse prevention activities', *Journal of Community Psychology*, 31(1): 25–38.

Pitcher, A., M. H. Moran and M. Johnston (2009) 'Rethinking patrimonialism and neopatrimonialism in Africa', *African Studies Review*, 52(1): 125–56.

Pflanz, M. (2014) 'Ebola rap warns West Africans of virus's dangers', *Telegraph*, 28 May, www.telegraph.co.uk/news/worldnews/africaandindianocean/liberia/10860045/Ebola-rap-warns-West-Africans-of-viruss-dangers.html, accessed 14 April 2015.

Plato (2012) *Republic*, London: Penguin.

Proctor, T. M. (2003) *Female Intelligence: Women and Espionage in the First World War*, New York: New York University Press.

Pugel, J. (2009) 'Measuring reintegration in Liberia: assessing the gap between outputs and outcomes', in R. Muggah (ed.), *Security and Post-Conflict Reconstruction: Dealing with Fighters in the Aftermath of War*, London and New York: Routledge, pp. 70–102.

Puniewska, M. (2015) 'Healing a wounded sense of morality', *The Atlantic*, 3 July, www.theatlantic.com/health/archive/2015/07/healing-a-wounded-sense-of-morality/396770/, accessed 12 July 2017.

Rahimian, N. (2013) 'Liberian street hit stirs the political pot', *Guardian*, 9 January, www.theguardian.com/music/2013/jan/09/liberia-music-pot-boiling, accessed 15 April 2016.

Rajan, V. G. J. (2011) *Women Suicide Bombers: Narratives of Violence*, London and New York: Routledge.

Reilly, C. (ed.) (1981) *Scars upon My Heart: Women's Poetry and Verse of the First World War*, London: Virago.

Reno, W. (2012) 'Anti-corruption efforts in Liberia: are they aimed at the right targets?', in D. Zaum and C. S. Cheng (eds), *Corruption and Post-Conflict Peacebuilding:*

*Selling the Peace?*, London: Routledge.
Reuters (2003) 'A diamond in the rough', *Taipei Times*, 27 August, www.taipeitimes.com/News/feat/archives/2003/08/27/2003065484/2, accessed 14 July 2014.
—— (2013) 'Liberia's education system "a mess" – President Sirleaf', Reuters, 29 August, www.reuters.com/article/us-liberia-education-idUSBRE97S0TO20130829, accessed 13 June 2015.
Rhodes, N. R. and E. B. McKenzie (1998) 'Why do battered women stay? Three decades of research', *Aggression and Violent Behavior*, 3(4): 391–406.
Rich, A. (1985) 'Notes toward a politics of location', in M. Díaz-Diocaretz and I. M. Zavala (eds), *Women, Feminist Identity, and Society in the 1980's: Selected Papers*, Amsterdam and Philadelphia, PA: Benjamins, pp. 7-22.
Richards, J. V. O. (1975) 'Some aspects of the multivariant socio-cultural rôles of the Sande of the Mende', *Canadian Journal of African Studies/Revue Canadienne des Études Africaines*, 9(1): 103–13.
Richards, P. (2005) 'To fight or to farm? Agrarian dimensions of the Mano River conflicts (Liberia and Sierra Leone)', *African Affairs*, 104(417): 571–90.
—— (2016) *Ebola: How a People's Science Helped End an Epidemic*, London: Zed Books.
Robinson, F. (2016) 'Feminist care ethics and everyday insecurities', in J. Nyman and A. Burke (eds), *Ethical Security Studies: A New Research Agenda*, London and New York: Routledge, pp. 116-30.
Rosen, D. M. (2005) *Armies of the Young: Child Soldiers in War and Terrorism*, New Brunswick, NJ, and London: Rutgers University Press.
Ruby, J. (1992) 'Speaking for, speaking about, speaking with, or speaking alongside: an anthropological and documentary dilemma', *Journal of Film and Video*, 44(1/2): 42–66.
Sachs, K.-J. (2001) 'Counterpoint', in S. Sadie (ed.), *The New Grove Dictionary of Music and Musicians*, 2nd edn, vol. 6: *Claudel to Dante*, New York: Grove's Dictionaries Inc., pp. 551–61.
Said, E. W. (1994) *Culture and Imperialism*, London: Vintage.
—— (1996) *Representations of the Intellectual: The 1993 Reith Lectures*, New York: Pantheon.
—— (2000) *Reflections on Exile and Other Essays*, Cambridge, MA: Harvard University Press.
Said, N. (2005) 'Tribute to my father', *Alif: Journal of Comparative Poetics*, 25: 21–5.
Salter, M. B. and C. E. Mutlu (eds) (2013) *Research Methods in Critical Security Studies: An Introduction*, London: Routledge.
Sassoon, S. (1983) *The War Poems*, London: Faber.
Scheper-Hughes, N. (1992) *Death without Weeping: The Violence of Everyday Life in Brazil*, Berkeley: University of California Press.
SCSL (Special Court for Sierra Leone) (2016) 'Homepage', Special Court for Sierra Leone, 21 June, www.rscsl.org/, accessed 21 July 2016.
Sen, A. (2009) *The Idea of Justice*, London: Allen Lane.
Seppälä, T. (2017) 'On "outsourcing" the political in political science', *Social Identities*, Published online, 21 February, pp. 1–16.
Shapiro, M. J. (2009) *Cinematic Geopolitics*, London: Routledge.
Shekhawat, S. and B. Pathak (2015) 'Female combatants, peace process and the exclusion', in S. Shekhawat (ed.), *Female Combatants in Conflict and Peace: Challenging Gender in Violence and Post-Conflict Reintegration*, Basingstoke: Palgrave Macmillan, pp. 53–68.
Shepler, S. (2002) 'Les filles-soldats: trajectoires d'après-guerre en

Sierra Leone', *Politique Africaine*, 88: 49–62.

Sheppard, J.-M. (2012) *Cracking the Code: The Confused Traveler's Guide to Liberian English*, Kindle eBook, Sheppard's Books.

Sheriff, A. (2008) 'Reintegration of female war-effected and ex-combatants in Liberia', *Conflict Trends*, pp. 26–33.

Sherman, N. (2010) *The Untold War: Inside the Hearts, Minds, and Souls of Our Soldiers*, New York: W. W. Norton.

—— (2015) *Afterwar: Healing the Moral Wounds of Our Soldiers*, New York: Oxford University Press.

Sherwood, H. N. (1917) 'The formation of the American Colonization Society', *Journal of Negro History*, 2(3): 209–28.

Silberschmidt, M. and V. Rasch (2001) 'Adolescent girls, illegal abortions and "sugar-daddies" in Dar Es Salaam: vulnerable victims and active social agents', *Social Science & Medicine*, 52(12): 1815–26.

Simić, O. (2010) 'Does the presence of women really matter? Towards combating male sexual violence in peacekeeping operations', *International Peacekeeping*, 17(2): 188–99.

—— (2012) *Regulation of Sexual Conduct in UN Peacekeeping Operations*, New York: Springer.

Simone, A. (2004) 'People as infrastructure: intersecting fragments in Johannesburg', *Public Culture*, 16(3): 407–29.

Singer, P. W. (2006) *Children at War*, Berkeley: University of California Press.

—— (2010) 'The enablers of war: causal factors behind the child soldier phenomenon', in S. Gates and S. Reich (eds), *Child Soldiers in the Age of Fractured States*, Pittsburgh, PA: University of Pittsburgh Press, pp. 93–107.

Sirleaf Market Women's Fund (2012) '"God first, second the market": a case study of the Sirleaf Market Women's Fund of Liberia', Sirleaf Market Women's Fund, wiego.org/publications/god-first-second-market-case-study-sirleaf-market-women%E2%80%99s-fund-liberia, accessed 19 June 2016.

Sivakumaran, S. (2007) 'Sexual violence against men in armed conflict', *European Journal of International Law*, 18(2): 253–76.

Sjoberg, L. (ed.) (2010) *Gender and International Security: Feminist Perspectives*, Kindle eBook, London and New York: Routledge.

Sjoberg, L. and C. E. Gentry (2007) *Mothers, Monsters, Whores: Women's Violence in Global Politics*, London and New York: Zed Books.

Sjoberg, L. and S. Via (eds) (2010) *Gender, War, and Militarism: Feminist Perspectives*, Santa Barbara, CA: Praeger.

Smith, D. (2013) 'All 25,000 candidates fail Liberian university entrance exam', *Guardian*, 27 August, www.theguardian.com/world/2013/aug/27/all-candidates-fail-liberia-university-test, accessed 6 May 2016.

Solomon, D. (2009) 'Madame President: questions for Ellen Johnson Sirleaf', *New York Times*, 23 August, www.nytimes.com/2009/08/23/magazine/23fob-q4-t.html?_r=0, accessed 30 December 2014.

Sontag, S. (1977) *On Photography*, New York: Farrar, Straus and Giroux.

—— (2003) *Regarding the Pain of Others*, London: Hamish Hamilton.

Sousanis, N. (2015) *Unflattening*, Cambridge, MA: Harvard University Press.

Specht, I. (2006) *Red Shoes: Experiences of Girl-Combatants in Liberia*, Geneva: International Labour Office.

Spivak, G. C. (1988) 'Can the subaltern speak?', in C. Nelson and L. Grossberg (eds), *Marxism and the Interpretation of Culture*,

Basingstoke: Macmillan Education.
—— 'Thinking about Edward Said: pages from a memoir', *Critical Inquiry*, 31(2): 519–25.
Stallworthy, J. (2008) *The Oxford Book of War Poetry*, Oxford and New York: Oxford University Press.
Standing, H. (1992) 'AIDS: conceptual and methodological issues in researching sexual behaviour in sub-Saharan Africa', *Social Science & Medicine*, 34(5): 475–83.
Steady, F. C. (2006) *Women and Collective Action in Africa: Development, Democratization, and Empowerment, with Special Focus on Sierra Leone*, Basingstoke: Palgrave Macmillan.
Sylvester, C. (2005) 'The art of war/ the war question in (feminist) IR', *Millennium – Journal of International Studies*, 33(3): 855–78.
Särmä, S. (2014) 'Junk feminism and nuclear wannabes – collaging parodies of Iran and North Korea', Doctoral dissertation, International Relations, University of Tampere.
Tamagnini, A. and T. Krafft (2010) 'Strategic approaches to reintegration: lessons learned from Liberia', *Global Governance*, 16(1): 13–20.
Tamale, S. (ed.) (2011a) *African Sexualities: A Reader*, Oxford: Pambazuka.
—— (2011b) 'Researching and theorising sexualities in Africa', in S. Tamale (ed.), *African Sexualities: A Reader*, Oxford: Pambazuka, pp. 11–36.
Thomas, M. E. (2009) 'Auto-photography', in R. Kitchin and N. Thrift (eds), *International Encyclopedia of Human Geography*, Oxford: Elsevier, pp. 244–51.
Tickner, J. A. (1992) *Gender in International Relations: Feminist Perspectives on Achieving Global Security*, New York: Columbia University Press.

Tucker, B. (2014) 'Beats, rhymes and Ebola', Hot Spots, Cultural Anthropology website, 7 October, www.culanth.org/fieldsights/592-beats-rhymes-and-ebola, accessed 16 May 2016.
Turshen, M. and C. Twagiramariya (eds) (1998) *What Women Do in Wartime: Gender and Conflict in Africa*, London: Zed Books.
Ukah, A. F.-K. (2003) 'Advertising God: Nigerian Christian video-films and the power of consumer culture', *Journal of Religion in Africa*, 33(2): 203–31.
UNICEF (United Nations Children's Emergency Fund) (1997) 'Cape Town Principles and Best Practices', UNICEF Publications, 30 April, www.unicef.org/emerg/files/Cape_Town_Principles(1).pdf, accessed 14 November 2015.
United Nations (1992) 'An agenda for peace: preventive diplomacy, peacemaking and peace-keeping', Report of the Secretary-General, 17 June, www.un.org/ruleoflaw/files/A_47_277.pdf, accessed 19 August 2016.
—— (2005) 'UN Doc. E/ICEF/2005/P/L.5', *Economic and Social Council: Draft country programme document: Liberia*, 4 April, www2.unicef.org:60090/about/execboard/files/05-PL5_Liberia2.pdf, accessed 4 March 2014.
—— (2006) 'UN Doc. E/ICEF/2005/P/L.5', *Internal Audit Report: UNMIL DDRR Programme. OIOS Audit No. AP2005/626/07*, 25 January, download.cabledrum.net/wikileaks_archive/file/un-oios/OIOS-20060125-02.pdf, accessed 14 June 2016.
—— (2011) 'Country programme: Liberia', UN Disarmament, Demobilizaton and Reintegration Resource Centre, unddr.org/countryprogramme.php?c=52, accessed 6 July 2011.
UNMIL (United Nations Mission in Liberia) (2015) 'An assessment

of human rights issues emanating from traditional practices in Liberia', *United Nations Mission in Liberia (UNMIL) Reports*, unmil.unmissions.org/sites/default/files/harmful_traditional_practices_final_-_18_dec._2015.pdf, accessed 7 June 2016.

UNODC (United Nations Office on Drugs and Crime) (2014) *World Drug Report 2014*, Vienna: UNODC.

UNOSAA (United Nations Office of the Special Adviser on Africa) (2007) 'Final report', Second International Conference on Disarmament, Demobilization, Reintegration and Stability in Africa, 14 June, www.un.org/press/en/2007/afr1551.doc.htm, accessed 22 July 2014.

UNSC (UN Security Council) (1992) 'UN Doc. S/23500', *Note by the President of the Security Council*, 31 January, www.securitycouncilreport.org/un-documents/document/PKO%20S%2023500.php, accessed 17 May 2016.

—— (1993) 'UN Doc. Resolution 866 S/RES/866', *Resolution 866*, 22 September, documents-dds-ny.un.org/doc/UNDOC/GEN/N93/513/89/PDF/N9351389.pdf?OpenElement, accessed 6 October 2017.

—— (1996) 'UN Doc. S/1996/858', *Nineteenth Progress Report of the Secretary-General on the United Nations Observer Mission in Liberia*, 17 October, www.un.org/en/ga/search/view_doc.asp?symbol=S/1996/858, accessed 6 June 2016.

—— (1997) 'UN Doc. S/1997/90', *Twenty-First Progress Report of the Secretary-General on the United Nations Observer Mission in Liberia*, 29 January, www.un.org/en/ga/search/view_doc.asp?symbol=S/1997/90, accessed 5 June 2016.

—— (2003a) 'UN Doc. S/2003/875', *Report of the Secretary-General to the Security Council on Liberia*, 11 September, www.securitycouncilreport.org/un-documents/document/Liberia%20S2003%20875.php, accessed 5 October 2017.

—— (2003b) 'UN Doc. S/RES/1509', *The Situation in Liberia*, 19 September, www.un.org/en/ga/search/view_doc.asp?symbol=S/RES/1509(2003), accessed 6 May 2014.

USAID (2016) 'Liberia: Education', *USAID Briefing*, 8 June, www.usaid.gov/liberia/education, accessed 6 May 2016.

US Army (2014) 'Careers and jobs: culinary specialist', US Army Home Page, www.goarmy.com/careers-and-jobs/browse-career-and-job-categories/intelligence-and-combat-support/culinary-specialist.html, accessed 24 August 2016.

US Department of State (2014_ 'Country Report: Liberia', *International Narcotics Control Strategy Report (INCSR)*, March, www.state.gov/j/inl/rls/nrcrpt/2014/vol1/222922.htm, accessed 7 July 2016.

Utas, M. (2003) 'Sweet battlefields: youth and the Liberian civil war', Doctoral dissertation, Uppsala University.

—— (2005a) 'Agency of victims: young women in the Liberian civil war', in A. M. Honwana and F. de Boeck (eds), *Makers and Breakers: Children and Youth in Postcolonial Africa*, Trenton, NJ, and Dakar: James Currey and Codesria, pp. 53–79.

—— (2005b) 'Victimcy, girlfriending, soldiering: tactic agency in a young woman's social navigation of the Liberian war zone', *Anthropological Quarterly*, 78(2): 403–30.

—— (2008) 'Abject heroes: marginalised youth, modernity and violent pathways of the Liberian civil war', in J. Hart (ed.), *Years of Conflict: Adolescence, Political Violence and Displacement*, New York: Berghahn, pp. 111–38.

—— (2011) 'Victimcy as social navigation: from the toolbox of Liberian child soldiers', in A. Özerdem and S. Podder (eds), *Child Soldiers: From Recruitment to Reintegration*, Basingstoke and New York: Palgrave Macmillan, pp. 213–28.

—— (2012) *African Conflicts and Informal Power: Big Men and Networks*, London: Zed Books and the Nordic Africa Institute.

Vaittinen, T. (2017) 'The global biopolitical economy of needs: transnational entanglements between ageing Finland and the Global Nurse Reserve of the Philippines', Doctoral dissertation, Peace and Conflict Studies, University of Tampere.

Van de Walle, N. (2014) 'The democratization of clientelism in sub-Saharan Africa', in D. Abente Brun and L. J. Diamond (eds), *Clientelism, Social Policy, and the Quality of Democracy*, Baltimore, MD: Johns Hopkins University Press, pp. 230–52.

Van Velsen, J. (1964) *Politics of Kinship: A Study in Social Manipulation among the Lakeside Tonga of Nyasaland*, Manchester: Manchester University Press.

Vastapuu, L. (2015) 'Study on the gendered impacts of Ebola in Liberia', Independent study commissioned by Finn Church Aid, 28 February, reliefweb.int/report/liberia/study-gendered-impacts-ebola-liberia-february-2015, accessed 7 July 2016 (published under the name Leena Kotilainen).

Vigh, H. (2006a) *Navigating Terrains of War: Youth and Soldiering in Guinea-Bissau*, New York and Oxford: Berghahn.

—— (2006b) 'Social death and violent life chances', in C. Christiansen, M. Utas and H. Vigh (eds), *Navigating Youth, Generating Adulthood: Social Becoming in an African Context*, Uppsala: Nordic Africa Institute, pp. 31–60.

—— (2009) 'Motion squared: a second look at the concept of social navigation', *Anthropological Theory*, 9(4): 419–38.

Vila, P. (2013) 'The importance of photo-interviewing as a research method in the study of identity construction processes: an illustration from the US–Mexico border', *Visual Anthropology*, 26(1): 51–68.

Vining, M. and B. C. Hacker (2001) 'From camp follower to lady in uniform: women, social class and military institutions before 1920', *Contemporary European History*, 10(3): 353–73.

Visvanathan, N., L. Duggan and L. Nisonoff (eds) (2011) *The Women, Gender and Development Reader*, London and New York: Zed Books.

Vogt, H. (2008) 'On the state of the IR art: problems of self-positioning and the absence of freedom: reflections of the outgoing president of the Nordic International Studies Association', *Cooperation and Conflict*, 43(4): 363–72.

Vuori, J. A. (2010) 'A timely prophet? The Doomsday Clock as a visualization of securitization moves with a global referent object', *Security Dialogue*, 41(3): 255–77.

Väyrynen, T. (2010) 'Gender and peacebuilding', in O. P. Richmond (ed.), *Palgrave Advances in Peacebuilding: Critical Developments and Approaches*, Basingstoke: Palgrave Macmillan, pp. 137–53.

WACD (West Africa Commission on Drugs) (2014) 'Not just in transit: drugs, the state and society in West Africa', *WACD Reports*, June, www.wacommissionondrugs.org/report/, accessed 4 June 2016.

Wagner, J. (2006) 'Visible materials, visualised theory and images of social research', *Visual Studies*, 21(1): 55–69.

Walker, P. G. T. et al. (2015) 'Malaria morbidity and mortality in Ebola-affected countries caused by decreased health-care capacity, and the potential effect of mitigation strategies: a modelling analysis', *The Lancet Infectious Diseases*, 15(7): 825–32.

Wander, P. C. (1971) 'Salvation through separation: the image of the Negro in the American Colonization Society', *Quarterly Journal of Speech*, 57(1): 57–67.

Wandia, M. (2016) 'Liberia needs to muster the courage to ban FGM', *Guardian*, 27 April, www.theguardian.com/global-development/2016/apr/27/liberia-courage-to-ban-fgm-ellen-johnson-sirleaf, accessed 21 June 2016.

Waugh, C. M. (2011) *Charles Taylor and Liberia: Ambition and Atrocity in Africa's Lone Star State*, London and New York: Zed Books.

Werner, G. (2016) 'Partnership schools for Liberia: building a better future for our children', Government of Liberia, 30 March, moe.gov.lr/site/pages3.php?pgID=137, accessed 7 June 2016.

Wessells, M. G. (2006) *Child Soldiers: From Violence to Protection*, Cambridge, MA, and London: Harvard University Press.

Wheelwright, J. (1989) *Amazons and Military Maids: Women Who Dressed as Men in the Pursuit of Life, Liberty and Happiness*, London: Pandora.

White, L. (1997) 'The traffic in heads: bodies, borders and the articulation of regional histories', *Journal of Southern African Studies*, 23(2): 325–38.

WHO (World Health Organization) (2015) *Report of the Ebola Interim Assessment Panel: Independent Report by a Panel Chaired by Dame Barbara Stocking*, World Health Organization.

—— (2016) 'Ebola situation report 30 March 2016', *WHO Situation Reports*, 27 March, apps.who.int/ebola/current-situation/ebola-situation-report-30-march-2016, accessed 22 July 2016.

Wibben, A. T. R. (2011) *Feminist Security Studies: A Narrative Approach*, London: Routledge.

—— (2016) 'Introduction: Feminists study war', in A. T. R. Wibben (ed.), *Researching War: Feminist Methods, Ethics and Politics*, Abingdon and New York: Routledge, pp. 1–16.

Willis, D. and C. Williams (2002) *The Black Female Body: A Photographic History*, Philadelphia, PA: Temple University Press.

Wilson, G. M. (1994) 'Edward Said on contrapuntal reading', *Philosophy and Literature*, 18(2): 265–73.

Wilson, R. and R. D. Brown (2009) *Humanitarianism and Suffering: The Mobilization of Empathy*, Cambridge and New York: Cambridge University Press.

World Bank (2012) 'World Development Report 2013: Jobs', *International Bank for Reconstruction and Development/The World Bank Reports*, September, siteresources.worldbank.org/EXTNWDR2013/Resources/8258024-1320950747192/8260293-1322665883147/WDR_2013_Report.pdf;, accessed 14 March 2015.

World Bank Group (2015) *The Economic Impact of Ebola on Sub-Saharan Africa: Updated Estimates for 2015*, World Bank Group.

Youthpolicy.org. (2014) 'Liberia: Factsheet', *Definition of Youth*, 28 April, www.youthpolicy.org/factsheets/country/liberia/, accessed 17 June 2016.

Özerdem, A. (2012) 'A re-conceptualisation of ex-combatant reintegration: "social reintegration" approach', *Conflict, Security & Development*, 12(1): 51–73.

Özerdem, A. and S. Podder (eds) (2011) *Child Soldiers: From Recruitment to Reintegration*, Basingstoke and New York: Palgrave Macmillan.

# Index

abduction, 1, 8, 31–2, 44, 45–7, 51, 60, 67, 70, 72, 80, 89, 90, 99, 102, 103, 129, 155
abortion, 129; forced, 76
Abuja II Agreement, xiv, 91
Adair, John, 25–6
adulthood, 116; as category, 3
advantages in joining armed forces, 51–2
Africanism, 13
agency, 170; of women, 28; spaces of, 17 *see also* tactic agency
agriculture, 119–21, 163; rejected as form of income, 120; study of, 105, 159
Akosombo Agreement, 91
alcohol, consumption of, 46, 65 *see also* drugs, use of
American Colonization Society (ACS), xiii, 150, 170
Amos, V., with P. Parmar, 'Challenging imperial feminism', 15
Amy, 30–4, 35, 121, 177
Angela, 1, 3, 48–9, 97, 147, 165, 176
Angeline, 48–9, 97, 138, 147, 165, 176
Anna, 87, 90, 96, 155
Annan, Kofi, 91
Annie, 77, 80
Anthony, 141
Anti-Terrorist Unit (ATU), 46, 52
Ariana, 152
Arjuna, a warrior, 108
Armed Forces of Liberia (AFL), xiii, xv, 1, 32, 51, 60, 70, 74, 89, 91, 102, 152
aspirations and dreams of women veterans, 4, 6, 7, 17, 26, 129–30, 147–66
auto-photographic research approach, 26
auto-photography, 5, 7, 21–41, 39, 171; as research method, 24–7, 40–1 (laborious and expensive), 171; use of term, 26
avenging death of a relative, 44–5 *see also* revenge

Baaz, Maria Eriksson, 74–5, 77
babies: delivery of, in fighting forces, 76; toted in front, 76 *see also* giving birth
Banerjee, Abhijit, with Esther Duflo, *Poor Economics*, 144
Basini, Helen, 86
battered women, 35
beauty salon, work in, 165
Belinga, Eno, 79
Belinga, Guyer, 79
big boys *see* gigolos
big men, 39, 65
Bintu, 28–9, 67–8, 78, 99–101
Black Diamond, 58
Blah, Moses, xv
Bledsoe, Carolyn, 78–9
bluff boys *see* gigolos
Bøås, Morten, 113
bodyguard services in armed forces, 52, 60
Bong County, 128–9
Boutros-Ghali, Boutros, 91–2; 'An Agenda for Peace...', 87
bribery *see* corruption
Bridge Academies, 151
Broh, Mary, 156, 176
brown brown drug, 126
Bullet Bounce, 70
bulletproofing, 57
Burnet, Jennie, 45
bush, 61, 155
bush doctors, 125, 129, 130
bush husbands, 55, 56
bush wives, 54–5, 70–1, 80
businesswomen, 131, 155–63

cameras, distribution of, 25, 122
camp follower, 52; problems with the term, 53, 54, 80–1; use of term, 43, 52, 54, 81
Camp Scheiffelin, 94
cannabis, 36
cannibalism, 57
cantonment, 93
Careen, 139
Carpenter, Charli, 77
cassava, cultivation of, 121, 131, 154, 161

Catherine, 96
Chantal, 51–2, 135–6
charisma, 67
Chea, Pa *see* Pa Chea
child care, 40, 52, 76, 99, 104, 130
child soldiers, 5, 6, 10–11, 36, 94, 106; estimated numbers of, 92; motivations of, 44; not taken into account in DDR, 85; studies of, 2; tactical agency of, 28
childhood, as category, 3
children: in DDR program, 93; of war veterans, futures of, 147–66, 170; presumptively non-combatants, 43 *see also* child soldiers *and* street children
Children Associated with Fighting Forces (CAFF), 52–3; non-use of term, 53; use of term, 81
Children's Assistance Progam (CAP), 106
Children's Law (Liberia, 2011), 3
Chowdhry, Geeta, 14
Christianization, 149
churchgoing, 164, 176
Ciata, 49
Citizens' Defence Force (CDF), xiv
civilized, use of term, 162
'civilized woman', 162
clientelism, 39
clothing *see* dress
cocaine, 67; crack, 57, 126, 128 (addiction to, 124)
'coco' drug, 133
Cold War, 86
'cold water', selling of, 99, 116, 156, 176
Collier, John, 25
colonialism, 173
colour coding of military factions, 60
combat service support, 53–6, 70, 72, 73, 74, 87, 89, 90, 91, 99, 129, 131; use of term, 54
commanders: criteria for choice of, 66–7, 73; differences between women and men, 73; good, definition of, 68–9; in DDR, 97–9, 110, 112; power of, 55–7, 60, 65–70, 73–4, 77, 88, 96; providers of protection, 77, 80–1; relations with generals, 66; sexual relations with, 46, 64–71, 79, 89; women as, 31–2, 48, 53, 58–60, 65–9, 73, 89, 99, 110, 126

commando, model of, 58
Comprehensive Peace Agreement (CPA), xv, 93
computers, use of, 158, 160
condoms, use of, 137
Conrad, Joseph, *Heart of Darkness*, 13
Constitution of Liberia, 120
consumer culture, 142
contrapuntal method, 9, 12 *see also* curious contrapuntalism
'contribution', 36, 38, distinct from corruption, 153 *see also* corruption
corruption, 36, 152–154; campaigns against, 143, of police, 37–8, 124, 157
Cotonou Agreement, 91
Coulter, Chris, 29, 80
counselling, 68, 81, 92, 100, 115, 123, 128, 131, 136, 175
counterpoint, use of term, 12–13
'country devil', activity of, 154–5
cow skin, selling of, 118–19
crack cocaine *see* cocaine
credit associations *see* susu credit association
Crenshaw, Kimberlé, 16–17
curfew, announcement of, 137
curiosity, feminist, 8–9, 10–12
curious contrapuntalism, 8, 14–18, 21, 23, 27, 86, 105, 170, 172

dark glasses, wearing of, 160
Datta, Ayona, 157
De Certeau, Michel, 28, 29
debt, chains of, 90–1
demobilization, 94
Desire, 56, 99
development, as social equalizer, 16
Development Alternatives Inc., 'Assessment of the Situation of Women and Children Combatants...', 85
disability, 36, 94, 159–60, 176; of child, 129–30, 143
disadvantage, reason for joining fighting forces, 44
disarmament, 86, 94, 95–6, 103 *see also* DDR
Disarmament, Demobilization and Reintegration (DDR), 85–114, 3, 11, 33, 152, 170; alternative views of, 105; as

INDEX 207

disarmament, disillusionment and remarginalization, 85; concept of, 87; multiple registrations of soldiers, 98; narratives regarding, 86; phases of, 92–3; program guidelines for, 88, 91; second program, 86, 88, 93–5, 104, 106, 107, 109–10 (basis of, 109–10; gender sensitization in, 111); Strategy and Implementation Framework, 106; use of term, 87; women veterans' non-participation in, 86; women veterans' views regarding, 87, 95

Disarmament, Demobilization, Reintegration and Rehabilitation (DDRR), 82; use of term, 87

'DK clothes', 149

Doe, Samuel, xiii; assassination of, xiv, 48

dog, dead, eating of, 64

domestic work, 31, 74

Don Bosco NGO, 123

Dorris, 115

dress, 57–60, 157–8; differences in, 162; fashionable, 141, 142, 144; of male soldiers, 51 (cross-dressing, 57, 59)

drip, prescription of, 127, 177

Drug Enforcement Agency (DEA), 36–7

drugs, 57; coming off, 127; consumed by police, 37; dealing of, 32–3, 36, 67; legislation regarding, 36; smoking of, 115, 124, 127–8, 133, 164; use of, 36, 65, 122, 130, 133, 176; withdrawal symptoms, 128

dual-sex system, 45, 59

*dubriagem*, 28

ear, loss of part of, 126

Ebola epidemic, 124–5, 136–7, 176; deaths of interviewees in, 175; gendered impact of, 136; preventative measures, 137, 143

'Ebola in Town' song, 125

Economic Community of West African States (ECOWAS), xiv, xv, 93

Economic Community of West African States Mission in *Liberia* (*ECOMIL*), xv

Economic Community of West African States Monitoring Group (ECOMOG), 49, 91, 92

education, 98, 100, 103, 122–3, 158, 159, 161, 166; and DDR, 92, 98, 112–13; as source of empowerment, 123–4; fees for schooling, 153, 157; history of, 149–52; opportunities of, 148–52; primary, 150, 151; secondary, 150; seen as mess, 152; statistics for, 151; tertiary, 149, 151, 175 *see also* Ministry of Education *and* vocational training

egg-nog, cannabis-spiced, 33

elections, xiii, xiv, 88

empathy, 23, 55, 80

employment status of women, post-war, 118

empowerment, gained from education, 123–4

Enloe, Cynthia, 8, 11, 14, 15, 18, 54, 57, 87, 110, 172

entertainment industry, 142

escaping from fighting forces, 88, 89–91, 159

Esther, 87, 91, 97–8

ethics, of photography, 26 *see also* research ethics

Evelyn, 64–5, 98

exile, concept of, 13

exiled voices, 14

exiting from the battlefield, 88–95 *see also* escaping from fighting forces

family reunification, 92

farming *see* agriculture

fashion business, 157–8

fashion plays, of women, 59

fathers, 147; of war veterans, 90, 145, 176 (reactions of, 101–2; relations with, 130–1)

female soldiers, use of term, 3; community's fear of, 104; gendered stereotypes of, 2,11, 28–9, 43, 45, 77, 80, 111; post-war lives of, 43–82; overlooked in DDR, 95 *see also* combat service support; commanders; fighters, Liberia's female *and* multitasking by women soldiers

femininity, 11, 16, 58, 112, 123

feminism, 172; black, 16; motivation for joining fighting forces, 45;

postcolonial, 15–18; Western, imperialistic roots of, 15 *see also* curiosity, feminist; intersectionality *and* curious contrapuntalism
feminist monitoring questions, 110–11
feminist peace research, 172
fighters, Liberia's female, 57–65
Foot to Foot, 65
Foucault, Michel, 21
Frances, 45–6
future objectives of women war veterans *see* aspirations and dreams of women

Galtung, Johan, 9
*gana gana*, 33
gaze, politics of, 17–18
Gbarnga, 128–31
Gbowee, Leymah, 107
gender-based discrimination; in aid industry, 123; in fighting forces, 74–7; in DDR, 96, 109, 110, 111; in studies of African youth 116, in vocational training, 123
gender, context-specific, xvi, 75
gendered terminologies, use of, 53
gigolos, 117, 133, 140
Gio people, xiii, 49
girl soldiers: definition of 3, 53; in the ranks, 43–82; non-participation in DDR, 86; overlooked in DDR, 95
girls: as child soldiers, 10–11; excluded from DDR processes, 85; made invisible, 2, 11; placed in supporting roles, 10
giving birth, 91, 147
glaucoma, 159, 176
Glebo ethnic group, 162
'godfathers' *see* sugar daddies
'godmothers' *see* sugar mommies
good life, idea of, 164
Grace, 1, 3
Graham, Dee, 55
Graham's Stockholm Syndrome Theory, 46, 55–6, 65, 81, 90, 129
grandmothers, 91
*grona* behaviour, 120, 126
guilt, 117
Guinea, xiv, 90
gun-carrying combatants, focus of DDR, 93
gunpowder, smoking of, 46
guns, 90; abandonment of, 51; acquired by women fighters, 73 (means of safety, 57); carried by women, 49, 65; collecting of, 94; methods of firing, 69; not carried by women, 95; not required for DDR registration, 88, 92, 94, 95, 96, 98; of women, increase sexual autonomy, 75; surrender of, 92 *see also* weapons-for-cash approach
'guns, camps and cash' approach *see* weapons-for-cash approach

hairdressing, 56, 112, 118, 123, 144, 156
hair salons, 156–7
hairbands, fashion for, 52
'having a job', meaning of, 119
Hawah, 101–2, 130–1; abduction of, 46–7
hell, as the lack of being heard, 2
heroin, 36 *see also* tar-white (brown heroin)
Heyerdahl, Thor, 27, 169
hipco music, 142–3, 177; as sensitization tool, 143
HIV/AIDS, 158, 176
Hoatha, 77
homegirls, category of, 132, 133
Honwana, Alcinda, 'Innocents ou coupables...', 27–8
hooks, bell, 17
hope, 8, 124, 135, 145, 164–5, 166, 176 *see also* aspirations and dreams of women; lack of, 128
housewives, 54, 162, 176
housing, 115–17, 170; 'dream house', 160–3; concrete, 160–3
human rights, abuses of, xiii, xv
hustlers, category of, 132
hustling, 132–45, 155

ID cards, provision of in DDR, 92
idleness, securitization of male, 109, 112, 113, 123
illustrator, role of, 19
Independent National Commission on Human Rights (INCHR), 94
Independent National Patriotic Front of Liberia (INPFL), xiv, 49, 50–1, 74, 97
indicators of success of DDR programs, 87; problematic nature of, 106

indoctrination rituals for joining armed forces, 47
inequalities in armed forces, 71–80
inheritance of property, by women, 120
injustice, as reason for joining armed forces, 48–9
institutions, as manifestations of justice, 107–10
institutions of justice, 87–8
intellectual: challenge of, 9; role of, 21, 170–1
Interim Government of National Unity (IGNU), xiv, 91
internal organs, damage to, 103
International Stabilization Force (ISF), 93
internet, photos posted on, 22–3
intersectionality, 16–18, 44, 71–2, 81, 170
interviewees: profiles of, 3; protection of, 23–4; selection of, 5–6, 25, 34; informal, 6,
interviews: as a research method 4, 34 *see also* photo-elicitation
intimacy, visual, 171

Jason, son of Angela, 165
Jauhola, Marjaana, 112
jeans, wearing of, 59
Jennings, Kathleen M., 94, 109, 132
Johnson, Prince, xiii–xiv, 50–1, 74

Johnson-Hanks, Jennifer, 79
*juju*, 57, 79, 81, 142
Juliet, 1, 3, 22–3, 60–3, 67, 80, 148, 156–7, 160–2, 165–6, 175
justice: concepts of, 87; institutional, 104–12

Kepler, Johannes, 105
kidnapping *see* abduction
killing of relatives and friends, 32, 44–5, 48, 49, 50, 64
Klein, Jacques, 104
Kpelle ethnic group, 78–9
Krafft, Teresa, 104
Krahn ethnic group, xiii, 50, 69
Krishna, 108

'labour made cheap', 9
languages, new, speaking of, 171
*lappa* cloth and clothing, 31, 62, 76, 144, 148, 157, 162, 166

law, customary, 120
legal system, dual, 120
Leontius, son of Aglaion, 22, 23
Liberia, settlement of, xiii, 149, 170
Liberia College, 149
Liberia Demographic and Health Survey, 151
Liberian Peace Council, xiv
Liberians United for Reconciliation and Democracy (LURD), xiv, xv, 1, 32, 58, 60, 66, 68, 69, 80, 98, 102, 129
life stories, telling of, 17
life-worlds, 41, 171; of female soldiers, 43–82
Lisa, 69–70
literacy, 31–2, 100, 149, 151; training in, 92
literature, value given to, 11
location, politics of, 15, 18, 19, 171
Lofa Defence Force (LDF), xiv
looting, 51, 68, 70; of UNOMIL premises, 91–2
love, 147, 175
love affairs, 56; involuntary, 54–5
'loving to', 46, 56, 79, 90, 127, 140; multiple partners, 141
ludo, playing of, 147

Machiavelli, Niccolò, *The Prince*, 53
Magdalena, 74
magic *see juju*
malaria, 63, 125
Mama P, 100
Mandingo ethnic group, 102, 131
Mano ethnic group, xiii
Mano river, xv
mapping of world phenomena, 172
Mariama, 59, 65, 68–9, 79, 126–8, 165; death of, 125–8
marijuana, 36, 122, 127, 133–4
market women, business categories of, 157
Marks, Zoe, 74–5
marriage, 131
Martha, 105–7, 122–4
Marthaline, 53
Mary, 72, 138
masculinity, 57–8; in vocational training, 112; militarized, 11, 105, 110–13, 115; versions of in the first civil war of Liberia, 58
masonry, learning of skills, 112, 123
Massa, 115–17, 126, 145, 176

Médecins sans Frontières (MSF), 125
medical studies, 152
medicine men, 57
medicines, 63
menstruation, 62
methodology of research, 4–7, 21–2, 169; visual participatory, 171
microcredit, seen as problematic, 158
militarism, as ideology, 11
militarization, 87; complexity of, as process, 11; tracking depth of, 110–12 *see also* masculinity, militarized
Ministry of Education, 149
missionary societies, 150
misuse of institutions, 96–9
Mohanty, Chandra Talpade, 'Under Western eyes', 15–16
Monrovia, 31, 32, 33, 34, 36, 117, 121, 128, 133, 145; arrival of Ebola disease in, 124; slum areas in, 100, 106, 156–7; street life in, 133–4
Montpellier Codex, 12
Moran, Mary, 57–8, 156; *Civilized Women...*, 162
mosquitoes, 125
mothers of combatants, 97, 101–2, 132; relations with, 131
motorbike taxis, 154–5
Movement for Democracy in Liberia (MODEL), xv, 60, 66
multitasking by women soldiers, 69–71

Nagel, J., with C. W. Snyder, 'International funding of education development', 150
National Commission for Disarmament, Demobilization, Reintegration and Rehabilitation (NCDDRR), 93
National Democratic Party of Liberia (NDPL), xiii
National Oil Company of Liberia, 123
National Patriotic Front of Liberia (NPFL), xiii, 32, 45, 48, 50, 64, 66, 69, 71; split in, xiii–xiv
National Patriotic Party (NPA), xiv
National Transitional Government of Liberia (NTGL), xv, 94
nationalism, 9

NEPI organization, 86
neo-patrimonialism, 39
New Kru Town neighborhood, 125
Nieminen, Emmi, 7
*niti*, 104–12
Nollywood soap operas, 142
non-governmental organizations (NGOs), 86, 156, 158, 159
numeracy, 100; lack of, 67
NVivo program, 6
*nyaya*, 104–12, 113
OB, 134
opium, 65
Oral, 89
Oretha, 48, 104
'Others': life-worlds of, 171; seeing as, 24; voices of, 21, 40–1; voices of, 21

Pa Chea, 32, 117, 121–2, 124, 125, 126, 176–7
pain: images of, use of, 23; of others, visualization of, 22–3
Partnership Schools for Liberia, 151
patience, 102, 132, 139
patriarchy, 17, 45, 73, 111, 142 *see also* big men
patrimonialism, 39
Peanut Butter, General, 91
peer pressure, 45, 51–2, 117, 128, 139, 140, 141
People's Redemption Council (PRC), xiii
perpetrator: gendered stereotypes of, 50 *see also* victimhood
photo-communication, practice of, 26
photo-elicitation, 5–6, 18, 21, 25–6, 60, 129, 130, 154, 165
photo-elicitation interviews; practice of *see* photo-elicitation
photography, 18, 22, 122, 124, 129–30, 135–6, 141, 147, 148, 152–3, 158, 159–60, 161; distribution of cameras *see* cameras, distribution of; for ID cards, 92; limited use of photos, 23; of women at DDR, 95, 97; participatory, 26; pluralist, practice of, 26; research use of, 4; used by police, 37; varying points of interest in, 25 *see also* auto-photography; ethics, of photography; *and* selfie photographs

photovoice, practice of, 26
pimps, 132
Plato, *Republic*, 22
play mothers, 38
playboys *see* gigolos
police, 37, 147; bribery of, 36, 38, 124, 157; consumption of drugs by, 37; lack of trust in, 34, 35, 36
Poro society, 155, 185
post-traumatic stress disorder (PTSD), 117
postcolonialism, 17, 21 *see also* feminism, postcolonial
poverty, 141, 142, 143-4
pregnancy, 46, 50, 64, 102, 129
pressure, parental, 140-1
Princess, 80
Priscilla, 30-4, 35, 37, 38, 39-40, 121, 124, 128, 164, 176-7
prison, 176
professional status, desirability of, 148
promiscuity, professional, 35
promotion in rank, criteria for, 67
prostitution, 32, 33, 35, 99, 106, 112, 118, 126, 132-45, 156, 165; concept of, 139; definition of, 140; for survival, 131; for the sake of children, 147-8; in Ebola epidemic, 136-7; in motels, 134; male, 6, 140; prices of, 137, 138; quitting of, 176; short-time, 133; 'sleeping', 134; survival, 145; under-age, 137-8
pseudonyms, use of, 7
psychological burdens of female soldiers, 63, 117
push and pull factors in voluntary recruitment, 45

race, analysis of, 17
radical empiricism, 4
radio, possession of, 143
rafting, 155 *see also* social rafting
rafts, balsa, flotillas of, 169
rafts of survival, 33, 39, 43, 57, 78, 79, 81, 90, 106, 113, 117, 128, 134, 137, 142, 148, 161-2, 170; flotillas of, 169; strengthening of, 34-8
rank: as foundational category, 72-4; criteria for promotion, 73; determination of, 72; determining factor in social status, 169-70; discrimination in, 74; does not translate into post-war power, 81 *see also* combat service support; commanders; fighters, Liberia's female *and* multitasking by women soldiers
rape, 32, 47, 48, 54, 64, 68, 71, 74, 76, 103; as weapon of war, 77; campaigns against, 143; threat to kill rapists, 74
reader, as vulnerable observer, 173
reasons of women for joining fighting forces, 43, 44-9
reconnaissance activities, 69, 70, 89
Red Light neighborhood, 127
Redemption Hospital, strike of nurses at, 125
reintegration, 81; failure of, 86; 'of whom and into what', 107
relations, killing of *see* killing of relatives and friends
rent, 115; payment of, 161
researcher, role of, 19, 41
research ethics, 4-5, 21-4, 26
resilience of women veterans, 166
respect, quest for, 57-65
returning home, joys of, 99-102
revenge, as motive for joining armed forces, 49-51
Revolutionary United Front (RUF), 74
Rhoda, 155
Rich, Adrienne, 15
ring, breaking of, 71
rivers of insecurities, 8, 17, 21-41, 116, 145
roles and duties of girls and women, 52-71
rope: placed on waist, 64; use of, 60-1
Rumi, 171
rumors, 57, 97, 102, 124, 136, 155
Rwanda, 45

safety and security, quest for, 7
Said, Edward, 8, 9, 12-14, 15, 18, 170, 172; *Culture and Imperialism*, 13
Samuel, 1
Sande society, 185
Sandy, 112
Santhiaba, 24, 25
Sara, 52
Sauvaire, Jean-Stephane, *Johnny Mad Dog*, 1-2

scholarships, 159, 175
Scramble for Africa, 13
securitization of reintegration, 112
security sector, budget allocation to, 111
security: militarized, 111; of poor people, 34, 38–40; of women war veterans, 43
selfie photographs, 124, 152–3, 163–4
Sen, Amartya, 87, 105, 107–9; *The Idea of Justice*, 108
Senegal *see* Santhiaba
sewing work, undertaken by women, 10
sex slaves, 43
sexism, analysis of, 17
sexual abuse, 2, 46, 47, 54, 73, 74, 75, 79, 80, 101, 102, 129; by UN staff, 137–8 *see also* rape
sexual mutilation, 77
sexual relations: components of, 139–40; in fighting forces, 68, 70–1; with prestigious figures, 72, 73, 79, 81 *see also* prostitution
sexual services, provision of, 54, 64, 70, 89 *see also* prostitution
sexuality, post-war, problems of, 76
sexually transmitted diseases, 75 *see also* HIV/AIDS
shame, 120, 126; of women war veterans, 95 (overcoming of, 102–4)
'showing me life', 46
sickness, in combat action, 62–3
Sierra Leone, 74
Simone, Abdoumaliq, 39
singing, in church choir, 176
Sire, 24, 25
Sirleaf, Ellen Johnson, 152
Sirleaf Market Women's Fund, 157, 158
sisterhood, global, idea of, 15–16
sleeping, in combat action, 61–2
slum clearance in Monrovia, 156, 176
small businesses, running of, 156
Snake in the Grass, 65
social class, 4, 16, 33, 44, 48, 81, 113, 132, 137,; determining role of, 113; in fighting forces, 53, 72, 80–1
social navigation, 7, 27–30, 77, 78, 169
social networks, 130; dependency on, 79 *see also* social relations *and* social rafting

social rafting, 7–10, 27–30, 30–4, 41, 78, 121, 145; concept of, 116; post-war, 115–45
social relations, importance of, 77–80
*soggetto*, 170; creation of, 18–19, 44
soldier: gendered stereotypes of, 2, 11, 28–9, 43, 45, 77, 80, 111
Sonia, 129–30, 143–4, 163
Sontag, Susan, 26
Sousanis, Nick, *Unflattening*, 26–7
South Beach prison, 38
Specht, Irma, 51
Special Court for Sierra Leone, xv
Spivak, Gayatri, 21, 40
spying *see* reconnaissance activities
Standing, Hilary, 139
statistics for female soldiers, 106–7
status, social, improvement of, 144
*see also* professional status *and* social class
statuses obtainable by women in post-war societies, 111
Stern, Maria, 75, 77
stigma, of female war veterans, 6–7, 22–3, 95, 116; overcoming of, 102–4
Stockholm syndrome, 55–6 *see also* Graham's Stockholm Syndrome Theory strangers, assistance of, 88, 90
street brothers, 31, 34, 80, 121, 122, 124, 134, 136, 166; as security providers, 38–40
street children, 134
street dwellers, 134–6
street sisters, 31, 39, 41, 80, 121, 122, 124, 134, 136, 166; as security providers, 38–40
subaltern *see* 'Others'
substance abuse *see* drugs, use of *and* alcohol, consumption of
sugar daddies, 118, 132, 139, 140
sugar mommies, 132, 140–1
*susu* credit associations, 118–19, 145, 156, 158

T-Girl, 134
tactic agency, 7, 28–9, 77–8; of child soldiers, 28
tailoring, learning of skills, 123
Tamagnini, Andrea, 104
tar-white (brown heroin), 36, 122, 126, 144

Taylor, Charles, xiii, xiv, xv, 74, 89
teaching, 154
Temama, 118–19
Teta, 30–4, 35, 37, 121, 177
theft, 135, 136
Theresa, 50, 154, 175
timeframes of reintegration, 107
Tolbert, William, xiii
Tracy, 115
training of female recruits, 60
transactional sex, 132, 137, 139–41 *see also* prostitution
transportation, costs of, 145
transvestism, 57, 59
trauma, 5, 50, 76, 116–17, 128 *see also* counselling
travel restrictions, on war veterans, rumored, 95, 97, 104
True Whig Party, xiii
Truth and Reconciliation Commission (TRC), 94
tuberculosis, 175
TV: possession of, 163; religious shows, 142

Uganda, 140
uniforms: as markers of masculinity, 58–9; color codes in the second civil war of Liberia, 60; in school, 132, 147–8, 155; vocational, 37, 152–3
United Kingdom (UK), xv
United Liberation Movement of Liberia (ULIMO), 66, 68, 91
United Liberation Movement of Liberia (Johnson) (ULIMO-J), xiv, 49, 74, 97
United Liberation Movement of Liberia (Kromah) (ULIMO-K), xiv
United Nations (UN), 94, 113; preventive diplomacy of, 86–7; sexual abuse by staff, 137–8
UN Children's Fund (UNICEF), 92, 94
UN Humanitarian Assistance Coordination Office (UN HACO), 91
UN Mission in Liberia (UNMIL), xv, 85, 91, 93, 107, 111, 138
UN Observer Mission in Liberia (UNOMIL), premises looted, 91–2

UN Security Council: Resolution 866, 91; Resolution 1325, 85, 93; Resolution 1509, xv
United States of America (USA), xv; business contacts with, 158; travelling to during the wars, 48; women in the military in, 54, 66
University of Liberia, 149, 151–2
urban environment, attraction of, 120
urinating in eyes, 159–60
Utas, Mats, 28–9; 'Victimcy, girlfriending, soldiering...', 77

Velsen, Jaap van, 78
Veral, 8, 70–1, 76, 87, 103, 141, 158–60, 163, 165–6, 175–6
victimcy talk, 5
victimhood, 29; change from victim to perpetrator, 65; gendered stereotypes of, 50
Vigh, Henrik E., 28
violence: against women, 35, 37, 46, 51, 52, 80, 89; being forced to witness, 50; entailed in recruitment indoctrination, 47; epistemic, 41; in prostitution encounters, 136; of urban development, 157; of female soldiers, descriptions of, 63–4; psychological, 69; sexual, against men and boys, 77; threat of, 36
virginity: loss of, 46; requirement of, 102
visuality, 27, 41; importance of, 17, 22
visuals, production of, as research method, 22, 171
vocational training, 92, 112, 122–3; for teachers, 154; in 'masculine' professions, 123 *see also* masonry *and* tailoring

war children, 76
war habit, 115
warscapes: as contrapuntal environments, 172–3; as viewed by women veterans, 172
washing: of clothes, 74; of self, during combat action, 62
water, drinking of, in combat action, 61
Watta, 69
wealth in knowledge, 79
wealth in people, 78–9, 90, 162

weapons *see* guns
weapons-for-cash approach, 112, 113
weight given to stories, gendered, 110
Werner, George, 151
Wessells, Michael, 113
West Point neighborhood, 30-1
'where are the women?', 10
whiteness, 2, 15, 17, 34-5, 138, 153
'wickedness', 73, 80
wives: protected, 75; unprotected, 75
Wlejii, 51
women: exclusion of, 112 (from DDR processes, 85, 110; from peace processes, 107); non-representation of, 1, 2; placed in supporting roles, 10; portrayed as non-violent, 49-50; presumptively non-combatants, 43 *see* also combat service support; commanders; fighters, Liberia's female *and* multitasking by women soldiers
Women Associated with the Fighting Forces (WAFF), 43, 52, 96;
non-use of term, 53; use of term, 53-4, 81
women of color, 15
Women of Liberia Mass Action for Peace, 107
women veterans: as social rafters, 7-10, 27-31, 115-45, 78, 169; non-participation in DDR, 86; views on DDR activities, 95-104; post-war life of, 115-46; aspirations of, 147-68
Women's Army Auxiliary Corps (WAAC) (USA), 66
Women's Artillery Commandos / Women's Auxiliary Corps (WAC), 66
Worth, Sol, 25-6

youth: as social status, 116; rights of, in farming sector, 121
youthhood, as category, 3

Zeid report, 137
zinc housing, 33

www.ingramcontent.com/pod-product-compliance
Lightning Source LLC
Chambersburg PA
CBHW030649230426
43665CB00011B/1010